Better Homes and Gardens®

Workshop
TOOLS & TECHNIQUES

Better Homes and Gardens® Books
Des Moines, Iowa

Better Homes and Gardens® Books
An imprint of Meredith® Books

Workshop Tools & Techniques
Editor: Christopher Cavanaugh
Contributing Editor: Kay Sanders
Associate Art Director: Lynda Haupert
Contributing Designer: Michael Burns
Copy Chief: Angela K. Renkoski
Copy Editor: Mary Helen Schiltz
Electronic Production Coordinator: Paula Forest
Production Manager: Douglas Johnston
Prepress Coordinator: Marjorie J. Schenkelberg

Meredith® Books
Editor-in-Chief: James D. Blume
Director, New Product Development: Ray Wolf

Vice President, Retail Marketing: Jamie L. Martin

Better Homes and Gardens® Magazine
Editor in Chief: Jean LemMon

Meredith Publishing Group
President, Publishing Group: Christopher Little
Vice President and Publishing Director: John P. Loughlin

Meredith Corporation
Chairman of the Board and Chief Executive Officer: Jack D. Rehm
President and Chief Operating Officer: William T. Kerr

Chairman of the Executive Committee: E.T. Meredith III

The projects in this book first appeared in the WOOD® Shop Library
Editor: Benjamin Allen
Produced by Cy DeCosse, Inc.

All of us at Better Homes and Gardens Books are dedicated to providing you with information and ideas you need to enhance your home. We welcome your comments and suggestions about this book of workshop tools and techniques. Write to us at Better Homes and Gardens Books, Do-It-Yourself Department, RW 240, 1716 Locust Street, Des Moines, IA 50309-3023.

Chapter 1 Planning and Organizing 6

Setting Up Shop 8

Measuring and Marking 10

Making Project Drawings 12

Enlarging Grid Patterns 16

Sharpening 18

Chapter 2 Woodworking Tools............22

Pushsticks and Featherboards 24

Tablesaw Basics 26

Saw Blades 30

Circular Saw 32

Scrollsaw Basics 34

Bandsaw Basics 36

Power Miter Box.....................................40

Sabersaw Basics 42

Router Basics...44

Lathe Basics..48

Stationary Power Sanders......................52

Drill Press Basics....................................54

Drill Bit Guide..58

Portable Drills 60

Handsaws 62

Hand Planes 64

Chapter 3 Woodworking Woods 68

Red Oak 70

Maple..72

Redwood...74

Walnut 76

Cherry 78

Buying Wood 80

Chapter 4 Hardware and Materials 84

Drawer Hardware...................................86

Hardware Guide 88

Hinges 90

Chapter 5 Shaping Wood **92**
Basic Bowl-Turning Techniques 94
Cutting Tapers...96
Basic Carving 98
Cutting Multiple Workpieces 102
Resawing Techniques............................104

Chapter 6 Joining Wood **106**
Box Joints 108
Dadoes and Rabbets.............................110
Miter-Joint Techniques and Jigs 114
Gluing and Clamping 118
Frame-and-Panel Technique 122
Biscuit Joinery.....................................124
Making Drawers 126
Basic Dowel Joints 130
Veneer Basics 132
Dovetail Joints.....................................136
Mortises and Tenons............................140

Chapter 7 Finishing Wood **144**
Water-Based Finishes 146
Finishing Products 148
Sandpaper 150
Painting Basics 152
Working with Plugs 154
Finishing with Oil................................156

Index **158**

Workshop Tools & Techniques is designed and illustrated to serve as an indispensable workshop resource for all woodworkers, beginning or expert. Here are techniques, tips, and information guaranteed to maximize your time and budget, and reduce your workshop frustrations.

The woodworking experts at Better Homes and Gardens Books provide ideas and practical tips for setting up and organizing your shop, so your work flow will be efficient, enjoyable, and safe. This book teaches you how to minimize mistakes with precise measuring and marking and how to work effectively with project drawings. You'll learn how to match the correct wood, hardware, and finishing products to your project.

We encourage you to use this book when you're shopping for new tools and accessories. Chapter two titled "Woodworking Tools" contains 44 pages of detailed data, buying suggestions, and set-up directions for stationary tools, portable tools, hand tools, and accessories. Follow the advice here to make wise buying decisions: properly powered tools with features and accessories you'll really use.

That's not all! This book teaches the techniques of woodworking: cutting, carving, drilling, sanding, routing, and turning. Step-by-step directions and photographs show 10 techniques for joining wood, from simple gluing and clamping to professional-style mortises and tenons. With these directions and practice, you can create almost anything from wood—workbenches and workshop jigs, toys, storage units, decorative accessories, and heirloom-quality furniture.

Our goal is your success.

CHAPTER 1

Planning and Organizing

First Things First

A master craftsman always puts pencil to paper before he puts tool to wood. He plans and plots. He measures and marks and redesigns. When you're eager to dive into a new project, careful planning may seem tedious. But it's a sure-fire way to prevent costly errors and triumph in the woodshop.

Organization and maintenance of your workstations and your tools also are critical activities, contributing to a safe and efficient environment. A well-organized shop and clean, sharp tools will save you time, reduce workshop stress, and boost enjoyment of your hobby.

Setting Up Shop 8
Measuring and Marking 10
Making Project Drawings...........................12
Enlarging Grid Patterns 16
Sharpening 18

Setting Up Shop

A little planning goes a long way when you're building or expanding your workshop.

Maintaining an efficient, functional workshop is a constant battle for most woodworkers. But with a little planning and foresight, you can keep control of your tools and space, making your workshop a more organized, pleasant, and safe place to spend your leisure time.

Work on your workspace

Begin setting up shop by focusing on the shop location itself. If you have more than one option for locating the workshop (for example, in the garage or in the basement), consider your choice of space carefully. Look for high ceilings, ample turnaround space for longer workpieces, good ventilation, and easy access for bringing in wood and machinery. Also look for a separate room nearby that you can use as a dust-free environment for finishing your projects.

If you're like most people, however, you don't have the luxury of choosing a workspace—you must make do with whatever space you can find.

Here are a few pointers to keep in mind while you analyze and plan your workspace:

• **Separation:** Keep harmony in your family by separating the workshop from the rest of the house (especially if it's a basement workshop). Insulate the walls and ceiling to keep sound from traveling, provide direct ventilation outdoors for fumes, and install a dust collection system.

• **Power:** Upgrade your electrical service, if necessary, so the workshop has at least one dedicated,

The rolling tool caddy *above* turns a simple tablesaw into a workstation. Organizing your shop around the workstation idea is a good method for planning.

20-amp circuit and plenty of wall and ceiling outlets. Few things are more dangerous in a workshop than extension cords and overloaded power circuits.

• **Lighting:** Make use of natural light whenever possible, and install ample, shadow-free ceiling lighting where needed. Commercial-grade 4' and 8' fluorescent light fixtures with protective screens are ideal for workshop use. Avoid incandescent lights.

• **Floor:** Finish the floor with a hard, smooth surface. Paint concrete floors with enamel or epoxy floor paint for easy cleanup, but also buy several rubber floor pads to cushion your legs and feet while you work, and to minimize

the risk of electrical shock.

• **Walls and ceiling:** Paint the room with light-colored enamel paint that cleans up easily and reflects light to brighten the room.

• **Ventilation:** For most workshops, installing a filtered, bathroom-type vent fan with ductwork leading outside is fine. The fan should have a CFM (cubic feet per minute) rating at least 5 CFM more than the total square footage of the workshop.

• **Dust removal:** If you plan to use your shop a lot, install a vacuum-based sawdust collection system that attaches directly to your stationary tools. If you'd rather not spend the money on a commercial dust removal system, at least use dust bags with your power tools, and buy a shop-vac with a blower attachment for easy cleanup.

• **Humidity control:** Many woodworkers prefer to dry their own wood stock, but even if you don't plan to do your own drying, a dehumidifier and a humidifier are critical for preventing warpage of your predried stock—especially in basements and garages. Buy a hydrometer, and use the humidifier and dehumidifier to keep humidity levels from fluctuating too much.

• **Heat:** Don't forget about heating garage workshops in colder climates. A good heating system allows you to putter away in your shop through the winter. Look for heaters that shut off automatically if tipped over. Never use heaters that have open flames or exposed heating elements.

• **Safety:** Safety cannot be overemphasized in the workshop. In addition to the safety suggestions provided throughout this article and by the manufacturers of your tools, be sure your shop has a fire extinguisher, a smoke detector, and a first aid kit. A telephone is a good idea in any workshop, in case you have an emergency.

• **Security:** Unfortunately, security is an important issue for many shop owners. Tools are a favorite target of thieves because they're easy to transport and easy to sell. Always make a record of the serial number of each new tool, and mark it with your name or another permanent identification marking. Build a heavy-duty cabinet with a padlock for storing your valuable hand tools, and, where possible, bolt stationary tools to the floor. Also consider installing a separate door with a deadbolt lock at the entry to garage workshops.

Organizing by workstation

Obsessive planning that requires each and every tool and accessory to be in a precise spot is not very practical for most of us. For most people, it's better to organize flexibly, following a few general, common-sense rules.

One good way to organize the

Make a schedule for upgrading your shop

These lists suggest the recommended tools for a basic, beginning-level workshop, and additional tools for the intermediate and advanced-level shops. Use the lists as a general reference only; talk to other woodworkers who do the same type of work you are planning to find out which tools they find most useful. Always invest in the best tools you can afford—in the long run, they are a bargain.

Beginning	Intermediate	Advanced
Tablesaw	Stationary jointer	Compound miter saw
Router & bits	Bandsaw	Lathe
Portable drill & bits	Scrollsaw	Parallel planer
Sabersaw	Radial-arm saw	Stationary shaper
Portable sander	Power miter saw	Power finishing
Circular saw	Portable planer	equipment
Miter box	Router table	Pneumatic/air tools
Coping saw	Stationary sander	Air compressor
Wood chisels	Drill press	
Hand plane	Biscuit joiner	
Clamps	Random-orbit sander	
Measuring tools		
Workbench		

tools, storage areas, and workspaces in your shop is by forming workstations. Each workstation should feature one stationary tool (tablesaws, lathes, scrollsaws, bandsaws, and drill presses are common candidates) surrounded by the specific jigs and accessories used with the tool.

Once you have determined what to include in each workstation, think about where in your shop

the station should go. Some tools are naturally used together, like a jointer and a tablesaw, or a scrollsaw and a stationary sander, so it's logical that they be positioned next to one another. Workstations that must share tools, jigs, or accessories, like a lathe and a carving bench, should also be close together.

With any workstation, try to provide appropriate access space for handling the largest materials you're likely to encounter. For a tablesaw workstation, for example, you'll need a minimum space of 12 × 16' if you're cutting full 4 × 8' panels, or a minimum space of 6 × 8' for cutting half-size panels. A mitersaw, radial-arm saw, or jointer workstation used to cut dimension lumber requires a narrow space at least 12' long if you'll be cutting 6'-long stock (or at least 16'-long space, if you'll be cutting 8' stock).

DESIGN TIPS

Pay close attention to clearances when you plan your shop:
• *Keep at least 8' of clear space for maneuvering materials at the entry to your workshop.*
• *Maintain a distance of at least 36" between stationary tools and the workbench for easy passage.*
• *Arrange stationary tools so their tables are at the same working height—the same height as the surface of your workbench is ideal. This lets you use the stationary tool tables for auxiliary support when working with extra-large stock.*
• *Maximum height for shelves and cabinets is about 80" for most people. If you need a stepladder to get at a storage space, make sure it's used for tools and materials you use only occasionally.*

TOOL TIP

In a small workshop, a good solution to the space problem is to mount your stationary tools and workbench on lockable rolling casters so the workstations can be rearranged according to your changing needs.

Measuring and Marking

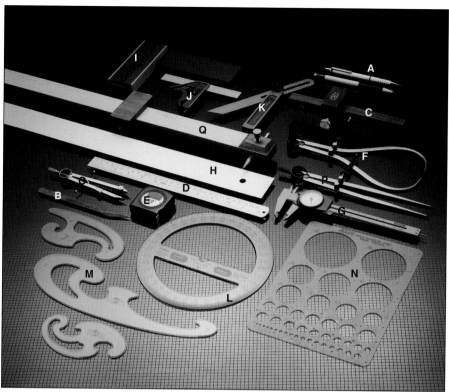

Using the proper measuring and marking tools (and using them correctly) is fundamental to achieving the best possible woodworking results. A basic measuring and marking kit, suitable for most woodworking projects, should include, at a minimum: a steel rule, a tape measure, a mechanical pencil and marking knife or awl, a marking gauge, a compass, a protractor, a straightedge, and a try square.

An almost unlimited variety of special-purpose measuring and marking tools can be purchased or made for specific projects.

Basic measuring and marking tools include: a mechanical pencil (A), marking knife (B), marking gauge (C), steel ruler (D), steel tape measure (E), outside calipers (F), micrometer (G), metal straightedge (H), try square (I), combination square (J), sliding T-bevel (K), protractor (L), French curves (M), circle templates (N), compass (O), dividers (P), bar compass (Q).

Marking tools

Even the most precise measuring tools are useless without an accurate marking instrument. For rough work and marking reference measurements that won't be cut, a lumber pencil is sufficient, as long as you keep it sharp, but a **mechanical pencil,** like those used in drafting, is a better choice. Some special marking pencils designed for woodworking (not shown) have replaceable, long-lasting carbide tips that fit into a steel body and never lose their sharp tip. A **marking knife** makes very accurate scored lines that help you make clean cuts by creating a shallow groove to guide cutting knives and saws. When marking, hold pencils and marking knives at about a 60° angle from the surface of the workpiece.

Marking gauges are available in a wide range of styles designed for specific measuring and marking jobs. A standard marking gauge, like the one shown above, has a pointed metal scoring spur or a graphite tip, and a slide that moves along a beam and locks into position to scribe a line the desired distance from the edge of the workpiece. Other special purposes for marking gauges include

Graduated marking gauges are mounted on a ruler, so you can scribe lines at an exact distance from the edge of a workpiece. Pushing a marking gauge produces a more accurate line than pulling.

marking mortises and following the edges of curved workpieces. Brass inserts in the beams of some models allow for very accurate calibration of scribing distances, and some gauges are mounted on rulers (see *photo,* above).

Measuring tools

For woodworking, a **steel ruler** 6", 12" or 18" long, calibrated to ½₂", is indispensable for making accurate measurements. Having one side calibrated in metric is helpful. When possible, set the ruler on edge so the calibration marks touch the workpiece.

For longer measurements, use a high-quality, 10' to 16' **steel tape measure** with a locking tape calibrated at least to ¼₆" inch. When using a tape measure, make sure the tape is taut and at a right angle to the end of the workpiece where the tape is hooked. Top-quality folding extension rules, usually 6' or 8' long, are preferred by some woodworkers, but lesser-quality ones are very inaccurate.

> **TOOL TIP**
>
> *Use the same measuring tools throughout a project. Because minor calibration variations are common, switching rulers or tape measures can lead to inaccuracy.*

Calipers are used to measure thickness, frequently for turning projects done on the lathe. The jaws of the calipers can be locked to let you duplicate and transfer thicknesses mechanically. Outside calipers are the most commonly used, but inside calipers are available to measure and transfer inside dimension—as with a cutout or hole. For more precise thickness measurements, a **micrometer** is the tool of choice. Whether they work electronically or mechanically, micrometers can measure and set thicknesses at tolerances of as little as .001". Micrometers are used most often in woodworking to match veneers for thickness.

Straightedges & squares

A well-machined metal **straightedge** quickly will become one of your most-used tools. Woodworkers' straightedges are sold in a variety of lengths up to 2 meters (78"), but typically, the longer they are, the larger the tolerances are. A good 24" steel straightedge, accurate to within .002", is a very versatile addition to your shop. A good metal straightedge also can be used as a guide for cutting and trimming and to check surfaces to see if they're flat. When using a straightedge as a cutting guide, clamp it to the workpiece to prevent slippage.

A **try square** is perhaps the most basic woodworker's square. Simply a blade attached to a handle at a 90° angle, try squares are used to set and check 90° and 45° angles. They are especially useful when marking stock for crosscutting at right angles and to make sure stationary saw blades are square.

A **combination square** is a calibrated handle and edge guide, often equipped with a bubble level, that holds a sliding steel ruler. The combination square can be used to check and set 90° and 45° angles and for taking very accurate height and depth readings. A **sliding T-bevel** is a simple angle gauge that adjusts easily to any angle between 0° and 180°. The T-bevel also can be used for complicated measuring tasks, like laying out dovetail joints. To use a T-bevel, set the blade at the desired angle, using a protractor as a guide, then secure the blade with the wing nut or thumbscrew. Butt the handle against the edge of the workpiece to transfer an angle.

A **protractor** is a circle or semicircle calibrated to set or measure angles. Seldom used directly on the workpiece, the protractor is usually used to set other tools, like T-bevels, for marking angles and checking measuring tools to make sure they are accurate.

Measuring & setting curves

Setting curves and circles is made easy with the right variety of measuring and scribing tools. Some tools, like a compass or a divider,

Use a French curve as a template for drawing irregular curves that give woodworking projects a decorative touch.

can be adjusted to set any curve or angle within the capacity of the legs of the tool. Other measuring tools, like French curves and circle templates, are nonadjustable patterns that can, in some cases, create asymmetrical forms.

French curves are sets of templates that can be used to draw complicated, irregular curves for making decorative shapes and cuts. A basic set of French curves contains three to seven templates of various sizes and shapes. Most often, a French curve is used to even out an irregular curve that was drawn freehand to the desired rough shape. To use a French curve, find the edge of the French curve that most closely matches the desired shape, then trace around that edge of the template.

Circle templates are sized in ¹⁄₁₆" increments, making it easy to mark almost any radius you'll need, especially when marking round-overs. Do not use circle templates to measure the diameters of dowels or other round objects, because they are oversized to allow for the thickness of the marking instrument.

A **compass** is the basic tool used for marking small- to medium-size circles and arcs. Compasses have legs ranging in length from 6" up to 16", and the radius of the circles and arcs they can create is roughly equal to the length of the legs. One leg of a compass is fitted with either a pencil or an awl, and some will take a crafts knife, letting you cut circles.

Dividers are similar to a compass, but they have permanent points at the tip of each leg. They are available in much larger sizes than the compass, and also can be used to mark parallel lines. When using a compass or dividers, set the legs to the desired radius, using a steel ruler as a guide.

An adjustable **bar compass** is used to make sweeping arcs and circles that are too large to be made with dividers or a compass. The bar compass is a straight beam, usually 24 to 36" in length, although there are no limitations on how long you can make the beam. The compass has a fixed, pivoting point at one end of the

A bar compass for scribing larger circles and arcs can be purchased or homemade.

beam and a sliding housing for your marking tool at the other end. A bar compass is a more reliable tool than trammel points, which are also attached (but not permanently) to a long beam.

Making Project Drawings

*Draw on these skills
to document your creative
woodworking ideas.*

To make accurate drawings, all you'll need is a simple drafting tool kit that includes: a smooth, flat drawing board, a T-square, artist's tape, a precise ruler, plastic triangles with 30°, 45°, 60°, and 90° angles, a compass, and drawing pencils.

As you become more skilled as a woodworker, you will eventually want to express your creativity by altering existing plans to your own taste, or by creating your own unique woodworking projects from scratch. But your creative ideas are little more than fantasy unless you can represent them on paper. Learning a few basic drawing skills can greatly enhance your creativity as a woodworker—especially if you plan to share or sell your project ideas.

Construction drawings for woodworking projects can be drawn two-dimensionally, as a series of front, top, and end views; or three-dimensionally, as *isometric* or *perspective* drawings. Two-dimensional sketches, which are fairly easy to draw, are all you need for many simpler designs. Three-dimensional sketches are more complicated to draw, but are very helpful for showing how all the parts in a detailed project fit together.

All construction drawings should be drawn to scale for accuracy (a 1 to 4 ratio, where ¼" in the drawing represents 1" in actual size, is a common scale for woodworking drawings).

DESIGN TIP

There are several different styles of lines used to create woodworking construction drawings. Visible lines (A) are solid; they show the edges of components. Break lines (B) are used to indicate that a drawing has been interrupted—usually to save space. Hidden lines (C) are dotted lines used to represent elements that are hidden from view. Dimension lines (D) are used to indicate precise measurements between points marked with crossing lines. Label lines (E) have either arrows or bullets on one tip, and are used to identify specific elements in a drawing. Centerlines (F) are drawn to mark the middle of project parts, providing a convenient reference for establishing measurements.

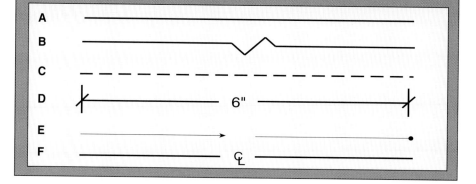

Elements of a construction drawing

In addition to the basic front, top, and end views, with each part of the project accurately represented to scale, a good construction drawing should include the following elements:

Identification of parts: All components of the project should be labeled with key letters that correspond to an itemized cutting list.

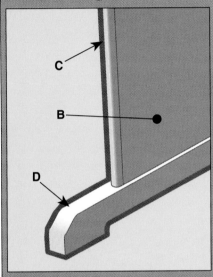

Cutting list: An item-by-item cutting list showing the exact finished size of each component in the drawing will simplify construction and helps you estimate costs of materials.

CUTTING LIST

Key	Qty.	Description & Size
A	2	**Panel top,** 1 × 5 × 64½"
B	2	**Panel bottom,** 1 × 8 × 64½"
C	2	**Foot post,** 3 × 3 × 38"
D	2	**Head post,** 3 × 3 × 44"
E	2	**Bed rail,** 1 × 5½ × 80"
F	4	**Cross rail,** 1½ × 3½ × 60"
G	16	**Foot slat,** ½ × 2½ × 16½"
H	16	**Head slat,** ½ × 2½ × 22½"
I	60	**Slat spacer** (inner), ½ × ½ × 1"
J	8	**Slat spacer** (outer), ½ × ½ × 1½"

Note: All wood is oak.

Misc.: Glue, ½ × 2¾" dowels, #10 × ¾" roundhead and flathead wood screws, keyhole hangers (8), bed-rail fasteners (4).

Measurements: All dimensions of the project should be labeled with exact measurements.

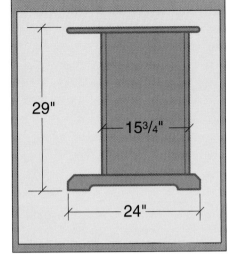

Joinery methods: The methods for constructing joints should be clearly indicated, using a close-up detail drawing, if necessary.

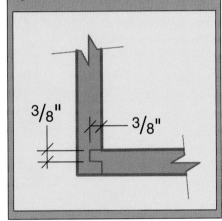

Details: Complex portions of a project should be illustrated with close-up detail drawings. Details are especially useful for areas with curves or unusual angles.

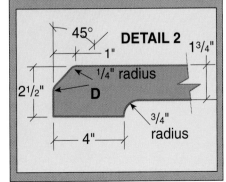

Pattern grids: For parts with elaborate curves or scrollwork, a scaled pattern grid is essential for laying out cutting lines.

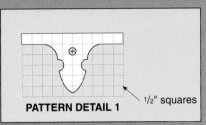

PATTERN DETAIL 1 — ½" squares

Hardware: All dowels, biscuits, screws, nails, and other hardware items should be indicated on the drawing. If it is not possible to show all hardware, use the label "typical" to indicate that the shown hardware item also represents others not visible.

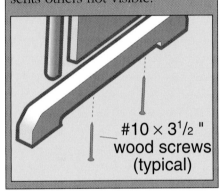

#10 × 3½" wood screws (typical)

Section views: Show the location of hidden components not visible in the standard two-dimensional views by making cross-section drawings.

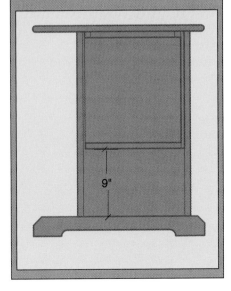

An easy-to-make drawing board can be constructed from rows of horizontal maple boards joined with glue and dowels, framed on each side by vertical boards that provide a straight edge for aligning your T-square (See *Gluing and Clamping, pages 118 to 121*).

Making construction drawings

A square, flat drawing surface is essential for making accurate construction drawings. You could buy a prefabricated (and expensive) drafting table to do your work, or you can build your own drawing surface by gluing up ¾" maple or birch stock. A handy, portable drawing surface should be at least 18" square and should be belt-sanded smooth so it is completely flat.

1 Tape a sheet of drawing paper to the center of your drawing board, aligning the edge of the paper with the edge of your T-square.

2 Choose a scale for your drawing. A scale of 1:4, where ¼" on the drawing actually equals 1" on the project, is a common scale for woodworking drawings.

your project in the lower left corner of the paper. Use the T-square aligned with the edge of your drawing board as a guide for drawing horizontal lines, and use a plastic triangle aligned against the T-square as a guide for drawing vertical lines.

4 Draw and label a top view of the project directly above the front view.

5 Draw a side view of the project directly to the right of the front view.

6 Use a compass, circle template, or French curve as a guide for drawing curved lines, like the rounded corners on a desk.

7 Make cross-section drawings to show any elements that can't be seen in the other views.

portions of the project. Mark the degree measurements of all angles and the radius measurements of all curves.

9 If your drawing is cluttered or messy, lay fresh tracing paper over the drawing and trace a clean outline of the drawing.

10 Add alphabetical key letters to identify the parts of the project.

11 Create a detailed cutting list showing the sizes of each piece keyed in the drawing.

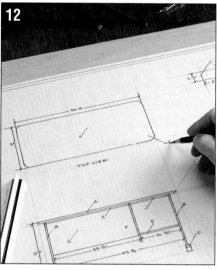

12 Draw in dimension lines and show all pertinent measurements in the drawing.

13 Indicate all hardware on the drawing, including screws, nails, brackets, dowels, biscuits, hinges, and handles.

14 If you wish, add shading to your drawing with colored pencils for a finished look.

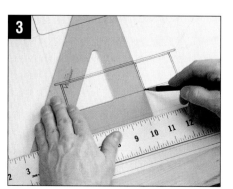

3 Begin your drawing by outlining the two-dimensional front view of

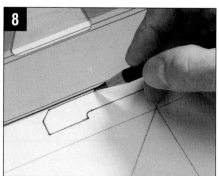

8 Make detail drawings to show close-up details of complicated

WOODWORKER'S TIP

To copyright an orginal woodworking design, obtain a copy of application form VA (visual arts material) from the federal copyright office (call Forms & Publications hotline, 202-287-9100). Complete the form, and send it along with the registration fee and one complete copy of your design to:

Register of Copyrights
Library of Congress
Washington, D.C. 20559

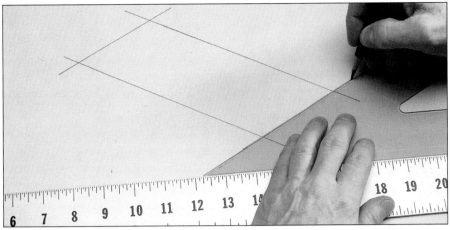

Most lines in an isometric three-dimensional drawing are made with the aid of a T-square and 30°-60°-90° triangle.

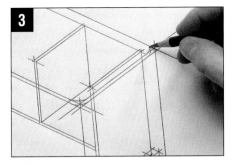

3 Sketch in the curved areas and unusual angles, like the rounded edges of a desk.
4 Shade the visible edges of the design so it will clearly show through when you trace the final outline.

Three-dimensional drawings

Although two-dimensional drawings are all you'll need for many woodworking projects, a three-dimensional drawing makes your design easier to understand, particularly with complex projects with many parts.

There are several styles of three-dimensional construction drawings, including perspective and isometric views.

Perspective drawing is most realistic, because lines converge as they move from foreground to background, making elements appear to get smaller as they get farther away from the eye. Mastering this drawing technique requires training.

Isometric drawing is considerably easier to learn. In isometric drawing, all the lines are drawn at set angles with the aid of plastic triangles (see *photo,* above). Lines that are parallel in real space are also parallel in the drawing. Isometric drawings look slightly unrealistic because there is no attempt to make lines converge, but are very easy to interpret.

1 Tape drawing paper to the center of your drawing board. Begin your three-dimensional drawing by sketching the foreground parts of the design (see *photo,* above). For most drawings, use a plastic triangle with a 30° angle as a guide for drawing the horizontal, receding lines (steeper angles, like 45° or 60°, will give the illusion of a higher viewpoint for the design).

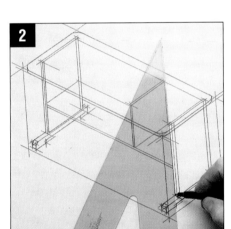

2 Continue the drawing by sketching the remaining parts of the project, working from foreground to background. Use dotted lines to indicate parts that are hidden from view.

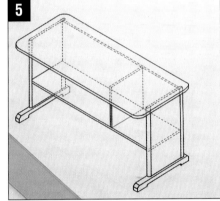

5 Lay tracing paper over the rough drawing and trace a final outline of the project.
6 Add alphabetic key letters to identify parts, measurement graphics, and hardware items. For a more finished look, shade in the parts using colored pencils (see *photo,* below).

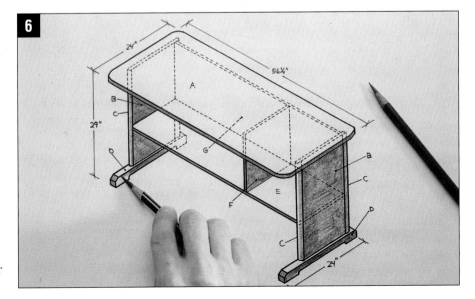

Enlarging Grid Patterns

Make full-sized patterns using old-fashioned or modern methods.

The grid patterns that accompany many woodworking articles are rarely printed full-size, unless they're for a small-scale project. Enlarging and reproducing a pattern to full-size is not difficult, and knowing how to do it gives you the flexibility to change the size of a project if desired. There are several different ways to do it, and the simplest method, transferring by hand, requires just a piece of paper with grid squares, a pencil, a ruler or other marking tool (see *Measuring and Marking,* pages 10 and 11), and an eraser (just in case).

Transferring by hand

Begin by checking the scale provided in the project grid pattern. If it says "each square equals 1"," for instance, you'll need graph paper with 1" squares to make a grid for the full-sized pattern. For simple patterns, you can easily transfer the pattern to the full-sized grid by eye, but for more complicated designs, follow these steps to ensure good results.

1 Buy graph paper, or use a straightedge to draw a grid for the full-sized pattern with squares that are the size needed according to the scale given.

2 Label the vertical lines in the project grid pattern alphabetically, and then label the corresponding lines alphabetically in the full-sized pattern grid.

3 Label the horizontal lines in the project grid pattern numerically, then number the corresponding horizontal lines in the full-sized pattern grid.

4 Looking at one square at a time on the project grid pattern, locate the points where the pattern lines intersect a grid line, and mark points at the same location on the full-sized pattern grid. Use the letters and numbers at the top and side of the grid to keep track of which square you're working on.

5 On the full-sized grid, draw connecting lines between the dots, using a straightedge or other marking tool, to complete the pattern outline.

Determining enlargements

If you have access to a photocopier, making a full-sized reproduction of a pattern can go more quickly than doing it by hand, but you'll still need to figure out what percentage to enlarge or reduce the original. You can do this by using either a ruler and calculator, or by using a handy tool called a proportion wheel.

Using a calculator, divide the scale size for each square by the actual measured size of each square. For example, if the project grid is keyed as one square equals 1", and the squares as shown are actually ½" wide, divide 1 by ½ to get 2. Press the percentage key (or multiply by 100) to see how much you'll need to enlarge the original grid pattern—it will be 200% in this case.

A proportion wheel is an inexpensive item (available at most art supply stores), and is often used to determine the percentage by which an image needs to be enlarged or reduced to fit a space.

1 Measure the actual length of one side of the project grid pattern, then find this number on the "Original size" scale on the proportion wheel.

2 Check the scale provided with the pattern, then multiply the number of squares, along the same side as you measured before, by this number. For exam-ple, if the project grid pattern has eight squares across and the scale given says each square equals ½", divide 8 by ½, which equals 16. Find this number on the "Repro-duction size" scale on the propor-tion wheel. Note: If you are customizing the size of the project, find the desired finished size number on the "Reproduction size" scale.

3 Line up the original-size and re-production-size numbers by rotat-ing the wheels; then read the percentage that appears in the "Percentage of original size" win-dow below them. This is how much the grid will need to be en-larged on the photocopier to cre-ate the desired finished size.

Making enlargements in stages

Once you've determined the en-largement needed to create a full-sized pattern, check the possible enlargement settings on your photocopier. Many photocopiers have a maximum enlargement capability (usually 150%), so you may need to make the full-sized enlargement in several stages. This generally means making an initial enlargement at the photo-copier's maximum setting, and then enlarging the enlargement again and again until you reach the desired full-sized enlargement.

It will be easier if you jot down the required calculations on a sheet of paper before making the enlargements. For the example presented here, we set out to make a 400% enlargement on a photocopier that could only make enlargements up to 150%. Follow these steps and substitute your numbers for those we've used, to achieve the desired results for your project.

1 Begin by dividing the total enlargement desired, 400%, by the photocopier's limit, 150%; in this case, it equals 2.67. If you multiply 2.67 by 100 to convert it to a percentage, the end result is 267%. This percentage is too large for the copier, so you'll need to divide again.

2 Divide the second percentage number, 267%, by the maximum copier setting, 150%—this equals 1.78, or 178%. Again, this percent-age is too large for the photo-copier's enlargement settings, so you'll have to divide again.

3 Divide the third percentage number, 178%, by the photo-copier's maximum setting, 150%, to get the next percentage size, in this case, 1.19, or 119%. The pho-tocopier can make enlargements at this percentage, so this will be the final percentage size.

4 Review your notes—count the number of times you had to di-vide a percentage number by the photocopier's maximum setting to reach the final enlargement size (it was 3 times in this example). For each instance (except the last), make an enlargement at the photocopier's maximum setting, using the most recent photocopy for each subsequent enlargement.

5 Enlarge the last photocopy at the final percentage size, 119%, to reach the desired finished size (400%) for your full-sized pattern.

Sharpening

Good sharpening skills allow you to get the most from your tools and dramatically improve the quality of your projects.

Maintaining a sharp edge on your woodworking tools is of the utmost importance for safety and performance. With the exception of drill bits and saws, most cutting tools are sold with a coarse, factory-made bevel and must be sharpened before use. Proper sharpening increases the life of the tool, improves the quality of the work, and eases the strain on the woodworker. There are many sharpening techniques and styles, and each requires a certain degree of skill and practice. The "correct" method is largely the decision of the individual woodworker.

Traditional Western sharpening methods usually begin by removing the blade's chipped or dull edge with a rough abrasive, often on a motorized grinder or wheel. This basic shaping creates a primary bevel and is followed by the initial sharpening, which removes the roughness through a combination of coarse and fine abrasives.

Natural Arkansas oilstones are excellent, and increasingly rare, sharpening stones. The cost of these stones is prohibitive, making synthetic waterstones a popular sharpening choice.

This step leaves a thin wire burr on the back of the blade. (The back is the side opposite from the bevel.) Instead of bench stones, rubberized abrasive wheels are often used after a bevel is ground onto a sharp edge. The rubberized wheels feature neoprene rubber with silicon carbide embedded in it. These wheels resist oil and water and, unlike conventional wheels, should rotate away from the user to avoid damage. If your grinder cannot reverse direction, sharpen tools on the wheel's side.

Combination grinders combine the qualities of low-speed whetstone sharpeners and high-speed grinders. One side of the machine contains an aluminum oxide wheel, while the other side features a clutch-operated whetstone with a water bath. Some machines feature an abrasive grinding belt. Belts do not heat as rapidly as stones and can be replaced when clogged with metal particles. The initial sharpening is followed by finishing the edge with a fine abrasive, creating a secondary bevel. Many woodworkers add a polishing step with a leather strop or extra-fine abrasives to complete the process.

Using motorized sharpeners

A fast-moving stone quickly removes unwanted metal from an edge. However, when a blade contacts the turning abrasive in dry grinding, considerable heat is produced, which can ruin the temper and damage the blade. To prevent overheating, pull the tool away every five seconds and dip it in water. Wet-grinding systems have a constant source of water or oil spilling on the stone, cooling both the blade and stone.

High-speed grinders are generally equipped with aluminum oxide grinding wheels. Use larger wheels (7 to 8") for the best results. Small-diameter grinding wheels tend to produce inferior bevels. High-speed grinders usually come with both a coarse- and a fine-grade wheel. An adjustable tool rest is also standard. Use the tool rest to brace the tool and stabilize the edge against the wheel. Bolt all high-speed grinders to a stable worksurface.

Motorized whetstones turn at a relatively slow 500 rpm; 1000-grit general-purpose stones are standard on these sharpeners.

Motorized whetstones rotate relatively slowly and are usually equipped with a lubricant reservoir to reduce friction.

Follow these general directions when grinding an edge.

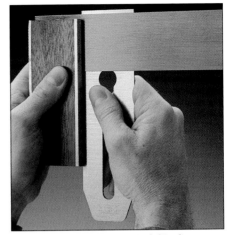

Use a square to ensure a straight edge.

1 Use a square to check the cutting edge. If it is uneven, draw a line square to the long edges across the front edge of the blade so you can grind away any nicks or dents.
2 Mount a medium or rough-grit wheel on the grinder.
3 Hold the blade against the tool rest so the blade touches the stone at a right angle to the surface.
4 With the blade on the rest, slide the blade back and forth across the wheel until the edge is shaped. Check for square.

Grind a chisel bevel to 20° for softwoods, 27° for hardwoods.

5 To cut a bevel on the blade, use a medium or fine-grit wheel. Hold the blade on the rest at the proper angle. Most tool rests will have a 20 to 30° surface suitable for chisel or plane blades. A chisel bevel should be 20° for softwoods

and 27° for hardwoods. For general-purpose chisel work, 25°

The secondary bevel, or microbevel, puts a sharp edge on the factory-ground angle.

is best. Plane blades and hand chisels are hollow ground, meaning a major bevel is ground first, followed by a small secondary bevel, or microbevel, to produce a sharp cutting edge.

6 Keeping the blade flat on the angled rest and perpendicular to the wheel, slide the blade up until it contacts the wheel. Then slide the blade back and forth to produce a slightly concave cut on the blade. The cut should not quite reach the cutting edge of the blade.

7 Do not press too hard on the tool and keep the blade cool by dipping it frequently in water. If the blade metal overheats and turns blue, you must grind the blade beyond this damaged area to recover the tool.

Synthetic waterstones match the quality of natural Japanese waterstones at a lower cost.

> ## WORKSHOP TIP
>
> *It is possible to sharpen saw blades and drill bits at home, but we recommend you either take these components to a professional, or simply purchase new ones.*

Using diamond sharpeners

Some sharpening stones are available with a diamond grid pattern. Diamond particles are embedded in a plastic base to create fine, coarse, and extra-coarse grits. Use diamond grid stones to flatten worn waterstones or natural oil-stones. Some woodworkers spray diamond particles onto specially made ceramic plates to create a fine grit, or slurry, for sharpening edges. Diamond spray, available in three standard grades, requires a separate piece of ceramic for each grade.

Using oilstones

The traditional Western sharpening tools, oilstones are rectangular blocks lubricated with honing oil. Kerosene is often used to lubricate Natural Arkansas stones, which are commonly considered the best of the oilstone group. Natural Arkansas stones can be categorized into the following groups. *Soft Arkansas* stones are gray in color and feature great coarseness for quick sharpening and rough metal removal. *White Hard Arkansas* stones hone blades to a sharp edge. For extra-fine sharpening, use the *Black Hard Arkansas* stones.

Natural Arkansas stones, though excellent sharpening tools, are becoming increasingly rare and expensive. Many woodworkers have turned to synthetic oilstones, which are made from aluminum-oxide or silicon-carbide grit. They are available in coarse, medium, and fine grades. Synthetic oil-stones are often sold as combination pieces, with two grades glued back to back.

Using waterstones

Waterstones are becoming increasingly popular because of their affordability and ease of use. Coarse waterstones must be stored in water or soaked for about 30 minutes prior to use. Fine waterstones do not require extensive soaking to perform adequately. A properly used waterstone leaves perhaps the finest edge available.

Famous and highly prized, Japanese waterstones are available in both natural and synthetic varieties. Japanese waterstones sharpen quickly with relatively little effort. They come in a wide range of grades, from an 800 coarse grit to an 8000 finishing grit.

Japanese waterstones are used in conjunction with Nagura stones,

> ## WORKSHOP TIP
>
> *A honing guide is recommended for anyone who has trouble holding the edge at a consistent angle while hand-sharpening. Clamp your blades and chisels into the guide at the desired angle and push the device up and down the sharpening surface. Many styles are available.*

which are rubbed onto the stone's sharpening surface prior to sharpening. Nagura stones produce a chalky mixture of water and very fine abrasives that forms a slurry. This slurry is an essential element in this sharpening process, especially on the finest Japanese finishing stones.

Hand-lapping blades & chisels

Flattening the back of a cutting edge is the first step in sharpening. To flatten the back, you must smooth, or lap, the back surface. This part of the process is often overlooked. No matter how much time is spent developing a sharp bevel with expensive stones or grinders, scratches on the back of the blade will prevent the edge from being smooth. To lap a cutting tool, follow these instructions.
1 Spread 280-grit to 600-grit silicon-carbide abrasive powder and oil on a flat piece of glass. Make sure the glass is large enough to lap the piece.
2 Rub the back of the blade against the glass in the mixture. This constant rubbing motion eventually breaks down the oil and abrasive mixture into a sharpening slurry.
3 Wipe away the used slurry. Spread a finer powder and some oil on the glass, and repeat until the back is completely flattened.

Hand-sharpening blades & chisels

Plane blades and chisels are sharpened in the same way, with one notable exception. Plane blades are rocked slightly against the sharpening stone to round off the edge corners. Before you begin sharpening, always make sure your stone is adequately lubricated.

Most bench plane blades and chisels are ground with a 25° bevel. This angle is too weak for hardwood. To put a secondary bevel at the very edge of the blade for increased strength or cutting ability, start with a medium-grade stone. Put the blade on the surface, bevel down, and rock it slightly until the bevel is flush with the stone. Lift the

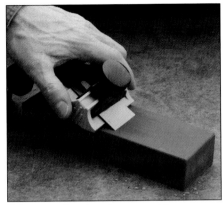
Put a secondary bevel on your chisel or bench plane blade to strengthen the cutting edge and improve performance.

blade slightly to make the secondary bevel. Rub the blade up and down the stone, being careful to maintain a constant angle. If the edge is wider than sharpening surface, turn the edge slightly so the whole piece is in contact with the stone. With smaller edges, such as narrow chisels, remember to use entire surface to avoid excessive wear in one section of the stone.

Once you create a secondary bevel, use a fine stone on the edge to raise a burr on the back side of your blade. Then hone the back of the blade to break the burr and create a sharp edge. For most applications, further polishing with a leather strop is completely optional.

Sharpening Gouges

To sharpen out-cannel gouges, rub the edges side to side across the sharpening stone in a figure-eight pattern to even the wear. Remove the burr with a slipstone or a Carver's stone, thin sharpening

A Carver's stone is designed to fit the varied shapes of carving tools.

stones designed for gouges. Sharpen an in-cannel gouge using the stones in reverse order. Use a slipstone or a Carver's stone for best results in honing the edge, then remove the edge burr by turning the gouge on a fine sharpening stone.

Maintaining stones

Proper care and maintenance of sharpening stones ensures long life and good results. Cover oilstones and waterstones when not in use to prevent dust buildup. When an oilstone gets clogged with oil and metal particles, clean it thoroughly with paraffin oil and coarse burlap.

Always store waterstones in water. Vinyl storage boxes are available to keep them moist.

True the waterstone by rubbing it along a piece of wet 200-grit silicon-carbide paper.

Sharpening stones have a tendency to wear down at their center from the constant wear. Keep your oilstone true by flattening it on a sheet of glass with lubricant and carborundum powder. A waterstone can be flattened by rubbing it with a piece of wet 200-grit silicon-carbide paper taped onto a piece of glass.

WORKSHOP TIP

One way to keep a blade cool when grinding on a wheel is to hot-glue a piece of sponge to the back of the blade near the cutting edge. Dip the blade in water. The sponge holds water against the back of the blade to draw off the heat. When the sponge gets warm, wet it again.

CHAPTER 2

Woodworking Tools

Tools of the Trade

Everything you need to know about tools and accessories is here! Our woodworking experts tell you how to buy them, how to set them up, and how to use them safely.

Without doubt, tools are the essential element of a woodworking shop. They also are the most costly. The information in this chapter will help you maximize your tool budget. It will help you decide which tools and accessories are essential and which are embellishments. To make wise tool-buying decisions, read the practical data and tips included on the following pages.

Pushsticks and Featherboards 24
Tablesaw Basics 26
Saw Blades 30
Circular Saw 32
Scrollsaw Basics 34
Bandsaw Basics 36
Power Miter Box 40
Sabersaw Basics 42
Router Basics 44
Lathe Basics 48
Stationary Power Sanders 52
Drill Press Basics 54
Drill Bit Guide 58
Portable Drills...60
Handsaws 62
Hand Planes 64

Guard removed
for clarity

Use a pushstick and a featherboard to cut narrow pieces on your tablesaw. The pushstick keeps your fingers at a safe distance from the blade, and helps guide your workpiece past the blade for a clean cut. The featherboard fingers flex and hold the workpiece against the fence.

Pushsticks and Feather-boards

Reach for these tools to lend a safe and helping hand.

Pushsticks and featherboards are simple, but extremely effective, safety accessories. Among seasoned woodworkers, a distinctive homemade jig is regarded as the signature of a true artisan. Coming up with your own designs is often rewarding.

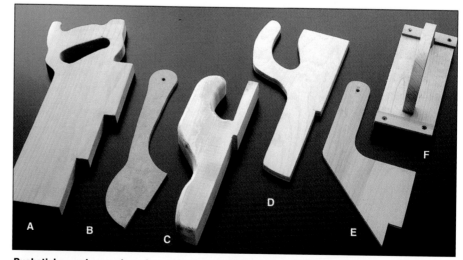

A   B   C   D   E   F

Pushsticks can be purchased or made in a wide range of styles and materials, as shown *above*. By making your own, you can design pushsticks that will fit your hand easily and securely, and will be practical for whatever job you're doing. For example, you may be more comfortable working with a pushstick with a handle that is set back from the notch when you're cutting smaller workpieces (A,B,D, and E). Or you may want the handle to be located over the notch to help you hold a workpiece down (C and F). It can be a satisfying challenge to come up with unique and creative pushstick designs.

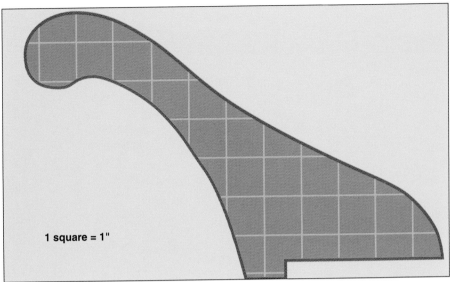

1 square = 1"

This pushstick design is best for cutting narrow strips of wood. The handle is positioned to give you good leverage and control over your work, while keeping you at a safe distance from the saw blade. It lets you safely hold the wood down and guide it forward at the same time.

Making a pushstick

Pushsticks can be as simple as a block of wood with a notch cut along one edge. But to be useful, a pushstick has to have a notch that is slightly less high than the thickness of the wood you're cutting. This way, the pushstick rests solely on the workpiece, instead of on the cutting surface. The pushstick also has to fit between the saw blade and the fence; take this into account when designing your own.

Make a pattern for your pushstick shape by drawing an outline on a piece of heavyweight paper. Tape the pattern to a piece of wood (we used pine), then cut

DESIGN TIP

Give the pushstick increased gripping power by cutting and gluing a small strip of sandpaper or rubber from a bicycle inner tube to the inner edges of the notch.

out the pushstick shape following the pattern, using a bandsaw or scrollsaw. Sand the edges to remove any rough edges. Because you'll generally be working with different wood thicknesses all the time, you're going to need a few different pushsticks for almost every project you do. Make several at a time so you'll have them.

Using a pushstick

Whether you're cutting materials on a tablesaw, jointer, planer, or a router table, it's very important to use the pushstick to guide the workpiece *all the way past the cutting blade.* Use the pushstick to press the workpiece forward and down. Otherwise you may run the risk of dangerous kickback.

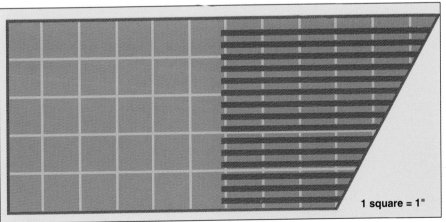

1 square = 1"

The width and length of the fingers affect how much flex and holding power the featherboard has. Keep several different ones around so they'll be handy for whatever work you're doing.

Making a featherboard

Featherboards have thin fingers that are cut off at an angle at the ends. The fingers flex slightly when the featherboard is clamped against a workpiece, which lets you move the workpiece forward while holding the workpiece

securely against a tablesaw fence or other brace.

To make the featherboard, cut a 5 × 10" piece of wood (we used maple). It should be laid out so fingers will be parallel to wood grain. Draw a line across the board, 6" from one end. Cut off the end of the board farthest from the line at a 30° angle. Using the line as a stopping point, cut the ¼"-wide fingers, using your tablesaw. Then, go back and cut along the center of each finger using a bandsaw. Sand the rough outer edges.

Using a featherboard

A featherboard can be used to keep your workpiece from shifting sideways or upward, depending on where you position it. Set your workpiece on the cutting surface, then push the featherboard against the workpiece, at the side or above, until the featherboard teeth bend slightly. Clamp it to the fence or cutting surface.

When you use the featherboard with your tablesaw, be sure to position it on the blade *infeed* side. Don't put the featherboard on the outfeed side of the blade, because it will pinch your workpiece against the saw blade. When you're using tools other than a table saw, make sure to position the featherboard parallel to, or just in front of, the cutting blade.

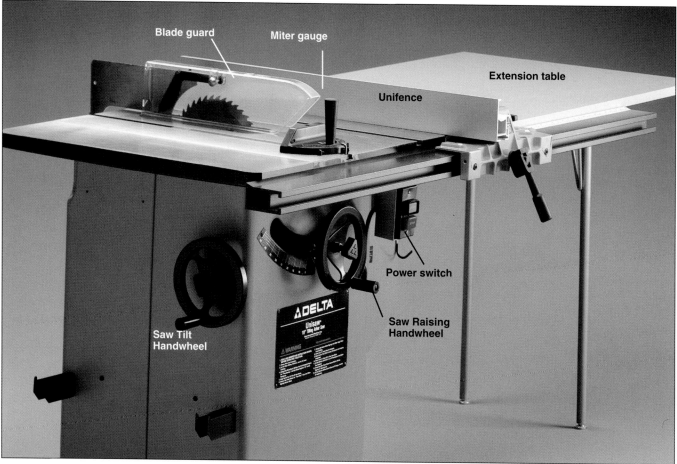

A top-of-the-line tablesaw forms the heart of the serious woodworker's shop. This 10", 2 hp. stationary saw has been equipped with an extension table to handle large sheet goods and a precision Unifence rip fence for increased accuracy.

Tablesaw Basics

The first power tool for woodworkers is still the most popular.

A tablesaw is possibly the most useful stationary tool the woodworker can own. If your budget or shop space can accommodate only one large tool, a good tablesaw is your best choice. A modern tablesaw, combined with a few jigs and accessories, can perform almost any woodworking task.

If you're choosing your first tablesaw, you'll need to consider the size of the tool, cutting capacity, the power of the motor the quality of the table, and the available accessories.

Tablesaw models are generally categorized as either portable or stationary. Portable saws, often called "tabletop" or "bench" saws, are a good choice for small workshops where the ability to rearrange workstations is needed. The motor and basic components of a good-quality bench tablesaw are in no way inferior to larger and more expensive stationary saws. Stationary tablesaws, however, do have larger table surfaces, and are more easily adapted to some accessories.

You'll also need to consider cutting capacity and blade size when choosing a tablesaw. Cutting ca-

pacity for a tablesaw is usually defined by the thickest lumber it can crosscut and bevel-cut—a measurement most directly related

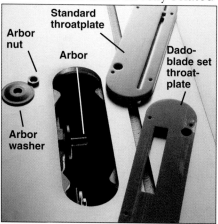

The throat plate on your tablesaw can be removed to provide access for attaching saw blades to the arbor. If you use specialty blades, like a dado-blade set or a molding cutterhead, you may need to make custom throat plates with slots that fit wider blades.

A benchtop saw can be stored out of sight until needed and carried to your work area easily when you're ready to work.

to the size of the blade. A tablesaw that uses a 10"-diameter blade (the most common type of woodworker's tablesaw) can crosscut wood up to 3⅛" thick (a few models can cut lumber up to 4" thick). With the blade set to bevelcut at 45°, a 10" saw can generally cut through stock up to 2⅛" thick.

By contrast, a tablesaw with an 8¼"-diameter blade will crosscut stock up to 2¼" thick, and will bevel-cut 1¾" stock at 45°. Cutting capacity varies considerably from saw to saw, even on saws with the same blade size, so check owner's manuals and manufacturer's catalogs for precise specifications.

Whether you choose a portable or stationary model, your tablesaw will be the main workhorse of the workshop. It should have a motor with adequate horsepower, especially if you use your saw daily, or in sessions that last several hours at a time.

Tablesaw models designed for home workshops generally have

motor horsepower ratings that fall between ½ and 3 hp. Although smaller horsepower saws are adequate for the occasional hobbyist, a larger motor operates with less strain through most sawing operations and will be more durable.

In some tablesaw designs, the saw is driven directly by the motor; others transfer power to the blade through a belt. Belt-drive construction generally puts less stress on the motor, and produces better cutting than direct-drive construction.

Most tablesaws are wired to plug into standard 120-volt household current, but some can be converted to 220-volt current. Operating at the higher voltage increases the motor's power output and lessens the strain on the motor.

A sturdy, smooth table surface made of cast steel or iron will resist vibration and allow you to cut accurately.

Next to the motor, construction of the table surface is the most important element in judging the quality of a tablesaw. Look for a smooth, cast-metal surface, with miter slots that are machined into the surface, not pressed. Test the miter gauge to make sure it slides

smoothly in the slot, and does not wobble. Lock the rip fence and make sure it doesn't move when you push against it.

Tablesaw accessories

Many accessories are available to make your tablesaw more versatile and more accurate. If you'll be acquiring any of these accessories, make sure to buy a saw that will accommodate them.

Auxiliary support tables and precision rip fences are expensive accessories that generally work best with larger, stationary saws.

Dado-blade sets and molding cutterheads let you use your tablesaw to make grooves and decorative shaping cuts. Most tablesaws, both portable and stationary, can accept these specialty blades, but you will need to remove the saw's throatplate and replace it with a purchased or homemade throatplate designed to fit the blade.

Setting up your tablesaw

Set up your tablesaw workstation so there is plenty of room around it for handling large workpieces. If you plan to cut plywood panels, this means at least 8' on the infeed and outfeed ends, 8' to the right side and 4' to the left side of the blade. Especially in small shops, it's helpful to have all the surrounding tables or benches at the same height as the saw table, so they can be used to support the work.

It's a good idea to install a separate, dedicated electrical circuit for your saw. A tablesaw motor takes quite a lot of power, especially under load. If powered by a circuit that also supports other large appliances, your tablesaw may overload the circuit, tripping the circuit breaker. Sudden power losses put considerable strain on your saw motor.

Install a large fluorescent light fixture over the spot where you'll do most of your cutting. (Fluorescent bulbs give light that is more even and shadow-free than incandescent bulbs.) Good lighting helps you keep an eye on the spinning blade and on your layout lines, and will lessen the strain on your eyes. If the lighting fixture you choose does not have a panel or guard over the bulb, make one from wire fencing or screening.

Once your tablesaw is in place, you'll need to adjust it before you start cutting. For accurate, safe cutting, the main components of your saw (table, blade, fence, and miter gauge) must be square and perpendicular to one another.

Most saws are relatively easy to adjust, but the adjustment techniques are also specific to each different saw model. Your best source of information on how to square-up your saw is found in the owner's manual.

A good tablesaw holds its alignment better than many other large power tools, but before each work session you should quickly check the blade and fence alignment, and make adjustments as necessary.

When checking blade alignment, make sure to position the blade of your square between the teeth so the angle (set) of the saw teeth does not affect the measurement.

Aligning the blade to the table:
For basic crosscutting and ripcutting, raise the blade to fullest height and set the bevel angle at 90°. Set one leg of a try square or small framing square flat on the saw table, and align the vertical leg with the flat surface of the blade. If the vertical leg of the square is not perfectly flush with the blade, you'll need to adjust the alignment according to manufacturer's directions. For bevel angles, use a plastic drafting angle (or a homemade jig cut to the desired angle) to check the blade angle.

Aligning the rip fence to the miter-gauge slot: Plane and cut a piece of 1½"-wide hardwood to the same width and length as your miter-gauge slot. Place the board

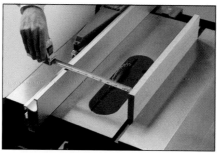

Aligning the rip fence to the miter-gauge slot ensures straight cuts.

into the the miter-gauge slot and move the rip fence against it. If any gaps appear between the fence and the board, you'll need to adjust your fence. Keep the board handy so you can quickly check rip-fence alignment before each work session.

Aligning the saw blade to the miter-gauge slot: This simple jig will help you quickly check to make sure your saw blade is parallel to the miter-gauge slot and rip fence. Cut a 12"-long piece of hardwood the same thickness and depth as the miter-gauge slot. Cut a 12"-long piece of ¼" plywood about 1" wider than the distance from the miter-gauge slot to the saw blade. Attach the hardwood strip to one edge of the plywood, exactly flush with the edge, using glue and wire brads. After the glue dries, lower the blade on your tablesaw so it is below the throat

plate. Place the jig in the miter slot so the plywood is over the blade. Turn your saw on and slowly raise the blade through the jig to its full height. (Hold the plywood down with a piece of scrap wood as you raise the blade.)

Turn off the saw, remove the jig, and measure the distance from the edge of the hardwood strip to each end of the cut. If the measurements are the same, the blade is square: Turn your saw on and pass the jig through the blade to trim it to final size. (If measurements differ, adjust the blade alignment and try again.)

To check the saw blade alignment before work sessions, simply lay the jig into the miter slot and check to make sure the blade is flush against the plywood with no gaps.

WOODWORKER'S TIP

Listen to the tablesaw as you cut. If your saw motor starts to lug down, you're probably feeding the wood across the saw blade too quickly. If the saw blade binds and starts to slow down, stop the motor immediately and remove the workpiece. Never try to force a pinched or warped workpiece through the saw; this often causes dangerous kickbacks.

Ripcutting

Ripcutting parallel to the wood grain is the single most common task for the tablesaw. Its broad, flat blade gives a far straighter rip cut than can be achieved on a bandsaw or other stationary saws.

To do ripcutting on your tablesaw, you'll need to use the rip fence and mount your saw with a rip blade or combination blade. Rip blades generally have larger teeth spaced farther apart than those on a crosscut blade.
1 Fit the rip blade in your saw and set the tilt at the desired angle. Set the blade just high enough so the tips of the teeth will clear the surface of the wood by ⅛". Setting the blade too high increases friction on the blade and wear on the motor.

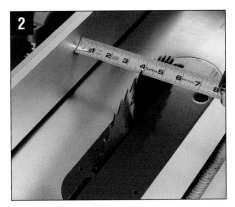

2 Adjust the rip fence to the desired width by measuring from the fence to one of the inward-set teeth on the blade. (It's a good idea to measure the width, even when your rip fence is equipped with a scale. Many fences are knocked out of adjustment quite easily, so the scale becomes inaccurate until it's readjusted.) Lock the fence in position, then before making the cut, check the width again.

Guard removed for clarity

3 Clamp a featherboard to the table on the infeed side of the blade to hold the workpiece against the rip fence (see *Pushsticks and Featherboards, pages 24 and 25*). Start the saw, and position the workpiece against the fence. Feed the workpiece smoothly into the blade, making sure the splitter on the blade guard slides into the kerf on the workpiece.
4 Guide the board through the blade in one smooth pass, using a pushstick to feed it across the blade. Don't pause, because the spinning blade may chip or burn the wood.

When ripping long stock, it's helpful to have extra support on the infeed and outfeed side of the saw table. One option is to build sawhorses to match the height of the saw table. Waxing the tops of the sawhorses lets materials slide more easily.

Crosscutting

Most crosscutting tasks are easily performed on the tablesaw. Because the saw must sever all the wood fibers, a crosscutting blade with smaller, more closely spaced teeth is the best choice.

Basic crosscutting is usually done with the tablesaw's miter gauge. When the gauge is properly squared, according to the owner's manual, and set at 90°, it holds the workpiece perpendicular to the blade. As with any cut, it is a good idea to test-cut scrap materials to ensure that the miter gauge is positioned accurately. For crosscutting long workpieces, a hold-down or miter gauge extension attached to the head of your miter gauge will help steady your work (see *Joining Wood, page 116*).
1 Set the miter gauge at 90°, and set the tablesaw blade so the tips of the teeth will clear the surface of the wood by ⅛".

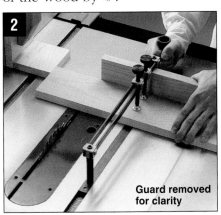

Guard removed for clarity

2 Mark a cutting line on the workpiece, then place the workpiece

against the miter gauge and position it so the blade is aligned on the waste side of the cutting line and the inward-facing saw teeth just touch the line (if you need to cut many pieces to the same length, a stop block clamped to your rip fence can help quickly cut identical pieces). To avoid kickback, never pinch a workpiece between the blade and the rip fence when crosscutting.
3 Tighten the hold-down on your miter gauge (if it is equipped with one) or grip it tightly to hold the workpiece steady, then turn on your saw and feed the workpiece across the blade.

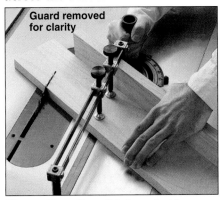

Guard removed for clarity

When cutting miters, it is important to use a miter gauge with a hold-down, because the workpiece has a natural tendency to slide along the head of the miter gauge as it is pushed across the blade.

Maintenance

Prevent overheating and prolong the life of your saw by frequently clearing sawdust from around the motor and control housings. Be sure to follow all the manufacturer's maintenance recommendations.

WORKSHOP TIPS

Because the tablesaw can be used for so many specific tasks, additional information on its use can be found throughout this book. Please see the following pages:
• *Woodworking Tools, page 24* (Pushsticks and Featherboards).
• *Shaping Wood, pages 96 and 97* (Cutting Tapers).
• *Joining Wood, pages 108 and 109* (Box Joints), *110 and 111* (Dadoes and Rabbets), *and 114 to 117* (Miter-Joint Techniques and Jigs).

Saw Blades

Choosing the right blade is essential to fine-quality woodworking.

Common circular saw blades include: carbide-tipped combination blade (A), hollow-ground planer blade (B), a steel alloy rip blade (C), plywood blade (D), and crosscut blade (E).

The success of any woodworking project depends on smooth, precise cutting of the individual pieces—a skill that begins with the choice of the right saw blade for the job.

Circular blades

Circular blades for tablesaws, radial-arm saws, and circular saws are first categorized by diameter, ranging from 6" to 12". Generally, you'll want to use saw blades that match the size specified by your saw, although most saws will let you mount smaller diameter blades.

Blade shape: The next important classification is based on the overall shape of the blade and its cutting teeth. For smooth cutting without tearout or binding, all circular blades are shaped so that they are slightly thicker at the outside diameter near the cutting teeth than they are in the center. There are three basic ways to achieve this effect: by "setting" the teeth at a slight outward angle to the blade; by flattening the ends of the teeth or attaching wider carbide steel tips; or by "hollow-grinding" the blade so the inner area is thinner than the outer portion of the blade.

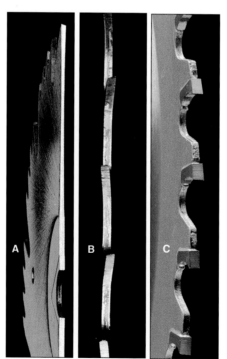

Three different shapes for circular blades include: the hollow-ground blade (A), the set-tooth blade (B), and a carbide-tipped blade with tips brazed onto the tooth face (C).

Type of cut: Blade designs also can be categorized according to the types of cuts for which they are best suited, or by the kinds of materials they cut best. These classifications are determined primarily by the shape, size, and number of cutting teeth, as well as the basic shape of the blade itself.

Combination blades feature sets of four or five beveled, crosscutting teeth that alternate with straight, ripcutting "raker" teeth.

Planer blades, sometimes called *precision-trim,* give glass-smooth, precise cuts for fine cabinetry. To minimize tearout, they are usually hollow-ground, and have teeth with little or no angle (set) to them. Deep gullets spaced every four or five teeth help the blade dissipate heat, clear chips, and prevent it from wobbling.

Rip blades have fewer, larger teeth than crosscut blades. The teeth are hooked forward sharply and are straight at the tips to quickly remove wood fibers.

Plywood blades, sometimes called *panel* blades or *trimming/parting* blades, have many small teeth, and sometimes are designed so the outer rim is thinner than the center of the blade. This design gives smooth cuts with minimal tearout.

BUYER'S TIP

For most blade types, you'll be able to choose among varying numbers of teeth. A 10" combination blade, for example, is available with as few as 18 teeth or as many as 80. In general, blades with more teeth will cut smoother, but slower, than those with fewer teeth.

WORKSHOP TIP

Most of today's tablesaws and radial-arm saws can be mounted with shaping head accessories, including dado-blade sets (see Joining Wood, *page 112).*

They are used for cutting plywood, veneer, and plastic laminates. *Crosscut blades* generally have medium-sized teeth spaced close together. The tips often are angled (set) to help the teeth slice through wood fibers without tearing. *Specialty blades:* A variety of specialty blades is available for cutting materials other than wood. Abrasive blades made of silicon carbide let you cut ceramics. Aluminum oxide blades are used to cut metals. Metal blades coated with nonstick Teflon work well for cutting green wood, treated lumber, or glue-saturated materials like particleboard.

The carbide-steel revolution

Saw-blade manufacturers are now offering a growing number of blades that feature carbide-steel cutting tips bonded to steel alloy teeth. Carbide-tipped teeth are available for most types of saw blades—crosscut, ripcut, combination, and precision-trim.

The different types of carbide-tipped blades look very similar at first glance, because the teeth themselves are shaped much the same. The difference between combination, ripcut, and crosscut blades lies in small variations in the shape of the carbide tips, so it's important to check labels closely to ensure that you select the right saw blade.

Although they are more expensive than steel alloy blades, carbide-tipped blades last much longer, and the performance is so good that many woodworkers will use no other type of blade. Don't try to sharpen carbide-tipped blades yourself, though; the tips are so hard and brittle that only a specialist with the proper tools can do this job.

Bandsaw blades

The best blades for bandsaws use "bimetal" or "flex-back" construction in which a thin strip of hard tool steel is bonded to a backing strip of more flexible spring steel. The result is a blade that is much less likely to break than older blade types.

Avoid bandsaw blades advertised as "soft-edge" blades that can be resharpened. Trying to sharpen bandsaw blades is usually a waste of effort; buy "hard-edge" blades and simply replace them when they get dull.

Size: Bandsaw blades are available in several widths, ranging from ⅛" to ¾". Wider blades will give you a straighter cut, making them a good choice for resawing lumber down to a smaller stock. Narrower blades are best for cutting curves.

Tooth shape: Bandsaw blades come in three different tooth shapes. *Regular-tooth* blades are the standard for general use. The teeth have a shallow hook, producing a relatively smooth cut in most woods. *Skip-tooth* blades have extralong notches (gullets) between teeth for better chip removal and faster cutting. The cut made by a skip-tooth blade, however, is rougher than that made by a regular-tooth blade. Skip-tooth blades are especially good for cutting very thick stock. *Hook-tooth* blades have teeth with a sharp downward angle. They cut very quickly (though roughly) and are good blades for cutting very hard materials.

Specialty blades you can use on your bandsaws include *knife-edge* blades to cut fabric, leather, and cork, and *abrasive bands* that let you use the bandsaw as a loop sander.

WOODWORKER'S TIP

When cutting curves, choose a blade width suitable for the minimum radius you'll be cutting:
- *⅛" blade for 5⁄16" radius*
- *¼" blade for 1" radius*
- *⅜" blade for 1½" radius*
- *½" blade for 2½" radius*

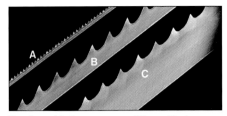

Bandsaw blades use one of three blade shapes: standard-tooth blade (A), hook-tooth blade (B), and skip-tooth blade (C). All three types of blade are available in widths ranging from ⅛" to ¾".

Sabersaw blades

The best sabersaw blades, like the best bandsaw blades, use the bimetal design that bonds hard tool steel to a more flexible strip of spring steel. Sabersaw blades for cutting metal generally have small, closely spaced teeth set at a shallow cutting angle. Wood-cutting blades have larger teeth set at a sharper angle.

Type of cut: Sabersaw blades are usually categorized as *fast-cutting* or *smooth-cutting,* depending on the number of teeth per inch (TPI). Fast-cutting blades for wood have fewer teeth per inch (usually 5 to 7) and give a rougher cut, while smooth-cutting blades for wood have more teeth per inch (10 to 15).

Blade width: Sabersaw blades are commonly available in standard widths (about 5⁄16" wide) and scrolling widths (about 3⁄16" wide).

Specialty blades available for sabersaw include *carbide-coated* blades for cutting ceramics and fiberglass, and *knife-edge* blades for cutting leather and rubber.

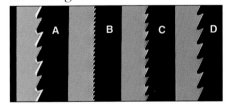

Typical bimetal jigsaw blades include: a 6 TPI blade with beveled (fleam-ground) teeth for very fast cutting in all woods (A), a 24 TPI metal-cutting blade (B), a 10 TPI fine-cutting wood blade (C), and a 6 TPI fast-cutting wood blade (D).

TOOL TIP

For information about scrollsaw blades see Woodworking Tools, *pages 34 and 35.*

Circular Saw

Carry this portable saw to the workplace for quick, accurate cuts.

When a workpiece is too cumbersome to cut on a stationary saw, or when you just want to make a fast, straight cut, use a circular saw. The circular saw's portability, large blade, and high cutting speed make it a valuable addition to your tool collection.

The circular saw consists of a cutting blade mounted on a motor-driven arbor with a fixed upper blade guard, a flat shoe plate, and a handle. For safety, most circular saws have a double-insulated plastic motor casing and a retractable lower blade guard.

You also can adjust the cutting depth on circular saws. The most common method of depth adjustment uses a pivoting shoe plate, hinged in the front. Change the cutting depth by raising or lowering the back of the shoe. On some circular saws, the entire shoe plate can be raised or lowered without tilting.

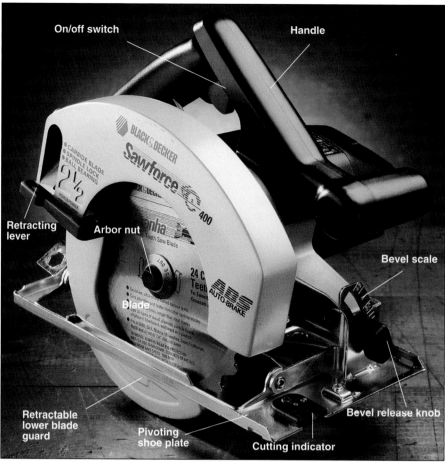

The plastic double-insulated motor casing helps protect the operator against electric shock and keeps the saw lightweight for easy handling.

BUYER'S TIP

• *A 7¼" saw cuts up to 2⅜" deep on square cuts and almost 2" deep on bevel cuts. This is adequate for most woodworking.*

• *If you plan to cut bevels, choose a circular saw with a shoe plate that pivots to the side from 0° to 45°.*

• *Select a saw with a quick-release mechanism for easy depth adjustment.*

• *For easy blade changing, choose a saw with an arbor-locking mechanism.*

• *You may want to get a saw with a dust port for sawdust removal.*

Choosing a circular saw

Gearing: There are two types of circular saws: helical-geared and worm-driven. Helical-geared saws are those most commonly found in households. The more powerful and more expensive worm-driven saws are generally found on construction sites. Either type of saw is effective for woodworking, but a helical-geared model should be adequate.

Size: Circular saws range from small trim saws (4½") to industrial saws (16¼"). The 7¼" saw is the most common and is able to cut through standard 1½"-thick stock.

Choosing a blade

Circular saws use the same type of blades as tablesaws and radial-arm saws, including a range of task-specific blades that vary according to the material you want to cut and the type of cut you want to make. For general woodworking use on a circular saw, use a carbide-tipped blade whose long-lasting cutting teeth make clean, fast cuts. For more information, see *Woodworking Tools,* pages 30 and 31.

Installing a blade

To install or change a blade, unplug the saw and loosen the arbor nut. Some circular saws have an arbor-locking mechanism to secure the blade while you loosen the arbor nut with a wrench. Always see the manufacturer's instructions for specific information on installing a blade in your model of circular saw.

Preparing to use the circular saw

Before you make any cut, unplug the saw and check the saw's settings. The cutting depth should allow the saw's teeth to protrude through the workpiece by about ⅛" during the cut. With the saw's power off, verify the depth by retracting the blade guard and holding the blade against the workpiece edge. Adjust the blade depth as needed. Always make sure all adjustable knobs are tightened before using the saw.

Clamp the workpiece to a worksurface for better cutting control. Also support any large waste portions during cutting. If you don't support a waste section, it can sag and pinch the blade or break off during the cut, causing the blade to bind or kick back toward you, as well as marring the workpiece.

Lay out your cuts so the saw is supported by the larger body of the workpiece, not the smaller one, during the cut. Resting the saw on the most stable surface will help you control your cuts.

Familiarize yourself with the sound of your saw as it cuts. Listen to the changes in the pitch of the motor when it is under no load, under a normal load, and under a heavy load. Learning to recognize these sound differences can help you know when you are overstressing the saw.

Using a guide strip

For the best results on long rip or crosscuts and to protect the workpiece, use a commercial or homemade guide strip.

To make a guide strip, cut a guide strip base from ¼"-thick lauan plywood, 18" wide and as long as your worksurface. Cut a pine 2 × 4 as long as the worksurface. Joint it on one edge and one face. Place the 2 × 4 on the guide strip base 3" from one edge. Keep the jointed face against the base and the jointed edge away from the near edge of the base. Drive screws through the guide strip base up into the 2 × 4, using ¾" wood screws. Drive them flush.

Run your circular saw along the jointed edge of the 2 × 4, cutting the base to the exact distance between your saw blade and the edge of your saw's shoe plate.

Because the distance between the saw blade and the edge of the shoe plate varies according to the kind of blade in the saw and the bevel angle of the blade, make different guide strips as needed for different blades and different angles.

Use a guide strip for long rip or crosscuts. Make sure the clamps don't interfere with the saw and hold the edge of the shoe firmly against the guide strip as you follow the cutting line.

To use a guide strip, clamp the guide strip onto the workpiece. Line up the edge of the guide strip base with the cutting line, keeping the blade kerf in the waste area. Cut along the edge of the guide strip, pressing the edge of the shoe plate against the 2 × 4.

Cutting crosscuts and rip cuts

Crosscuts are the most common cuts made with a circular saw, and rip cuts are made the same way. Cut either freehand along a mark (especially on short cutoff work) or cut along a guide strip.

1 Line up the saw or guide strip at the cutting mark so the blade kerf is in the waste area.

2 With both hands on the saw's handle, turn on the saw. Let the blade reach full speed before contacting the workpiece. Position yourself so you are not in line with the cutting path of the blade. Make the cut, moving forward steadily without forcing the saw.

3 As you finish the cut, move completely through it until the lower guard snaps into the safety position. Release the trigger switch

and wait for the blade to stop before setting the saw aside.

Cutting bevels: A circular saw can make bevel cuts if it has a shoe plate that tilts to the side. Unplug the saw. Then set the bevel scale for the angle of your cut. Lock the bevel knob in place, and change your cutting indicator (if your model has an adjustable one) so you can see the cutting point.

Cutting miters: Cut miters the same way as crosscuts. Clamping a straight guide strip to the workpiece at the miter angle gives the best cutting results.

Plunge-cutting: When you need to make a cut inside a workpiece, plunge-cut with your circular saw.

Use a 2 × 4 as a saw guide, clamping it to the workpiece exactly as far from the cutting line as the distance between the blade and the edge of the shoe plate. Then, with the power off, retract the lower blade guard and tilt the saw forward so it rests on the tip of the shoe. The tip of the shoe should also be against the guide strip, but don't let the blade touch the workpiece. Then turn on the saw. When it reaches full power, gently lower the blade into the workpiece until the shoe plate rests completely flat on the workpiece. Move forward along the guide strip. When you reach the end of your cut, release the trigger switch and wait for the blade to stop before removing it from the workpiece. Then square the ends of the cut with a handsaw.

Plunge-cutting is most practical on larger workpieces because the cut-out area must be at least as long as the blade. Use a saw guide clamped onto the workpiece to keep the saw straight as you enter the cut.

Scrollsaw Basics

Making delicate, intricate cuts is a breeze with your scrollsaw.

Similar in appearance to its relative the bandsaw, the scrollsaw is a stationary machine used to cut shapes and curves in wood, metal, or plastic. The scrollsaw specializes in cutting intricate curves too sharp for a bandsaw blade, cutting fine lines, and making internal cuts without making an entry cut into the side of the workpiece.

Scrollsaws cut on the downstroke, with a short, thin blade that reciprocates between an upper and lower clamp. The most common type of scrollsaw today is the constant-tension saw, which has a pair of movable arms that hold the blade and provide the cutting motion. Unlike the old rigid-arm saws, these constant-tension saws maintain blade tension by pulling on both the upstroke and the downstroke. The cutting motion has a slight forward pitch to it, so the blade enters the workpiece more aggressively. This type of cutting action reduces blade wear and makes a faster, cleaner cut.

Choosing a scrollsaw

The size of a scrollsaw is measured by its throat depth, which is the distance between the blade and the base of the arm. The throat size determines the maximum board width that can pass through the saw. Throat depth measurements vary quite a bit from model to model, but most are between 15 and 24". Choose a saw with a throat only as deep as the largest workpiece you envision yourself using. Keep in mind that some blades can be turned 90° in order to feed long workpieces past the blade from the side.

Most scrollsaws have a maximum cutting depth of 2" and come

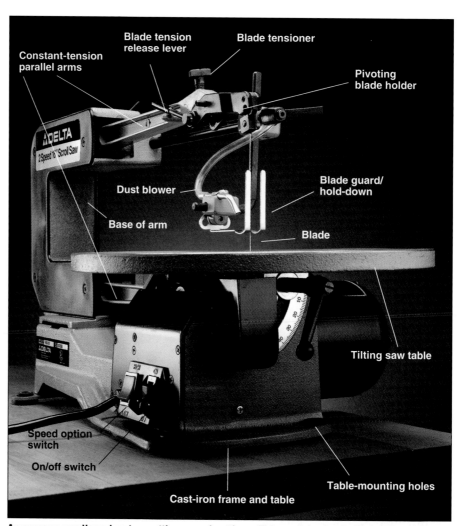

An average scrollsaw has two cutting-speed settings. This model cuts at either 850 or 1725 cutting strokes per minute, but the speed settings vary from model to model. Some saws have variable speed settings that allow you to choose the exact setting within their cutting range.

equipped with a blade guard, hold-down, and tension adjustor. While dust blowers are also fairly standard, not all models have them.

Depending on the model, scrollsaws have one set cutting speed, several set speeds, or a variable speed control. Most cutting is done at high speed, but slowing down gives you greater control over cuts, and also makes it easier to cut veneers, plastics, or metals.

Saw stands and antivibration pads also are available. These effectively cut down on excessive vibrations that can make controlling your cuts difficult.

Scrollsaw blades

Scrollsaws take two different types of blades, which have either

straight ends that clamp into a blade holder or pin ends that hook into slots in each blade holder. Some scrollsaws accept either kind, but be sure to buy the type specified for your scrollsaw.

Blades are categorized by a universal numbering system according to specific width, thickness, and teeth per inch (TPI). Blades range from about ⅛" to ¼" wide and between ⅟₆₄" and ⅟₃₂" thick. Saw blade manufacturers give blade specifications and will best inform you on the wide range of blade sizes, but a 15-TPI blade is good for general use.

Choose the best blade for the material you're cutting. If your cutting pattern has loose curves, fairly straight stretches, or if you are cutting a hard workpiece, use a wide, thick blade. However, a workpiece with very sharp turns requires a shallow, narrow blade. Using a heavier blade helps minimize the tendency for the saw blade to wander from the line and follow the wood grain. Essentially, you must use the widest and thickest blade possible that will allow you to follow the intricacy of your cutting pattern while producing a stable cut and desired kerf.

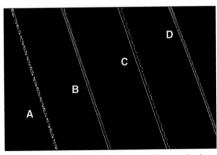

Common scrollsaw blades include: a spiral blade (A), a reversed blade (B), a standard skip-tooth (C), and a metal-cutting blade (D).

Tooth patterns of saw blades also vary. Skip-tooth blades are good for fast cutting without clogging the blade with sawdust, making them

Make simple cuts on the workpiece first to clear out as much waste material as possible. Then, return to make the more intricate cuts and curves.

good general-use blades. A reverse-tooth blade is similar to a standard blade, but has several teeth set in the opposite direction at the bottom end of the blade to prevent tearout on the underside of a workpiece. Spiral blades cut in all directions, so you don't have to rotate the work; however, they do cut a wider kerf. Metal-cutting blades are also available for cutting thin sheet metal or other hard materials.

Basic use

Prepare your workpiece by planning and marking a cutting path. Plan ahead to avoid interrupting your cut and backing the blade out of the kerf. While this is sometimes necessary, a steady forward pace makes cleaner cuts. Prepare for sharp curves and tight spots by drilling holes in the waste area next to the curve.

Before you begin, unplug the saw and check the movement and tension of the blade. The blade should move up and down freely, without bending or twisting, and the cutting teeth should point down. To reduce vibration, adjust the hold-down to secure the stock to the saw table.

Guide the workpiece slowly, with

Well-placed pilot holes in the waste area of your work make turning easier. Drill pilot holes ahead of time at sharp turns and hard-to-reach areas.

both hands, keeping your fingers out of the direct line of the blade. Apply moderate pressure as you feed, neither forcing nor rushing, and keep the blade on the waste side of the cut. To prevent uneven cutting or blade twisting, cut more slowly through thick materials or sharp turns.

Internal cuts

To make an internal cut without cutting into the side of the workpiece, drill starter holes in the waste area. Remove the blade from the upper clamp. Thread the blade through the starter hole and reattach it to the upper clamp. Readjust your hold-down and make your cut.

Bandsaw Basics

This sturdy machine makes it easy to tackle a wide range of jobs.

The bandsaw is a powerful and versatile machine. With a few adjustments, you can use it to cut curves, straight lines, bevels, and miters in both thin and thick materials, and even for crosscutting and ripcutting or re-sawing stock.

A bandsaw consists of a narrow, steel strip blade that runs in a loop around two or three large wheels, called band wheels, that are driven by a motor or belt-and-pulley system. The mechanisms are encased in a metal housing. The blade is mostly concealed by the housing and by an adjustable blade guard that moves up or down to accommodate the thickness of the material you're cutting. Adjustable guide blocks or bearings located both above and below the cutting area support the blade on its sides and back and keep it from slipping off the band

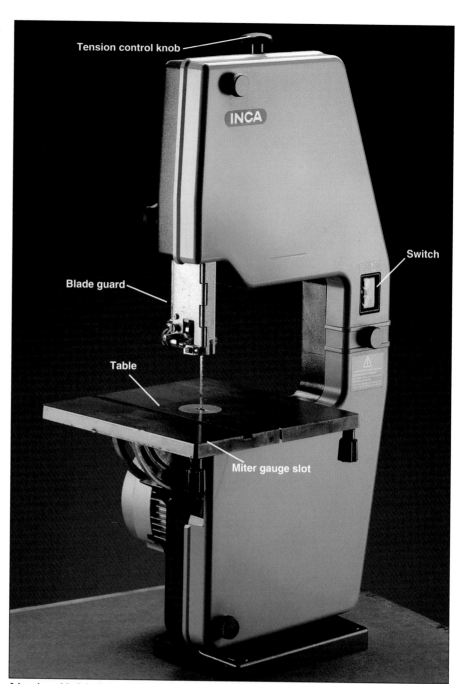

Tension control knob

INCA

Switch

Blade guard

Table

Miter gauge slot

A bandsaw blade's downward motion gives it an aggressive cutting action that can get through thick or hard materials quickly. It also eliminates the risk of kickback common to other saws, making it a fairly safe power tool.

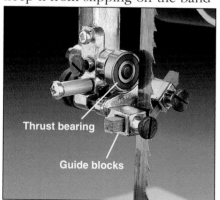

Thrust bearing

Guide blocks

Guide blocks keep the blade from drifting from side to side or twisting in a cut. Thrust bearings hold the blade from behind.

BUYER'S TIPS

- *Look for saws with blade guides that can be adjusted quickly and accurately.*
- *Choose a bandsaw with a built-in cleaning brush to remove sawdust and resin buildup.*
- *Buy a model with at least ¾ hp. if you plan to cut curves in stock thicker than 2" board.*
- *A table with the blade slot on the side, instead of the front, makes blade changing easier.*
- *Save money by selecting a model with a fence and miter gauge as standard features—it will cost more if you decide to add them later.*

wheels, or wandering from the cutting line.

Choosing a bandsaw

In addition to stationary floor models, there are benchtop bandsaws available. These smaller units are less expensive and can be easily stored out of the way when not in use. They are, however, less powerful and offer more limited features. The important features to consider when purchasing a bandsaw include its speed, throat capacity, cutting depth, and possible table settings. Keeping these points in mind will help you to select a saw that suits your basic work requirements.

The speed of a bandsaw is measured in terms of how many feet the blade will travel in a minute (called Surface Feet Per Minute, or SFM). Most bandsaws have a top speed in the range of 2500 to 3000 feet per minute, depending on the model. Most wood cutting is done using the top speed settings, but some machines have slower speed settings for cutting other materials, like metal, plastic, or hard, thick woods.

Throat capacity, which determines bandsaw size, refers to the distance between the cutting blade and the back arm of the saw, and indicates what width material can be cut. This number can range from 10" to 20", but a bandsaw with a 14" throat capacity is a good choice for general-purpose work. A three-wheel bandsaw will have greater throat capacity than a two-wheel saw because its blade has to travel back to the third wheel, leaving more room behind the blade. These models have the drawback of taking up more floor space, however, and they tend to wear blades out faster. A three-wheel saw may be worth it, however, if you plan to be cutting a lot of wide stock.

The cutting depth of a bandsaw is also an important feature to consider. Most bandsaws will cut material up to 6" thick, but this also varies from model to model, so look for a saw that has the clearance you'll need. Some manufacturers offer riser kits that increase the cutting depth.

Bandsaw tables are generally square and fairly small, ranging in size from 10 × 10" to 20 × 20". Most models allow you to tilt the table to 45°, making it possible to use the saw for bevel and mitercuts. Better models allow you to adjust the table at a range of increments and have knobs or other devices that help to make precise adjustments and then lock the position securely. Also look to see if the table comes with a miter gauge or rip fence, or has slots to accept them.

Bandsaw blades

The size, shape, and placement of the teeth in bandsaw blades vary widely (see *Woodworking Tools*, pages 30 and 31).

Blade widths range from ⅛" to ¾". Wide blades work better than narrow ones for cutting thicker material or straight lines, because they're stiffer and tend to stay on track better. Always choose the widest blade possible for the radius of the curve you're cutting.

The number of teeth per inch also affects how well a blade will cut material. Use a blade with more teeth per inch for cutting hardwood and other dense materials. Use blades with fewer teeth per inch for cutting softwood or thicker pieces.

Different band wheels accommodate different blade thicknesses, or gauges. Using a gauge not intended for the band wheels will cause premature wear on the blade. Check the manufacturer's recommendations for the correct gauge.

Installing a blade

1 With the saw unplugged, open the frame housing and loosen the tension on the blade guides and bearings. Carefully remove the blade from the band wheels.
2 Center the new blade over the top wheel, then around the lower one, making sure the teeth are pointing downward.
3 Adjust the tension of the wheels

by raising the upper wheel until there is no slack in the blade.

4 Check the tracking of the blade by turning the wheels by hand. As you turn the wheel with one hand, turn the tracking knob with the other to adjust the tilt of the wheel's axis. Adjust it until the blade stays true, running in the center of the band wheel rim.
5 Make the final adjustment on the blade tension. Some bandsaws have a tension indicator that tells the proper setting for a particular blade width. If yours doesn't, adjust the tension so the blade can flex no more than ¼" from side to side. Double-check the tracking once more.
6 Adjust the top and bottom guide assemblies by first setting the thrust bearing. The thrust bearing should just barely contact the back of the blade so the blade will neither slide backward nor grind against the bearing.
7 Next, align the guide blocks (or bearings, depending on the model) by setting the upper and lower guide on the left side first, checking with a square to ensure they're aligned equally and aren't bending the blade. Space the guide blocks so there is a paper-width gap between each block

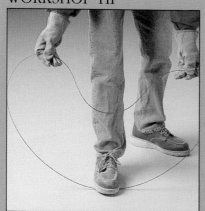

Coil bandsaw blades for easy storage. To coil a bandsaw blade, hold the blade (wearing protective gloves) with the teeth pointing away from you so it forms one large loop in front of you. Hold one end of the loop down with one foot, and let the top of the loop bend toward you. As the loop falls toward you, bring your hands together and cross the blade over on itself to form the coils. Lower the blade to the floor, and gather and tie the three coils together.

and the side of the blade. When the left guides are set, adjust the right guides to the same paper-width distance from the blade.
8 Last, set the guide blocks so they line up equally with the concave points in the teeth of the blade, called the gullets. Positioning the guides here will give the blade optimum side support without bending or touching the teeth.

Basic bandsaw use

Always keep your hands behind or to the side of the blade as you guide the work. Also be sure to lower the blade guard down to within ½" of the stock to be cut before you begin any cut. Readjust the guard each time you change workpieces.

Turn on the bandsaw and begin the cut, feeding the work at a steady pace. Because the bandsaw blade makes rough cuts, it's best to work on the waste side of your cutting line. Rough edges can be sanded later. Work patiently, to avoid forcing the workpiece or twisting the blade in the kerf.

Cutting freehand curves

1 Lay out the path of the cut. Prepare turning points by drilling pilot holes, or by making parallel straight cuts into the waste area to create maneuvering room for your blade (see *photos below*).
2 Guide the work with both hands, using one hand to guide the workpiece from behind the blade. The blade will have a tendency to wander from the line during freehand cutting, so pay close attention.

Crosscutting

Most bandsaws have a miter gauge resembling those used on a tablesaw, which can be used for crosscutting and miter-cutting. To crosscut long pieces, you may need to attach a miter-gauge extension to the the head of the

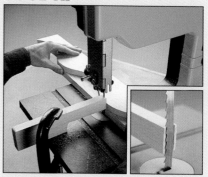

This L-shaped pivot block made from 1 × 4" hardwood is useful for cutting parallel curves or cutting with a template. It is also useful as a guide when resawing stock. The ends of the pivot block are rounded over and cut with a shallow notch just large enough for the bandsaw blade to fit (inset).

miter gauge (see *Joining Wood*, page 116).

Ripcutting

Because it leaves a very narrow kerf, a bandsaw wastes little material, which makes it a good choice for resawing lumber into thinner stock. However, a bandsaw cuts less smoothly than a tablesaw, so you'll probably need to run the cut edges through a planer or jointer after cutting them.
1 Position the rip fence and clamp it in place. (For tall stock, attach an auxiliary fence to the standard rip fence.)
2 Make test cuts on scrap stock to see if the blade wanders away from the cutting line. If so, clamp

To make cuts in tight corners, drill pilot holes to remove waste wood where the blade needs to change direction sharply, then cut toward each corner along the outline.

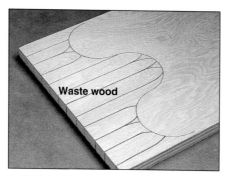

For tight inside curves, make a series of parallel cuts in the waste wood up to the layout line; remove each section to create room for maneuvering the blade.

For tight outside curves, make a series of tangential cuts in toward the curve outline so the blade does not have to turn as sharply to complete the curve.

your pivot block to the table as a guide and angle the workpiece slightly to keep it parallel to the natural path of the blade.
3 Smooth one face of the stock on a planer and joint one edge.

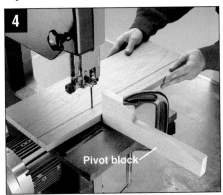

4 Position the workpiece with the planed face against the table and the jointed edge against the pivot block. Feed the workpiece into the saw blade.

Using a template
Make a template to use with your L-block to cut several workpieces with the same shape.
1 Transfer the pattern of the shape you're cutting to a piece of scrap ¾" stock, and cut out a template using your bandsaw, sawing just to the waste side of the lines. Sand the rough edges.
2 Set the uncut workpiece on the saw table and attach the template to it with hot glue or double-sided masking tape.
3 Clamp the L-block to the table of your bandsaw, perpendicular to the blade, so the blade fits inside the notch at the tip of the block.

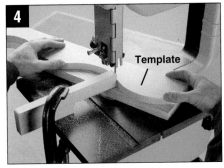

4 Guide the workpiece so the L-block stays in contact with the template at all times. Unclamp the workpiece and sand the edges.

Cutting parallel curves
Rocking chair feet and chair backs are examples of pieces that have parallel curves.
1 Lay out both cutting lines on the workpiece. Make the first cut freehand, then sand the cut edges.
2 Determine the distance between the parallel lines. Clamp your L-block to the table of your bandsaw, so the distance between the saw blade and the tip of the L-block equals the distance between the parallel layout lines.

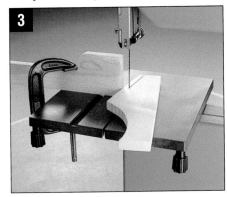

3 Make the parallel cut by guiding the cut edge tight against the tip of the pivot block as you feed the wood into the blade.

Bevel-cutting
Tilt the bandsaw table to cut bevels and chamfers. Most bandsaws have a gauge under the table that indicates the angle of the tilt,

but it is a good idea to double-check the angle with a protractor and make test cuts on scrap material to avoid expensive mistakes.

Cutting compound curves
The bandsaw is ideal for cutting workpieces with curves on more than one plane, like cabriole legs for a table or chair.
1 Lay out the cutting lines on each face of the workpiece.
2 Make cuts on the top face of the workpiece, saving the waste sections to use when cutting the other sides of the piece.

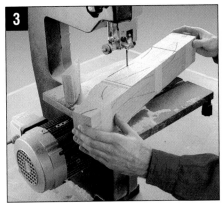

3 Tape the waste sections back to the workpiece to keep the outer surfaces flat, then rotate the workpiece a quarter turn to make the cuts on the adjacent side.
4 Repeat steps 2 and 3 to cut the remaining sides.

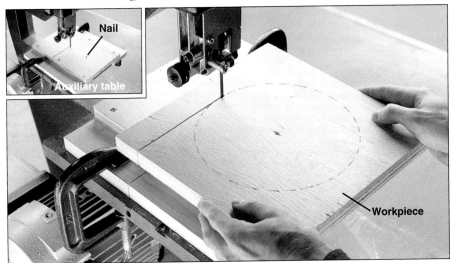

To cut circles, use an auxiliary table with a short finish nail or screw driven up through the bottom to serve as a pivot point. The distance between the blade and the nail should equal the radius of the circle. Make a freehand entry cut up to the edge of the circle, then thread the workpiece around the bandsaw blade and press the workpiece onto the nail. Rotate the workpiece on the nail to cut the circle.

Power Miter Box

Make quick work of your crosscutting with a portable power miter box.

The power miter box is one of the handiest portable saws you can own. Like the radial-arm saw, it makes accurate crosscuts, miter-cuts, and bevel cuts. However, the power miter box costs less, is safer to use, and needs adjustment less frequently than a radial-arm saw.

Power miter boxes, available in many styles, come in 8", 10", and 12" models. The simplest type, the angle-only power miter box, works well for cutoff work and making simple miter and bevel cuts. Compound and sliding compound power miter boxes also cut compound angles (miters and bevels simultaneously). Sliding compound power miter boxes have a larger crosscutting capacity, typically 12" wide, instead of 6" wide on a standard 10" saw.

Construction

The power miter box is essentially a circular saw mounted on a light aluminum, cast-iron, or plastic

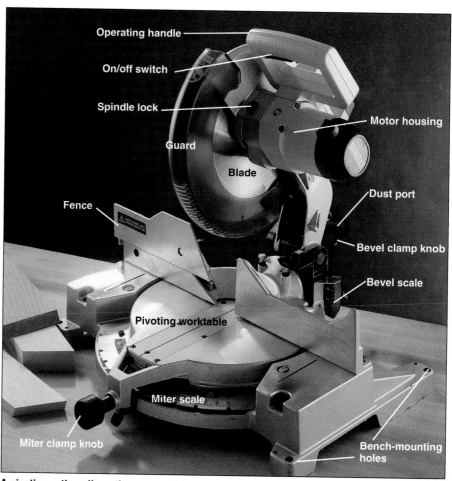

Operating handle — On/off switch — Spindle lock — Guard — Blade — Fence — Motor housing — Dust port — Bevel clamp knob — Bevel scale — Pivoting worktable — Miter scale — Miter clamp knob — Bench-mounting holes

A pivoting action allows the power miter box blade to swing down onto the workpiece. This is why a power miter box is often called a "chop saw."

worktable. Compact size and accurate miter and bevel scales all contribute to this tool's efficiency and precision.

Most models have quick-release clamps or levers to adjust the saw easily for miter and bevel cuts. The blade can be set and locked at any angle position from 0° to 45° for both miter and bevel cuts. Most models have preset stops for common miter and bevel angles, and very sophisticated models even feature laser-guided cut lines.

Power miter boxes usually have an automatic braking system that stops the blade a few seconds after shutoff.

Saw blades

The power miter box uses the same type of blades as those used in tablesaws and circular saws. (For more information on saw blades, see *Woodworking Tools*, pages 30 and 31.)

Setting up

Several of the power miter box's movable parts need periodic inspection and adjustment. To verify that the blade is set perpendicular to the table, set the blade in the zero position and place a precision square on the table bed. Press the square against the blade, but do not touch the teeth with

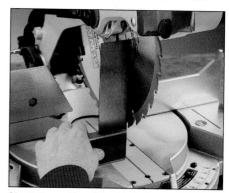

Check the angle of the blade in relation to the table. With the blade set at the zero position, the square should be perpendicular to the table.

the square. Examine the angle and adjust it as needed. To check the angle of the blade in relation to the fence, set the blade in the zero

miter position. Place one edge of a precision square against the fence and the other upward against the blade, again without touching the teeth. Check the angle and make any needed adjustments. Also, check the accuracy of the miter and bevel gauges by making test cuts on scrapwood, then verifying the angles using a protractor. Refer to the manufacturer's instructions for information on adjustments.

Using the power miter box

Follow these directions in crosscutting.

1 Clamp or hold the workpiece against the fence, with your hands well clear of the cutting area. Always clamp small workpieces.

2 Set the blade at zero on the miter scale for a straight crosscut. Line up the blade at the cutting mark on the workpiece, placing the kerf on the waste side of the mark.

3 Turn the power on and let the blade reach full speed. Lower the blade slowly to make the cut. (For a sliding compound miter saw, grasp the handle firmly and pull it at an upward angle before

turning on the blade and lowering it into the workpiece.) A slow and even cutting stroke produces the cleanest cuts. Cutting too fast can cause tearout.

4 As soon as you finish the cut, release the on/off switch and raise the arm to the neutral position. Make sure the blade is raised and stopped before handling the workpiece.

Cutting miters: The procedures for miter-cutting and crosscutting are the same. However, the saw's miter-cutting capacity is shorter than its crosscutting capacity. To cut miters, loosen the miter clamp knob and release the miter latch. Turn the miter arm to the desired angle by sliding the miter clamp knob to the left or right. Lock the miter arm position by tightening the miter clamp knob. Then make your cut.

Cutting bevels: With the saw unplugged, loosen the bevel clamp knob and tilt the saw to the desired bevel angle. Lock in the desired angle on the scale with the bevel clamp knob. Lower the blade to check for cutting clearance. On a compound miter saw you may have to adjust the left fence to give the blade guard clearance. Plug in the saw and lower the blade to cut.

To cut compound angles, set and lock the miter arm at the desired miter angle. Set and lock the bevel angle according to the bevel scale. Then make your cut.

Cutting compound angles: Cutting accurate compound angles for making frames or boxes with slanted sides can be

difficult. The compound power miter box works well because it cuts miters and bevels easily and adjusts precisely. Run test cuts on scrapwood to ensure correct settings.

Cutting crown molding: The compound power miter box cuts any type of crown molding well. Draw cutlines on your workpiece, make test cuts on scrapwood, and cut the molding.

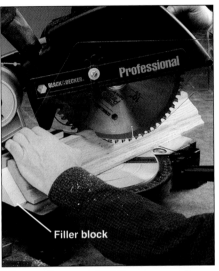

Filler block

When cutting crown molding on an angle-only miter saw, make sure the flat pieces on the back (which will press against the ceiling and wall) are pressed against the fence and table. You can use a filler block for support.

It is possible to cut compound angles on an angle-only miter s aw. For example, to cut crown molding with an angle-only power miter box, you must flip the piece upside down, with the finished side still facing you. To cut a left-hand angle, put the molding in this position and make a right-handed cut (see *Photo, left*). To cut a right-hand angle, you must flip the piece upside down, with the finished side still facing you, and make a left-handed cut.

Sabersaw Basics

Lightweight and portable, the sabersaw is perfect for both curved and straight cuts in hard-to-reach places.

Whenever a woodworking project has you in a tight spot, reach for your sabersaw—the tool that combines the ease and accuracy of a power saw with the portability of a hand-saw. Use the sabersaw to cut curves and irregular shapes, make interior cuts, and trim large work-pieces that are too big for your stationary saw tables.

Features

Sabersaws are available from light-duty to heavy-duty or professional strength, generally ranging from 3.0 to 6.0 amps. The amperage of the motor affects the longevity of the saw, but the cutting power of the saw, for short bursts, is better measured by the stroke length. The sabersaw works by plunging the blade up and down in the same manner as a reciprocating saw, and saws with longer stroke lengths (up to 1") can cut harder, thicker material more easily.

Sabersaws are small enough to hold and operate with one hand, although it's recommended that you use two hands whenever possible, especially when cutting freehand. Some sabersaws have a handle mounted to the top of the body, while others are designed with a saw body meant to be gripped. Note: When holding the body of an operating sabersaw, be careful not to cover the motor vents in the sides—overheating of the motor can result. Some saws have a handle mounted above the blade or on the side of the body for applying steady pressure.

Sabersaw blades cut on the

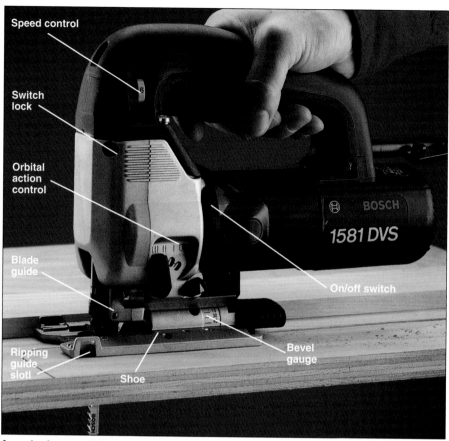

A good sabersaw with a standard blade will cut wood up to 2" in thickness, and metal up to ¼". With the proper blades, they'll also cut fiberglass, leather, rubber and other materials.

Labels: Speed control; Switch lock; Orbital action control; Blade guide; Ripping guide slotl; Shoe; BOSCH 1581 DVS; On/off switch; Bevel gauge

upstroke, usually with an orbital cutting motion. Saws with orbital action push the blade into the workpiece slightly on the up-stroke, where the cutting is done, then retract the blade from the kerf on the downstroke, making cleaner cuts and preserving blades. Some sabersaw models have variable orbital action set-tings, allowing you to set the blade forward for making fast cuts in soft materials, and at a near ver-tical position to make fast cuts in hard materials.

The scrolling sabersaw has a pivoting chuck, so the saw blade can be turned from side to side, usually by turning a knob located directly above the blade. The scrolling sabersaw is good for cutting tight curves.

Sabersaw blades

Sabersaw blades are usually categorized by the type of material they're designed to cut. Wood, metal, laminate, fiberglass, leather,

BUYER'S TIPS

•A good sabersaw has at least a 3.0-amp motor, with an adjustable stroke rate ranging from 500 to 3,000 strokes per minute (SPM).

•Look for a sabersaw with a stroke length of at least ¾"—longer strokes are more powerful.

•Saws with "orbital" or "oscillating" cutting action make cleaner cuts and preserve blades.

•A scrolling saw has a knob that can be turned to adjust the blade from side to side to make tight cuts.

and ceramic are common blade types. Blades can be as narrow as ¼" (scrolling blades) and as wide as 1" (offset blades). A standard blade is ⅜" wide. Typical metals used include inexpensive high-speed steel and more durable carbide-tipped blades. The num-ber of teeth per inch (TPI) for wood-cutting blades ranges from 5 to 15—lower TPI results in faster,

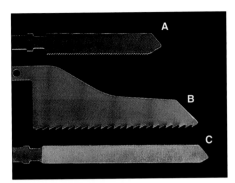

Some specialty blades include: a knife-edge blade for cutting leather and rubber (A), an offset flush-cutting blade (B), and a tungsten carbide-coated blade (C).

rougher cuts. For more information on saw blades, see *Woodworking Tools,* pages 30 to 31.

Basic sabersaw use

With sabersaws, it's very tempting to try to speed up a cut by pushing the saw forward with too much force. As when using any power tool, forcing a cut with a sabersaw will result in uneven cuts, burning, and undue strain on the saw and the blades. To make sabersaw cuts, clamp the workpiece to a worksurface to minimize vibrations. Always cut on the waste side of a marked line to allow for the blade kerf.

Straight cuts: The most important aspect of making straight cuts is to keep the saw straight and even, preventing the blade from wandering. Use a guide when making straight cuts with a sabersaw. Most sabersaws will accept a ripping guide (see *photo, right*), similar to a router edge guide, that attaches to the shoe. Otherwise, secure a straightedge to the workpiece or the workbench to guide the shoe of the saw. Use at least a ⅜"-wide saw blade, because wider blades are less likely to wander.

Turn on the saw before contacting the workpiece with the blade.

WOODWORKER'S TIP

Because sabersaws cut on the upstroke, prevent tear-out by cutting with the good side of the workpiece face-down. Another solution is to sandwich the workpiece between two scrap pieces of wood.

Make sure the waste material is supported as you near completion of the cut. To reduce the chance of tearout, finish the cut working very slowly.

Curved cuts are easiest to make in multiple passes. Use the first pass to cut away excess waste, but leave the hard-to-reach sections for last.

For cutting tight curves, make relief cuts through the waste areas of the stock, just as you would for similar cuts using a bandsaw or scrollsaw.

Circle-cutting can be done freehand or by attaching a ripping guide to the shoe, then securing the guide around a pivot point at the centerpoint of the circle. For larger circles, simply tie a string to the pivot point, attach the other end to the shoe, and make the cut, keeping the string taut.

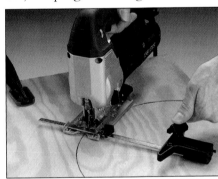

A ripping guide is a useful tool for cutting circular shapes, as well as for making straight cuts.

Bevel-cutting: Most sabersaws have an adjustable shoe that can be positioned from 0° to 45° on either side of the blade, making it ideal for bevel-cutting. Always

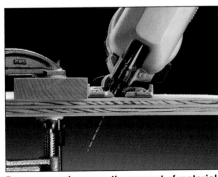

Because you increase the amount of material to be cut, the cutting capacity of the saw is reduced when bevel-cutting. Use a straightedge guide for accurate bevel-cuts.

make a practice cut first on a piece of scrap wood to make sure the angle of the bevel is correct.

Plunge-cutting: With its short, stiff blades, the sabersaw is capable of making *plunge* cuts, which are interior cuts started without a blade start hole. Plunge cuts are

Use the front edge of the saw shoe as a pivot point when plunge-cutting.

especially useful for interior cuts on plywood and other softer materials.

To plunge-cut, position the tip of the saw blade just above the workpiece, inside the cutting line; then tilt the saw forward so the tip of the shoe rests on the workpiece. Hold the saw firmly, and, with the blade in a horizontal position, turn on the saw. Slowly pivot the saw downward, using the the shoe as a pivot. As the blade moves up and down, it will "drill" its own guide hole. Let the blade work its way through; then finish the cut.

Scrolling simple curves can be cut with a standard sabersaw and blade. Work slowly, and make sure the kerf is kept clear of sawdust. A scrolling sabersaw with a ¼"-wide blade is a better choice for tighter, more complex curves.

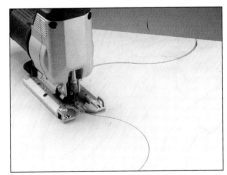

Scrolling, or following a contour with the sabersaw, can be done with either a regular saw or a scrolling sabersaw. A ¼"-wide, fine-toothed blade produces good results.

Router Basics

A true jack-of-all-trades tool, the router is an indispensible part of any shop.

The router is known best for its versatility: It can do many of the jobs that planers, shapers, and even tablesaws and sabersaws do. If you don't happen to have a shop full of equipment, the router is an especially economical tool to own. The modern router does more than just cut grooves, rabbets, and dadoes. It may be used for shaping, joinery, mortising, and following templates. With the proper jigs, routers can be put to more advanced uses, such as carving, lathe work, and following stencils and freehand drawings.

Choosing a router

Choosing the right router for your shop can be a surprisingly pleasant experience, mostly because there are so many well-equipped tools to fit just about anyone's budget.

The first (and most important) feature to consider is power. Routers vary in size and power, ranging from flashlight-sized ¾ hp models used for trimming and delicate work, to heavy-duty, 3 hp models for cabinetmaking or shaping work. Middle-range routers with 1 to 2 hp motors are good for general use.

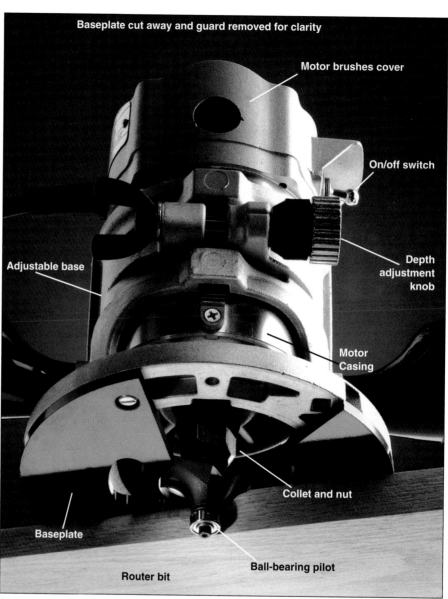

Baseplate cut away and guard removed for clarity

Motor brushes cover

On/off switch

Adjustable base

Depth adjustment knob

Motor Casing

Collet and nut

Baseplate

Ball-bearing pilot

Router bit

The router is a high-speed motor with a free-turning collet. It uses a variety of ornamental cutting bits to make clean, accurate cuts.

As with any tool, bottom-of-the-line quality is not the best investment, and won't provide satisfactory results. A router that's underpowered for the job will bog down, chatter through cuts, and burn up bits. If you can, test a friend's router to get a feel for specific power and performance.

The collet size of your router is another consideration. Pick a model with interchangeable collets or adaptors that accept ¼" and ½" bits. Bits for ½" collets have thicker shanks and are less likely to break. They also cut more steadily than the thinner bits, which is especially important for heavy work.

WOODWORKER'S TIP

A good router should have a removable base and casing, making it easily accessible for servicing and regular maintenance. Familiarize yourself with all of its parts, including how to open the casing to replace the motor brushes.

BUYER'S TIPS

Power: For general use, pick a router with at least 1½ hp and between 6.5 to 9 amps.

Speed: A fixed speed of 25,000 rpm's will meet the needs of most woodworkers. Also, look for minimal-torque start-up (the motor builds speed slowly, instead of jerking to a start).

Depth control: Should be accurate and easy to read and adjust.

Controls: Look for an on/off switch that's accessible without removing your hands from the handle.

If you like to use mortises and stopped rabbets and dadoes in your wood joinery, consider a plunge router. These models are also good for template routing and cutouts. A plunge router has a motor housing that slides up and down along two posts. Spring tension keeps the motor and bit raised off the work. To use, align the router over the work, release the locking mechanism, and push the housing straight down with the handles. The spinning bit lowers directly into the work to begin the cut, rather than being tilted into the cut like a fixed-base router. The housing can be locked into the lowered position. Plunge routers cost a little more than fixed-base routers, but offer precise stopped cuts and blind starts.

Some top-of-the-line routers are equipped with electronic variable speed (EVS). Electronic circuitry governs the motor and maintains a constant cutting speed when the motor is under a heavy load, like when you cut hard materials. This helps prevent the router from bogging down or burning the wood. If you use bits of 1½" diameter or larger for shaping, operating the router at lower speeds is especially important to avoid burning the wood and bits.

Owning several routers is ideal. Aim for getting a small laminate trimmer, a medium-sized router with 1½ to 2 hp, and a fixed-base router you can leave mounted in a router table.

Common router bits include: a multifluted trimmer bit with a ball-bearing pilot (A), an HSS pilotless straight bit (B), a V-groove bit with a ¼" shank (C), a dovetail bit (D), a rabbet bit with a fixed pilot (E), a carbide-tipped Roman-ogee bit with a ½" shank (F), a double-fluted round-over bit (G), a core-box bit (H), and a single-fluted veining bit (I).

Router bits

Most router bits are made from high-speed steel (HSS) or HSS with carbide tips. HSS bits are more common and cost less than carbide-tipped bits, but don't stay sharp as long. Tipped bits also make smoother cuts than the HSS bits. If you need a specific bit for a one-time job, consider the HSS bit, but the carbide-tipped bits are a better long-term investment.

Router bits have single, double, or multiple cutting edges (flutes). Double-fluted or multifluted bits cut more smoothly because they have more blade surfaces and make more cuts per revolution.

Most edging bits have a guide, called a pilot, which can be a solid extension of the bit or a guide bushing with ball bearings. Bits with ball-bearing pilots cost more than those with fixed pilots, but are useful because they smoothly follow the contours of your stock and don't burn or gouge the wood like a fixed-pilot bit can. However, fixed-pilot bits will sometimes follow contours better than the wider guide on ball-bearing pilots.

Tool tips

When installing a bit, place it in the collet so it touches bottom, then retract it about ⅟₁₆" to avoid tightening the collet around the curved end (fillet) of the bit. A poorly seated bit can wobble as it cuts or may vibrate loose.

If your bit jams in the collet as you change bits, remove the collet assembly and insert a nail set through the back end of the collet. Tap the nail set on a workbench. Also, clear any sawdust or accumulated grit from the collet fitting.

WOODWORKER'S TIP

Good care of your bits can extend their use. Clean your bits occasionally with lacquer thinner, then add a light coat of oil to prevent rusting or pitting. Store bits by standing them up in holes drilled in a block of wood. This makes them easy to identify and prevents nicking and dulling from contact.

Basic router use

Before you put the router to the wood on any project, do a little planning and testing. Consider the type of wood you will be cutting. If you have hard wood, you can expect slow going. Also check the sharpness of your bits.

Always make a test cut on scrap material of the same size and hardness as the workpiece. Check the depth of cut and the profile, and adjust the cutting depth (and fence, if applicable) until correct.

Routers can be guided in several ways, the most common being by a fence, the bit, or an edge guide. In the example below, we used a piloted bit as our guide.

> **WOODWORKER'S TIP**
>
> *Simplify your edge-routing by attaching a small piece of scrap the same thickness as the workpiece to the bottom of the router base. Screw the strip to the outside edge of the base, so the router is equally supported by the workpiece and the strip. Instead of having to balance the router by hand while making cuts, you can slide it easily along the workbench surface.*

Edge-cutting with the router

When you edge-cut, you will cut either with the grain or across it. If you are edge-cutting both the sides and end of a piece of wood, cut the cross-grain edges first. By making the grain cut last, you will smooth out any rough or torn edges on the ends. If you are only cutting the ends of a piece (cross-grain), make it a practice to clamp scrap blocks on the edges of your workpiece, to ensure your finished piece won't suffer tearout.

1 Clamp a workpiece to your workbench, so the working area overhangs the edge of the bench by several inches. Make sure the clamps aren't in the routing path.

2 Insert an edging bit into the router and set the cutting depth to between ⅛" and ¼".

3 Hold the router with both hands, about 1" away from the workpiece, then turn it on. Let it reach full speed before engaging the

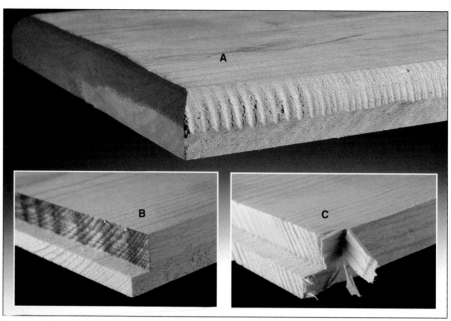

Proper feed speed ensures a smooth profile when routing. The rippling effect shown above (A) was caused by routing too quickly, and occurs particularly on harder woods like the maple shown. A steady, moderate pace will help you rout cleanly in all woods. Feeding too slowly can burn the wood (B), or working too fast can cause splintering (C), as in these oak boards.

workpiece. Routing is generally performed left to right on a workpiece, as you face it. The router bit spins clockwise, so you should move the router counterclockwise, against the direction of the bit. This prevents wandering and directs the force of the cut against your workpiece.

4 Begin the cut, holding the router lightly but firmly against the workpiece. Feeding too slowly can cause the bit to burn the wood, but feeding too fast may cause the router to bog down or the bit to ripple. Keep the router perpendicular to maintain a consistent profile on the wood. If you tilt it at all, the angle of the profile you're cutting will change. Listen to the motor and get a sense of the load. You will hear the pitch of the motor deepen if it bogs down. Make a steady through-cut, keeping your attention on your work as you follow through. Be careful not to round off the corner of the workpiece as you finish.

5 Turn the router off and wait for the bit to come to a complete stop before setting the tool down.

6 Inspect the edge you've just cut. Deepen the cutting depth of the bit by ⅛ to ¼" for your next pass.

With most cuts, you'll need to make several passes to reach your final cutting depth. If you try to make a deep cut in one pass, you'll bog down the motor and possibly burn up the bit tip. Repeated shallow passes create a clean cut.

Freehand routing

In addition to the guided work routers can do, the portable router can also be used in a freehand manner. This requires the patience and technique found in practiced hands, since the router will cut without remorse in any direction unless carefully guided. For those with patience and practice, the router can provide fine decorative carving or lettering.

> **WOODWORKER'S TIP**
>
> *For edge-cutting a narrow workpiece, like a strip of quarter-round, start with material that is several inches wider than the desired finished piece. A wide workpiece can be clamped to a workbench without interfering with the routing path, and is less likely to break. After you rout the edge, resaw the piece to the desired width.*

Jigs

Router accessories and jigs make using the router simpler and create more accurate, consistent results. Many worthwhile accessories can be purchased ready-made, but as you gain experience with your router, you'll discover the importance and convenience of handmade, special-purpose jigs. Make your own jigs to last so they can be reused, and label them carefully.

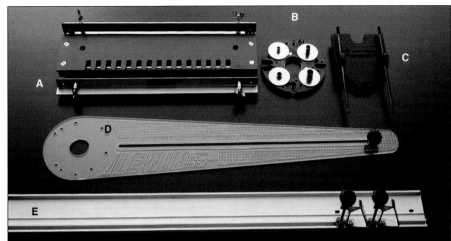

Common router accessories include: a dovetail jig (A), guide bushings for following templates (B), an edge guide (C), a circle jig (D), and a straightedge guide (E).

By mounting the router upside down in a router table and using a fence to guide the workpiece, you can cut a wide variety of profiles safely and quickly.

Router table

When mounted in a router table, the router becomes a stationary shaper. Also use a table-mounted router for projects with a series of cuts, or when a portable router would be less effective, such as in molding thin workpieces. A router table produces consistently accurate cuts more easily than routing long cuts with a portable router that must be steadied by hand.

Most routers can be mounted in commercial router tables or in a home-built table. Use a fixed-base router in the table, as plunge routers are generally difficult to use when table mounted.

Straightedge guide

A long straightedge guide is critical to accurate router work. The straightedge provides a stable, straight cutting guide for both short and long cuts, and it ensures consistency in repetitive cuts. Often, more than one straightedge is necessary to accomplish a routing job, such as cutting a wide dado.

Edge guide

An edge guide, often supplied with the router, is a short, adjustable side fence connected to two parallel rods that attach to the router base. The edge guide slides along the rods and can be butted against the workpiece to cut inside grooves or outside edges. With its quick setup time and ease of use, this is an indispensible routing aid.

Circle jig

Some edge guides can be used to cut circles, using a guide nail driven through a centered hole bored in the edge guide. To do this, sink a guide nail into the centerpoint of the planned circle on your workpiece. By adjusting the length of the edge guide, you can control the circle's circumference.

If you don't want to drive a nail into the workpiece, glue a small piece of scrap wood to the circle's centerpoint and drive the guide-nail into the scrap. When you are done cutting, remove the block and scrape and sand off the remaining glue.

If you don't have an edge guide that serves as a circle jig, or if you need a larger circle than your edge guide will allow, you can make or buy a circle jig (see *photo, above*).

Dovetail jigs

Commercial dovetail jigs for half-blind and through dovetails enable you to create perfect dovetail joints. These do require a bit of setup time, but once set, you can quickly and easily make accurate and attractive dovetails.

Following a template (A) is a very common use for routers. Templates are useful for duplicating a specific pattern, such as for parts of furniture, or for consistently reproducing identical results such as lettering for a sign.

Following a template

If you need to make repeated similar cuts or you're reproducing a specific shape, routing against a template simplifies your job. Templates should be made of sturdy materials, such as hardboard, plastic, or plywood. Template guides, which are small collars that slide over the bit and seat against the base of the router (see *photo, top*), protect the template from the bit and guide the router, much like a ball-bearing pilot bit.

Install a template guide in the router and make sure your template is clamped firmly to the workpiece. Your template must be slightly smaller than the desired finished piece to allow for the width of the guide bushing.

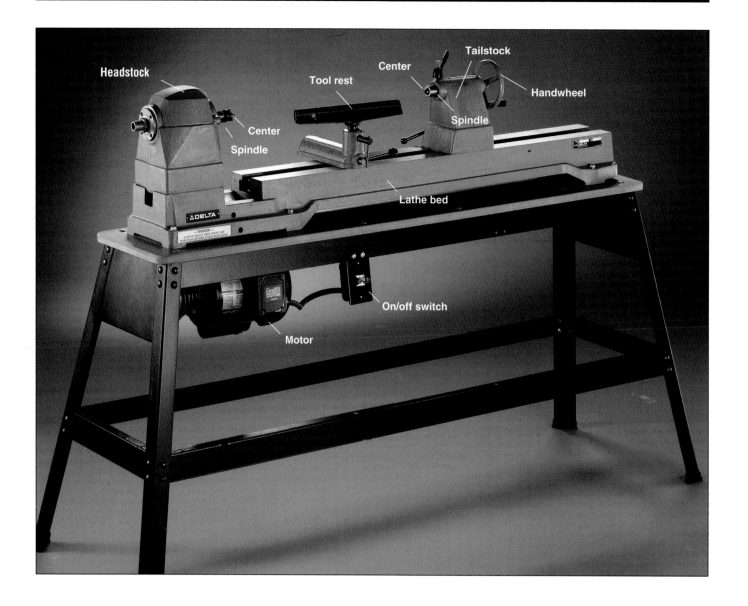

Lathe Basics

Transform blocks of wood into artful shapes with a lathe.

Symmetry and grace characterize a piece turned on a lathe, whether it be a chair leg, a stairway spindle, or other workpiece. The lathe does not do any cutting or shaping itself, but is used to hold and turn a piece of wood as a cutting tool is applied to it. Depending upon the cutting tool used, you can add details like coves and beads, with varying profiles and contours.

The most common lathe work, called between-center turning, involves mounting a piece of stock between spindles located at the two ends of the lathe—the headstock and tailstock. The headstock houses a motor that rotates the spindle and attached stock. It is connected to the tailstock by the lathe bed, which is usually made of metal. The headstock is sometimes called the "live" stock because it spins, while the tailstock is known as the "dead" stock, because it does not turn. The stock is mounted to the headstock spindle and then the tailstock is positioned against the other end, just

BUYER'S TIPS

• *36" between centers and 12" between the spindle and the lathe bed will allow you to turn a variety of projects on the lathe.*

• *¾ horsepower or 10 to 12 amps will turn stock up to 4" in diameter.*

• *A sturdy cast-iron bed is best for reducing vibration while working.*

• *A 4-step pulley and belt system with a 400 to 2000 rpm range is ideal for most home woodworkers.*

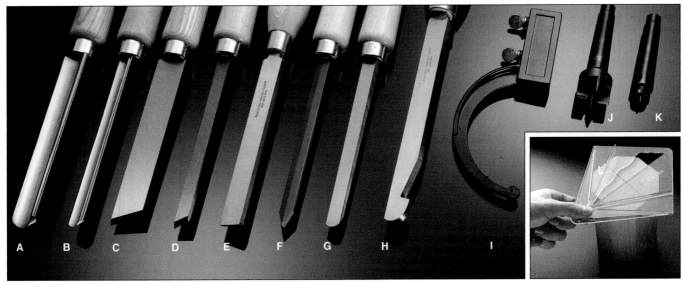

Some of the turning tools you'll need include: 1" gouge (A), ½" gouge (B), 1" skew (C), ½" skew (D), square nose chisel (E), parting tool (F), round nose scraper (G), side cutting scraper (H), sizing tool (I), headstock center (J), tailstock center (K), center finder (L).

tightly enough to hold the stock while letting it still rotate. A tool rest, attached to the lathe bed, is used to brace the cutting tools as they are applied against the turning stock.

Choosing a lathe

Capacity: The length of stock a lathe can accommodate is based on the distance between the lathe centers. Depending upon the model, this distance ranges from 12" to more than 48".

The distance between the spindles and the lathe bed, which is usually referred to as the "swing" of the lathe, determines the diameter stock the machine can handle—this can vary from 6" to more than 16". Some lathes have a recess in the bed, just below the headstock spindle, that increases its swing and makes it possible to turn pieces of slightly greater diameter. For larger faceplate turning projects, lathes may have either an auxiliary spindle located on the outboard side of the headstock, or a headstock that may be pivoted 90° so you can attach the faceplate to a larger blank. For more information on faceplate turning, see *Shaping Wood,* pages 94 and 95.

Bench-mounted vs. free-standing: Bench-mounted lathes are

most common in the home workshop, and they have a wide range of capabilities. Smaller benchtop models, called mini-lathes, are perfect for the hobbyist whose main interest is miniature furniture or dinnerware. Free-standing lathes that incorporate a sturdy worktable, can handle larger workpieces and are more powerful. If you plan to do a lot of turning, they may be a worthwhile investment.

Attaching the stock

The stock is held between the headstock and tailstock by two pieces known as centers, which fit into the spindles at each end. The headstock center has prongs or teeth that are driven into the end of the stock, while the tailstock center has a dull point that is not attached to the stock, but fits in a hole drilled in the tail end of the stock that is oiled or waxed so the friction is reduced. Note: Some tailstock centers have ball-bearings that make the oil or wax unnecessary, but they are less common. Leave at least 1" of extra length at each end of the stock to avoid striking the lathe with your tools as you cut near the end-points of the stock.

1 Mark the centerpoints on the ends of your stock. To find the center on square stock, draw diag-

onal lines between opposite corners. Use a center finder for round- or odd-shaped material (see *photo inset, above*).

2 Drill ⅛ × ½"-deep holes at the centerpoints on both ends of the stock.

3 Cut ⅛"-deep kerf lines along the diagonal lines of the stock.

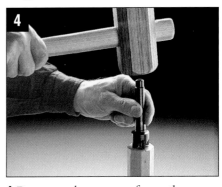

4 Remove the center from the headstock spindle. Align the headstock center prongs with the diagonal lines cut into the stock and drive the center straight down into the stock, using a mallet.

5 Fit the headstock center and attached stock onto the spindle.

6 Place a drop of machine oil in the hole at the tail end of the stock and slide the tailstock in so the center fits in the hole.

7 Apply moderate pressure to the stock by turning the handwheel then lock the tailstock spindle in place. Test the fit—you should be able to turn the stock by hand.

Roughing the stock

The turning mechanism of the lathe generates considerable force. For this reason it is important to prepare and work carefully. Adjust the tool rest so it is no closer than ⅛" from the stock, and before turning on the lathe, turn the stock by hand to be sure it clears the rest. Adjust the tool rest height so the gouge will contact the workpiece just above its centerline. Once you begin cutting, reposition the tool rest as necessary to roughen the length of the workpiece. To prevent injury, be sure to brace the blade of the cutting tool against the tool rest before it touches the spinning workpiece, and keep it braced against the tool rest at all times—otherwise the blade will be pulled downward and out of control. Move your body to follow the direction of the cutting tool as you work along the length of the workpiece.

To achieve the best results, use an overhand grip to hold the cutting tool while roughing the stock, and switch to an underhand grip for finer detail work. The overhand grip helps to counter the force of the cutting tools as it hits the ragged edges of the stock,

Always wear safety glasses or a face shield when using the lathe. To avoid injury, stand away from the lathe as you turn the motor on—just in case the stock works itself loose and flies out from the machine. To begin work, stand close enough to the machine so you can work without leaning off balance. Keep your elbow tucked in against your body and hold the cutting tool with the handle extending out from your forearm.

while the underhand grip provides greater control for precise cutting. With the cutting tools braced against the tool rest, slowly raise the tool handle upward so the blade cuts into the work. Apply pressure to the gouge gradually to obtain the cut you need. If the workpiece begins to chatter, ease up on the pressure. Roll the gouge as you work to use the entire cutting edge and to keep a sharp surface cutting the wood at all times. Resharpen tools as often as necessary to keep the tools from tearing the workpiece.

1 Begin roughing out the stock to a cylindrical shape, with the lathe set at roughing speed (see *Tool Tip*) using a 1" gouge. If tapering the workpiece, begin with the thick end at the headstock and work down towards the thin end.

2 To smooth the rough cylinder, use a square-nose chisel and increase the turning speed (see *Tool Tip*). Use an overhand grip on the first pass, then change to an underhand grip for fine tuning.

Defining the shape

Once the cylinder is smooth, turn off the lathe and mark the location of detailing like beads, coves, and the shoulders in between, called fillets, by drawing short marks in pencil on the cylinder.
1 Turn on the lathe at medium speed and use a parting tool to scribe the marked lines into the wood. Stop the lathe and remove the tool rest.

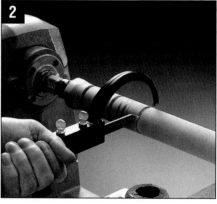

2 Clamp the sizing tool to the parting tool. For each line, set the parting tool to the desired depth, then hook the sizing tool over the scribed line. Turn on the lathe at medium speed and use a firm two-handed grip to guide the parting tool into each cut. Keep the sizing tool fitted in the groove, taking care not to let the parting tool jump out of the groove and make a jagged cut.

Cutting details

Begin cutting the deepest details, like coves, first. This allows more room to maneuver the tools when cutting the other features. Work at finishing speed (see *Tool Tip*) and use an underhand grip. Use calipers and dividers to check the sizing of details as you work.

1 Use a ½" or smaller gouge to cut coves. Start working from the center of the cove, then sweep the gouge to each side. Roll the gouge in the direction of the cut as you cut the cove.
2 Use the round nose scraper for the final shaping of the cove. Make sure to keep the handle parallel to the floor.
3 Cut fillets with an angled skew. Use the long point to reach across the cove to cut each fillet.

4 Start a bead by cutting a notched groove at each end. Form the bead with the heel of the skew, rolling the blade smoothly to each side to make the cut.

WOODWORKER'S TIP

Save worn sanding belts. Even well-used belts can be torn into strips and used successfully for sanding on the lathe.

Sanding on the lathe

Leave your workpiece on the lathe for quick and easy sanding.

Sand at the highest finishing speed recommended for the diameter of your workpiece (see *Tool Tip*) and keep the sandpaper moving constantly to avoid burns. Folding stiffens the paper so it can be used to smooth gentle curves. The very edge of a sheet will reach into tight areas.

1 Remove the tool rest, then begin sanding with 100-grit sandpaper. Continue with increasingly finer grits of sandpaper. 220-grit sandpaper is a good finishing paper for coarse-grained woods, while 400-grit paper will add a high polish to tight grains.
2 Burnish the piece with the non-abrasive side of the sand paper, or hold the leftover shavings from the workpiece against the workpiece to polish it further.

Completing the piece

The spinning action of the lathe makes it easy to apply smooth, even coats of finish. It can be a messy job however, so cover the work area and wear safety glasses to protect your eyes.

1 Turn on the lathe at finishing speed (see *Tool Tip*) and use a soft bristle or foam brush to apply finish to the workpiece. Work smoothly in one direction. Let the finish dry.
2 Waxes and oils may be applied with rags or pads and buffed to a high gloss.

3 Use a parting tool to cut a groove at the narrower end of the workpiece first. Cut the groove as deeply as possible without danger of breaking. Stop the cut when the blade is within ¼" of the center of the piece.
4 Repeat the cut at the other end of the workpiece. Stop the lathe and remove the workpiece.
5 Use a handsaw to cut the waste from the workpiece, then sand the saw marks out.

TOOL TIP

While turning speeds vary from lathe to lathe, most fall within the range shown below. Always follow the manufacurer's recommendation for the lathe you are using.

Stock diameter	Roughing	Shaping	Finishing
2 to 4"	600 rpm	1,200 rpm	2,000 rpm
4 to 8"	400 rpm	800 rpm	1200 rpm
Over 8"	200 rpm	800 rpm	800 rpm

Stationary Power Sanders

Smooth out your sanding jobs with a stationary power sander.

Sanding may be an inevitable part of woodworking, but it doesn't have to be tedious. If you want to make sanding easier, then it's probably time to consider getting some help from a stationary power sander. Power sanders don't eliminate finish- or hand-sanding, but they do save a lot of time and labor.

A variety of stationary power sanders is available, including belt, edge, disc, and strip sanders. These sanders are often paired together in different combinations to make a power sanding station. The most common combination, which we'll look at here, is the belt-and-disc sander.

Construction

The belt sander consists of a continuous belt that rotates around two rollers. One roller is driven by the motor, while the other is free-turning. The rest of the belt body rests against a flat, hard surface that is the sanding work area.

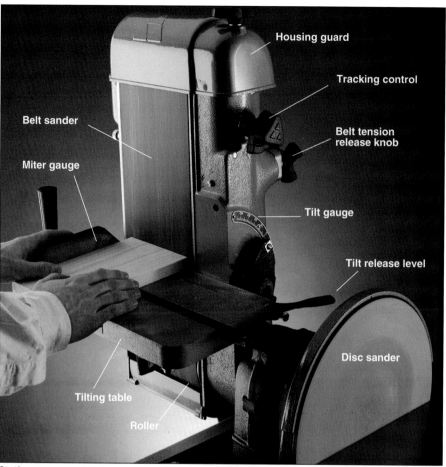

Housing guard

Tracking control

Belt sander

Belt tension release knob

Miter gauge

Tilt gauge

Tilt release level

Disc sander

Tilting table

Roller

Stationary power sanders have greater sanding surfaces than portable tools. In a single workstation, you can sand end and face grain, edges, curves, and irregular shapes.

The disc sander is a flat, round sanding plate set up adjacent to the belt sander. It is driven by the same motor as the belt sander.

Belt-and-disc sanders have either a single worktable that can be used for both sanders or two separate worktables. Most worktables tilt to any angle between 0° and 45°, and have a miter-gauge slot.

Belt & disc installation

It's important to keep the sanding belt on track and perfectly straight. To check whether a belt tracks straight, quickly turn the power on and off. If the belt shifts to one side, use the tracking adjustment controls to gradually tilt one roller until the belt remains centered.

The method of accessing the sanding belt and releasing belt tension to change a belt varies according to model. Follow the manufacturer's instructions to install a belt.

Methods of installing sanding discs

also vary from model to model. Some sanding discs are self-adhesive, while others require you to apply an adhesive. Check your owner's manual for the proper selection and application of discs.

Basic use

The belt-and-disc sander handles a variety of sanding jobs. Some jobs, like sanding end grain, can be done on either sander. Here's a look at the different ways you can use this tool.

Disc sander: The disc sander is used mostly for sanding end grain and the edges of a workpiece.

The circular motion isn't recommended for sanding large items or the face of a workpiece, because it leaves swirl marks on the wood. However, it is a good choice for sanding smaller workpieces.

Disc-sand using the left half, or down side, of the disc only, at or below the disc's center line. The disc's rotation pulls the workpiece down to the table surface, for better sanding control.

Use the miter gauge to ensure that you sand the end grain of a workpiece evenly.

1 Hold the workpiece firmly against the miter gauge, then contact the sanding disc. Sand lightly, without forcing the workpiece into the disc. The motor has ample power for most sanding jobs—pushing too hard will burn the wood and wear down your sanding pad fast.

2 Keep the workpiece moving across the sanding surface by sliding the miter gauge along its slot, so the wood doesn't burn.

Round workpieces: The disc sander can also sand the edges of round workpieces. Use this pivot-sanding jig to simplify the job.

1 Cut a 15 × 15" auxiliary table from plywood, then cut a 1" dado in the center from front to back.

2 Cut a hardwood strip to fit the dado, then attach a pivot nail 1" from one end, for positioning the

workpiece. Cut a second strip of wood that fits the table's miter slot.

3 Attach the second strip to the underside of the jig, so it fits in the miter slot and sets the jig ⅛" away from, and square to, the sanding disc.

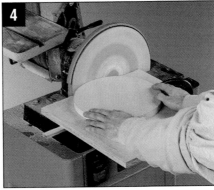

4 Clamp the jig to the table, with the pivot nail centered on the down side of the disc. Center the workpiece on the pivot nail. Slide the workpiece against the sanding surface and rotate it at a steady pace. Reposition the jig occasionally to avoid uneven wear of the sanding disc.

Belt sander: The belt sander works well for sanding large surfaces, parallel to the grain. It can be set in the horizontal position for surface and edge sanding, or in the vertical position for sanding end grain.

You can use the belt sander with a miter gauge or guide fence, or for freehand sanding. Use a guide when you want to ensure flat, even edges.

Sand large surfaces parallel to the grain, with the belt sander set in the horizontal position.

1 Set the table perpendicular to the belt, to act as a guide fence.

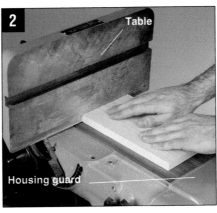

2 Sand with the end of the workpiece up against the table. Keep the workpiece moving for even sanding.

For long workpieces, keep the belt sander set horizontally, but move the table aside. Clamp a fence to the table, parallel to the belt. (Some models have a housing guard that must be removed first.)

Using the miter gauge, you can sand compound bevels on the end of a workpiece. Set the miter gauge to the desired miter angle and the table to the desired bevel, then contact the work with the sanding surface.

To sand end grain, set the belt sander vertically. With the workpiece flat on the table and flush against the miter gauge, contact the sanding surface. Use the miter slot to keep the workpiece moving.

Most belt sanders can be locked in any position between 0° and 45°. You can easily sand any beveled edge by tilting the belt, table, or both.

To sand the edges of a workpiece, set the belt up vertically, with the table perpendicular to the belt. Place the workpiece flat on the worktable and move the edges across the belt surface.

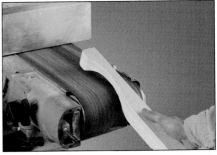

By removing the housing guard from the end of the roller, you can sand inside curves and some irregular shapes.

Drill Press Basics

Countless uses turn the drill press into the most interesting of boring tools.

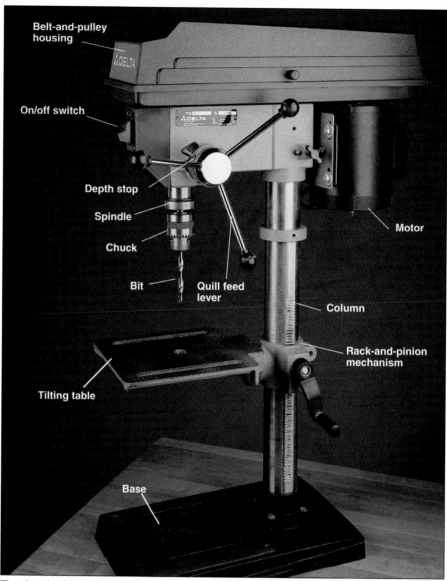

Belt-and-pulley housing

On/off switch

Depth stop

Spindle

Chuck

Bit

Quill feed lever

Tilting table

Base

Motor

Column

Rack-and-pinion mechanism

The size of a drill press is defined by the largest workpiece that can be placed on the table and centered under the drill bit. The 12" bench drill press shown *above* will drill the center of a 12"-wide workpiece.

Although the drill press is a less glamorous tool than some other stationary tools, its precision and the availability of a wide range of accessories make it a true workshop workhorse. A drill press gives you exact control of the diameter, depth, and angle of a hole. Whether you're drilling holes for a dowel joint or counter-sinking pilot holes for screws, you'll rely upon it constantly for its accuracy and consistency.

In addition to precision drilling, you can sand, mortise, grind, and shape with the drill press. With the proper accessories and supporting setups or jigs, the drill press will perform as precisely in any of these other applications as it does for drilling.

BUYER'S TIPS

• *Motors range from ¼ to 1 hp. For general-purpose use, buy a drill press with a motor that is at least ⅓ hp.*

• *Get a drill press large enough to handle your work comfortably. The capacity of the drill press is limited to the distance between the column and the bit (see photo, above). A 12" drill press (that will drill the center of a 12"-wide workpiece) is a good choice for general use.*

• *Choose a model with a rack-and-pinion table adjustment mechanism on the column. This system offers smooth and precise table movement, and won't slip.*

Construction

The ability of the drill press to do precise work begins with its construction. A cast-iron base and sturdy steel column support the adjustable table and the motor and drill head assembly in exact alignment. The large spindle and chuck can hold almost any type of drill bit or drill accessory with shanks up to ½", or even ⅜", in diameter.

The chuck and spindle are raised and lowered by the quill feed lever, which includes a depth stop that lets you control boring depths exactly. The depth of hole you can bore depends on the maximum quill stroke and the length of your

The drill's spindle speed is set by the way you arrange the belts on the pulleys. Small models typically have two pulleys with five speed settings, ranging from 450 to 2500 spindle rpm. Larger machines typically have three pulleys with 12 speed settings, ranging from 250 to 3000 rpm.

drill bits. Most models have a quill stroke range between 3" and 5".

The chuck and spindle are rotated by an adjustable V-belt and pulley system connected to the motor. By moving the V-belt to different slots on the pulleys, you can control the speed of the drill to suit the material you are drilling, whether it's wood, metal, or plastic (see *photo,* opposite).

Choosing a drill press

Drill presses come in a variety of sizes, typically ranging from 8" to 20", and are available as bench models or floor models.

Bench models, while smaller, often perform identically to floor models. They can be mounted on a workbench or any stable surface, but are too heavy to be truly portable.

A floor model's longer column provides a work area that accommodates larger workpieces without sacrificing table space, but they cost about $50 to $100 more.

Most drill presses also have tables that tilt to one or both sides, to let you drill at different angles. To get the most out of your drill press, make sure you get one with a tilting table that can lock in any position from 0° to 90°.

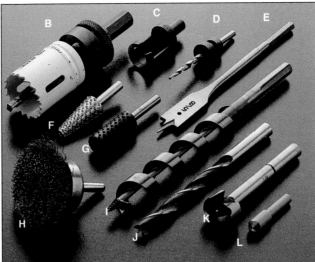

Typical drill press bits, specialty bits, and accessories include: a mortising attachment (A), holesaw (B), plug cutter (C), drill-and-countersink with bit stop (D), spade bit (E), rotary rasps (F, G), wire brush (H), power auger (I), brad-point bit (J), Forstner bit (K), and countersink (L).

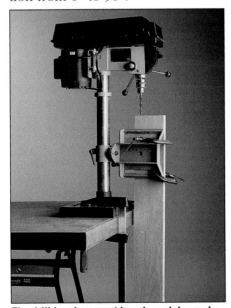

The drill head on most bench models can be turned sideways (relative to the base) to accommodate extra-long workpieces. Like the table, the base is slotted and machined flat, so it can also function as a worksurface. You can also work between the chuck and the floor.

Drill press bits

Drill presses can use the same standard bits used in a portable power drill, as well as bits with thicker shanks. A host of specialty bits and attachments are also machined specifically to fit in a drill chuck (see *photo,* above), enabling you to perform a variety of tasks beyond basic drilling.

Any bit or accessory will likely perform the best mounted in a drill press, simply because of the tool's accuracy. Specialty bits such as drill-and-countersinks, counterbores, and Forstner bits, already designed to enhance the quality of your work, excel in a drill press.

Basic drill press use

Before you use your drill press, adjust the speed setting for the material you're cutting. Drilling at too high a speed can burn up your bits, so be sure to refer to the manufacturer's setting information. A speed setting chart is commonly found on the inside of the pulley housing cover.

1 Clamp the workpiece to the table to prevent accidents or mistakes. The force of the spindle in motion can make holding a workpiece by hand difficult.

2 Mark the drilling point or points on your workpiece.

3 For precise depth setting, mark the depth on the side of the work-

piece. (Otherwise, you can use the depth gauge.) Lower the quill next to the workpiece and align the tip of the bit with the mark on the workpiece, then set and lock your depth stop.

4 Center the drilling point under the bit, then lower the bit until it almost contacts the workpiece. Make any further adjustments, then turn on the drill and let it reach full speed. Lower the bit into the workpiece to cut the hole. Raise the bit and turn off the drill.

Drilling in a cylinder: To drill accurate holes in the sides of a cylindrical workpiece, make a V-block (see *photo,* below) to cradle the cylinder. Make sure the sides of the block are squared up, and the angle of the "V" is between 50° and 90°.

Clamp the workpiece to a V-block, then install a pilot-pointed bit or set a location mark in the workpiece, using an awl. Make sure the bit and the bottom of the V-block are vertically aligned to ensure centered holes.

Compound angles: Boring compound angles can be tricky, but the drill press and the right jig can simplify the job. Essentially, the jig is an auxiliary table pitched at one of the angles of the compound angle. This auxiliary table can also be attached to the underside of a larger auxiliary table if you need to support a large workpiece.

1 Cut two pieces of plywood about the same size as your drill press table.

2 Cut two wedges to match the first angle of your compound angle (for instance, 15°) from scrap wood, then attach them with screws to one piece of plywood. To accurately arrive at the desired compound angle, make sure both ends of the wedges are flush with the edges of the plywood pieces.

3 Dry-fit the other piece of plywood on top and check the angle to verify that it is still the desired 15°. Screw the plywood top in place.

4 Add a straight strip to the jig to form a fence.

5 Clamp the auxiliary table to your worktable, and verify that it is perpendicular with a try square.

6 Tilt the table to match the second half of your compound angle, then recheck the compound angle. Next, drill your hole.

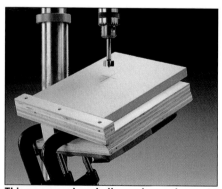

This compound angle jig can be used repeatedly for compound angles, using interchangeable wedges cut to match one part of the desired compound angle. The table is tilted to form the rest of the compound angle.

Drilling end grain: To drill the end of a piece of stock, tilt your table 90°, until it is vertical. Stand the workpiece vertically, then clamp it to the table. Center the pilot marks on the workpiece under the drill bit, then drill the hole.

Drilling deep holes: If you need to drill deep holes or drill completely through a thick workpiece, you may find yourself unable to complete the job if your quill stroke is too short. Long bits or bit extensions are available, but you can still only drill as deep as your quill stroke will allow in one pass.

With long bits or bit extensions, you can get around this limitation by working in stages. Drill the hole as far as the quill stroke will allow, then raise the quill all the way up. Next, instead of lowering the bit into the workpiece, raise the table until the bit bottoms out in the hole you just drilled. Then you can bore the distance of your quill stroke once more. This method can be used up to the length of the bit.

> **WOODWORKER'S TIP**
>
> *When you're drilling at an extreme angle, sometimes the sides of the bit will engage the workpiece before the sharp point of the bit can make contact and establish the hole. To ensure the bit makes a clean entry, clamp a scrap block to the workpiece so it slightly overlaps the entry point on the workpiece. This way, the bit will contact the scrap first and establish a cutting path.*

When you drill deep holes, work in stages, rather than drilling as deep as possible in one pass. Interrupt your work to raise the bit and clear chips and sawdust. This produces cleaner holes and keeps the bit from burning up.

Spherical workpieces: If you need to drill a hole in a spherical workpiece, first drill a hole in a piece of scrapwood just slightly smaller than the diameter of the workpiece. Place the workpiece in the hole in the scrap, clamp it in place, and drill.

> **WOODWORKER'S TIP**
>
> *Make very small workpieces easier to handle by clamping them in a handscrew. Secure the handscrews to the table with a clamp for safe and accurate drilling.*

> **WOODWORKER'S TIP**
>
> *To protect the drill table and prevent tearout, clamp a piece of scrap to the backside of the workpiece.*

Cutting tenons

Tenon-cutters, plug cutters, and plug-and-tenon cutters are ideal for use in a drill press, because of its accuracy for repetitive work. It's a simple matter for you to cut any number of uniform plugs from the wood of your choice, instead of settling for commercially cut plugs cut from wood that doesn't always match the workpiece.

While the drill press is capable of using many different accessories, some of them do require the aid of a jig. Cutting tenons on a drill press, for example, is best done with the help of a jig and a bit of preparation ahead of time.

To cut repeated tenons for fitting spindles in chairs or benches, make a jig to save yourself repeated setup time. The jig we made is basically a plywood frame that surrounds the spindle blank and holds it in place while you cut the tenons at each end. This jig works best with spindle blanks with square sides, before they are shaped on a lathe or with a spokeshave.

1 Cut two extra spindle blanks, making them 2" shorter than the rest. These will be used to form the sides of the jig.

2 Cut the front and back pieces for the jig from plywood, making both pieces as long as the short spindle blanks, and about 4" wide.

3 Cut a small hole in the plywood front piece, centered on its baseline, so dust won't clog in the bottom of the spindle slot of the assembled jig.

4 Clamp a spindle blank between the side pieces, then attach front and back jig pieces to the sides with glue and finishing nails. Take care not to get any glue on the middle spindle. Remove spindle after glue dries.

5 Cut a base for the jig from plywood, then attach it to the jig with glue and finishing nails. It is now ready to use.

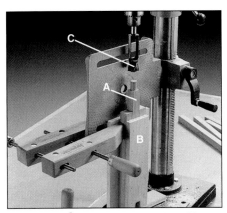

To use the tenon-cutting jig, tilt the table to the vertical position. Insert a spindle blank (A) in the jig slot, then clamp the jig (B) to the table, as well as to the base. Install a tenon cutter (C) in your drill press, then cut the tenon.

Mortising

There are several ways to mortise using a drill press. You can use precision mortising accessories or standard bits and a chisel.

A commercial mortising jig provides the most accurate method of mortising. When this mortising jig is clamped to the worktable, its rigid frame stabilizes and guides the hollow mortising chisel for very precise mortising. A hollow chisel mortiser, which is basically an auger bit centered within a sharp, hollow, square chisel, is used in conjunction with the jig.

If you prefer mortising without the expense or setup time of a commercial mortising jig, you can also use the hollow chisel mortiser alone. With the workpiece clamped to a fence, you can mortise quite effectively.

If you don't have a hollow chisel mortiser, you can mortise using any standard bit, as follows:
1 Measure and mark the mortise, then clamp the workpiece to a fence on the worktable.
2 Drill the two end points of the mortise with a bit diameter that matches the mortise width.
3 To clear out the mortise, use a bit slightly smaller than full width of the mortise and bore out repeated holes.
4 Finish by chiseling out the remaining waste to square up the sides and ends of the mortise.

Drum sanding

Drum sanding is another effective use for the drill press. Drum sanders are good for sanding the contours of curved shapes, sanding inside cut-out areas, and freehand sanding. Sanding drums range in size from ½" to 3" or more.

When you drum sand, the workpiece often only contacts a very small portion of the sanding surface near the bottom of the drum. To use all of the drum's sanding surface, build a jig like this one which accomodates all sizes of drums.
1 Cut two 7 × 7" auxiliary tables from plywood. Then, cut two 4 × 7" pieces of plywood for the sides of the jig.
2 Scribe a 3½"-diameter circle near the upper left-hand corner of one 7 × 7" piece. At the base of the circle, draw a line across the workpiece perpendicular to the left edge of the workpiece.
3 Scribe a 2"-diameter circle adjacent to the first on the same baseline, leaving ¼" between circles. Using a straightedge, draw lines connecting the contours of the two circles.
4 Clamp the workpiece to the drill press and use holesaws to cut the holes. Next, cut out the waste between the holes.
5 On the second workpiece, repeat steps 3 and 4, substituting ⅞" and 1¾" holes, respectively.
6 Glue the four workpieces together to form a box, so the drum slots are in the upper left-hand corner on both faces of the box.

To use the drum sanding jig, install a drum sander in your drill press, then align the jig so the drum has about ¼" clearance from the near edge of the jig hole. Clamp the jig to your drill press table from either side, then begin sanding.

Other accessories

The drill press can use a number of other accessories made for mounting in a drill.

Wire brushes in a range of gauges are available for the drill press. These are useful for removing dirt or rust from metals, cleaning tools, or burnishing a metal surface.

Rotary rasps are designed for carving or cutting. Use these to cut away hard-to-reach areas and inside corners of a workpiece, and for decorative carving. Rasps leave a rough surface that will generally require sanding.

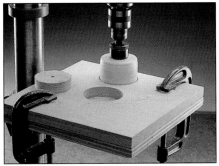

To cut perfectly round, clean holes from ⅝" up to 6" in diameter, use a holesaw. Holesaws mount in any drill, but the high speeds and stability of the drill press make it perfect for driving this cutting bit.

You can also use your drill press as a grinder by mounting a grinding wheel for sharpening tools or grinding metal.

If you don't have a router, the drill press can be used for some routing or shaping, when used with a special router chuck and router bits. Because routers turn at much higher speeds, your drill press won't be as effective as a router.

If you do use your drill press as a router, set it on its highest speed setting. Feed a workpiece more slowly than normal when routing, and remove stock with a lot of shallow passes.

WOODWORKER'S TIP

Avoid the struggle of balancing long or large workpieces on your small worktable by temporarily attaching an auxiliary tabletop to your worktable. Cut the auxiliary table from medium-grade plywood, and keep several sizes on hand.

Drill Bit Guide

Twist bit (A), Brad-point bit (B), Spade bit (C), Holesaw (D).

Typical bits

These bits can be used in hand drills, power drills, and drill presses unless specified otherwise.

Twist bits: These bits are the only ones featured that drill metal. Use lubrication when doing so. These bits also drill wood, but they produce some tearout. Extra-long twist bits, called extension bits, drill long holes for applications like running lamp wires through spindles. Sizes: 1/16" to 1" diameter.

Brad-point bits: Related to twist bits, brad-point bits have a sharp center point for precise positioning and sharp edge flutes for clean-edged holes and minimal tearout. Sizes: 1/8" to 1" diameter.

Spade bits: A long center point (spur) positions the bit, and horizontal cutting edges bore with a scraping action. Don't use these in hand drills. Sizes: 1/4" to 1½" diameter.

Holesaws: The holesaw consists of an outer cutter with serrated teeth mounted on a mandrel attached to a center twist bit for positioning. Don't use these in hand drills. Sizes: 5/8" to 4" diameter.

Forstner bits: These bits create flat-bottomed holes. A spur guides the bit, and a circular rim creates a smooth-sided hole. Sizes: 1/4" to 2" diameter.

Multi-spur bits: Similar to Forstner bits, multi-spur bits cut veneers and laminated products extremely well. Sizes: 3/8" to 3½" diameter.

Auger bits: These bits have a screw-tipped point to pull them into the wood to drill deep holes. They should never be used with drill presses. Sizes: 1/4" to 1" diameter.

Fly cutters: Adjustable holesaws, fly cutters are used only on the drill press. They cut circles ranging from 1" to 6" in diameter.

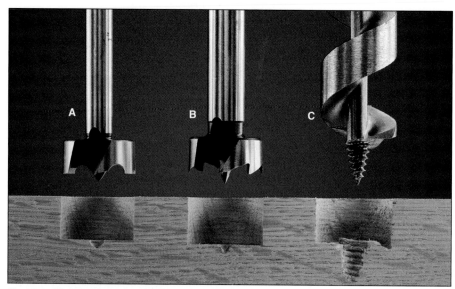

Forstner bit (A), Multi-spur bit (B), Auger bit (C).

Fly cutter *(above).*

Counterbore bit

Countersink bit

Adjustable counterbore bit

Plug cutter

Dowel cutter

Mortising bit

Vix bit

Router bit

Specialty bits

A variety of bits and accessories are available for jobs that require special drilling.

Countersink bits: These bits' cone-shaped cutters create recesses into which flat-topped screws are driven flush with the surface. Sizes: ¼" to ¾" diameter.

Counterbore bits: These contoured bits create pilot and shank holes for a wood screw while simultaneously creating the counterbore. Available for screw sizes from #5 to #16.

Adjustable counterbore bits: Each of these bits' setscrew fittings create counterbore holes of different lengths for one size of wood screw. Available for screw sizes #5, #6, #8, and #10.

Plug cutters: For use with a drill press, plug cutters create plugs for filling counterbore holes. Sizes: ¼" to 1" diameter.

Mortising bits: For use with the drill press only, mortising bits consist of a hollow, four-sided chisel with a drill bit in the center for chip removal. Sizes: ¼" to ½" diameter.

Router bits: These shaped bits for the drill press turn the tool into a router. The router bit shown in the *photo, left)* cuts hanger slots in picture frames.

Dowel cutters: Similar to plug cutters, dowel cutters' hollow bits cut cylindrical dowels or tenons. Sizes ¼ × 1¼" long to 1 × 3½" long.

Self-centering (Vix) bits: A hardened steel guide sleeve automatically centers the bit when drilling pilot holes for mounting hinges and other hardware. Sizes: ⁵⁄₆₄" bit for #3 and #4 screws; ⁷⁄₆₄" bit for #5 and #6 screws; ⁹⁄₆₄" bit for #8, #9, and #10 screws; and ¹¹⁄₆₄" bit for #12 screws.

BUYER'S TIP

When buying drill bits, do not buy the cheapest ones you can find. Cheap drill bits are made of soft metal that dulls quickly. Sometimes they even are ground incorrectly. Buy the best drill bits you can afford, even for a basic starter set.

The three basic portable drill types are (from bottom) the brace and bit drills, hand drills, and power drills.

Portable Drills

Basic drilling skills can make all the difference on home projects.

There are three main types of portable drills: the hand drill, the brace and bit drill, and the power drill. All three have a place in the woodworker's shop.

Types of portable drills

Hand drills: Also known as eggbeater drills, the hand drill is defined by the size of its chuck capacity. The chuck is the portion of the drill that holds the shank, or noncutting end, of the bit.

Hand drill bit shanks are cylindrical and vary in size, usually matching the size of the hole cut by the bit. Hand drill chucks are usually no larger than ¼", which means that they will hold drill bits whose shanks are ¼" or smaller. Hand drills with ⅜" chucks are also available but less common.

Brace and bit drills: Brace and bit drills are defined by the size of the sweep. The sweep is the amount of space it takes to sweep

the handle of the brace around one revolution. Most sweeps range from 6 to 14". A good size brace for general use is 10". The bits used with a brace have a square tang instead of a rounded shank, and the V-shaped jaws inside the brace chuck grip the square tang. Brace bit tangs are usually the same size, regardless of the size or type of bit.

Most braces have a ratchet mechanism behind the chuck which allows you to bore in close spaces. Even if it's not possible to make the full sweep of the brace, using a brace with a ratchet mechanism allows you to sweep as far as possible, back the brace handle up without disturbing the bit, then sweep again. Braces' bits bore holes from ¼ to 3" in diameter.

Power drills: Power drills come in both plugged-in and cordless varieties. Power drill sizes are determined by the size of the chuck. The three most common chuck sizes are ¼", ⅜", and ½". When chuck sizes increase, torque also increases to allow the drill to cut effectively with the larger bits. But when torque increases, speed decreases. To reach a good balance between speed and torque, choose a ⅜" power drill for general workshop needs.

Most power drill bits have rounded shanks whose sizes vary according to the size of the bit. When changing bits, be sure to use a chuck key to tighten all three chuck holes before drilling.

Power drills also can have various user-determined speed options: single-speed, two-speed, and variable-speed. The variable-speed variety lets you adjust the speed along a continuum by adjusting a sliding lever. Some power drills also have a reversible option so that they can remove screws or back out of a hole in a jam. A good woodworking drill should be reversible and have at least two speeds.

Cordless drills are rechargeable power drills, usually sold with wall storage units that recharge the drill when it is stored. Most cordless drills can drill a hundred holes or screw in hundreds of screws on one charge. If you need more power than that, you can purchase extra battery packs or buy fast-recharging drills, which completely repower themselves in one hour instead of 3 to 12 hours normally required for recharging.

Accessories

Because the power drill was the first and most widely available hand power tool on the American market, accessories to turn a power drill into a drill press, a sander, a buffer, a rasp, and even a lathe crowd the shelves of home centers. Depending on your frequency of need, it is probably best to purchase a task-specific tool such as a lathe rather than rely on a power drill attachment. But several of the accessories available for the power drill are worthwhile.

Drill guides can help you drill perfectly aligned holes.

Drill guides: Many types of drill guides are available. When used correctly, drill guides keep bits centered on the workpiece. When using these tools, be sure they are securely attached to the worksurface. Always protect the worksurface with a piece of scrapwood to prevent damaging drill-through.

Sanders: Your power drill can become a disc or drum sander with sander attachments. This is useful when the workpiece is too large or awkward to work with on your stationary sander. For accurate straight sanding, however, you should use a stationary sander.

Depth stops: To prevent drilling too far into the workpiece, either buy a commercially available depth stop that affixes to the drill (stiff piece of metal or a spring that touches the surface of the workpiece when desired depth is reached), or attach a stop collar to the bit to reach the desired depth.

Doweling jig: A doweling jig attaches to the edge of the workpiece and guides the drill for creation of straight, perfectly perpendicular dowel holes. Some doweling jigs also regulate the spacing between dowel holes.

Screwdriver bits: All portable drills can be turned into either Phillips or standard screwdrivers with special bits. You can purchase special screwdriver attachments. These specialized chucks have multiple depth settings with a clutch that automatically releases when the desired depth is reached.

Basic drill use

1 When determining hole placement, mark the location of the center of the hole. Use a pencil, straightedge, and measuring tape to draw an X in the correct spot. The center of the X should be the center of the hole.

2 After determining the starting point for the hole, use an awl to punch a small hole in the wood at the center of the X. This starter hole keeps the drill on track.

For both hand drills and brace and bit drills, use some of your body weight to steady the drills. Do not twist the drills, though, because the bits may break.

3 When drilling, verify that you are keeping the drill straight. Check the angle visually or, on a horizontal surface, set a try square near your drill and try to keep the drill straight in relation to the try square. If you have one, use a drill guide to keep a power drill straight.

4 If you are boring a large hole, remove the bit from the hole periodically to remove the waste wood and to allow both the wood and the bit to cool off.

5 When drilling an auger hole, do not finish the entire through hole in one pass. When the brad point of the auger bit protrudes through the other side of the board, remove the bit from the hole, turn over the workpiece, and pick up the hole from the other side, using the brad point exit hole as your starting point.

6 To prevent tearout on through holes, clamp a piece of scrapwood onto the exit side of the board. Drill the hole through the board, into the scrapwood.

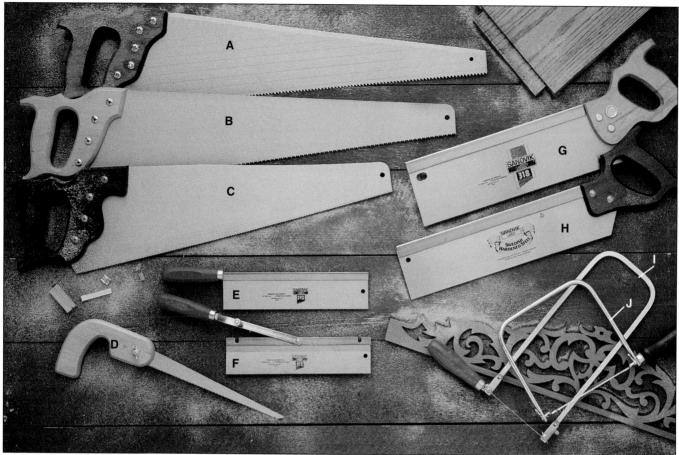

Common handsaws include: a ripsaw (A), crosscut saw (B), panel saw (C), compass saw (D), dovetail saw (E), offset dovetail saw (F), backsaw (G), tenon saw (H), scrollsaw (I), and coping saw (J).

Handsaws

Use handsaws to add a more personal feel to your work.

In a high-tech world with impressive power saws, it's easy to forget the usefulness of handsaws. Many woodworkers swear by handsaws, and hand tools in general, because they allow the woodworker to slow down and lose the production mentality that can arise when turning out projects on power tools. Also, by the time you set up, adjust, check, and use various power saws, you may not have saved as much time over using a handsaw as you might think. Finally, some cuts just can't be made with a power saw.

Saw characteristics

Each different type of handsaw comes in a variety of points per inch (ppi) or teeth per inch (tpi). The number of ppi or tpi a saw has serves as a prime factor in the quality and speed of the cut it makes. The more ppi or tpi, the finer and slower the cut. As with tablesaw blades, crosscut handsaws have more ppi than ripsaws.

Ripsaws

Ripsaws cut with the grain using chisel-edged teeth that remove wood fibers from the kerf. Half-ripsaws, slightly smaller than ripsaws, serve the same purpose as full ripsaws but are intended for use on thinner boards. Ripsaws are the largest handsaws, approximately 26" long, with 5 to 7 ppi.

Crosscut saws

Crosscut saws cut across the grain with knife-edged teeth that sever wood fibers in the kerf.

Panel saws are crosscut saws for use on thinner and man-made boards. Typically 22 to 26" long, crosscut saws have 10 to 12 ppi.

Backsaws

Backsaws are any saw with a reinforcing strip of metal along the top edge of the blade. The reinforcement spine adds weight and stability to the fine blade, which cuts thinner kerfs. Backsaws' thin blades are perfect for cutting dovetails and tenons, although they also function well on general crosscut work. Often 12 to 14" long, backsaws have approximately 15 ppi.

Tenon saws: Backsaws for general bench work, tenon saws come in a variety of lengths from 10 to 14", and their blades are usually 4" wide with 13 to 15 ppi.

Dovetail saws: Backsaws for very fine joinery, dovetail saws are smaller than tenon saws (8 to 10" long with a 3½"-wide blade) and have finer teeth (16 to 21 ppi).

Offset dovetail saws: Differing from dovetail saws only in the handle, the offset dovetail saw does flush cutting with a fixed or reversible offset handle.

Curve-cutting saws

Curve-cutting saws have narrow blades that usually adjust for changes in cutting direction.

Coping saws: These saws cut thin woods, plastics, composites, and softer metals. They have a frame, between the ends of which a thin, 12 to 20-ppi blade is attached. *Fret saws*, which are coping saws with larger frames, cut deeper materials.

Scrollsaws: Coping saws for cutting very tight curves or for cutting man-made boards or veneers, scrollsaws' deep frames work well on larger pieces of wood. Their quite fine (up to 32 ppi) blades break easily.

Compass saws and keyhole saws: Frameless curve-cutting saws, compass saws have pistol-grip handles, while keyhole saws usually have turned handles. These saws can also be used for internal cuts by inserting the blades into a drilled hole and cutting from there. Both have backless, tapering blades, the compass saw with 8 to 10 ppi, and the keyhole saw with 12 to 16 ppi.

Japanese saws

Japanese saws cut on the backstroke (the pull instead of the push stroke), which prevents the blades from buckling. This allows Japanese saws to use finer, thinner blades for a much thinner kerf. The centers of Japanese saw blades are ground thinner than the blade edges, giving them better kerf clearance. The steel in Japanese saws, harder than that in Western saws, can be made sharper than Western saws, but it breaks more easily.

Kataba: Used for rough cutting work, the kataba's thin blade still produces fine cuts. The flexible cutting blade is available with ripping teeth or crosscutting teeth.

Ryoba: Also used for rough cutting work, the ryoba also has a flexible cutting blade. But the ryoba has two cutting edges on it—one for ripping and one for crosscutting. The double cutting edges require that the ryoba be used at only a slight angle so that the cutting edge not in use doesn't enter the workpiece. For this reason, the ryoba is better for

cutting stock thinner than the saw's blade width.

Dozuki: A Japanese backsaw, the dozuki makes fine, accurate cuts and joints. It has a 7 to 10½" blade and 18 to 25 ppi.

Hugihiki: An extra-flexible kataba, the hugihiki makes extremely accurate flush cuts. To achieve the flush cut, rest the highly flexible blade flat on the workpiece and bend the blade to create tension.

Basic handsaw use

Ripsaws and crosscut saws: Grip the handle and extend your index finger along the handle to steady and guide your sawing stroke. Start the cut with a few backward cuts to establish the kerf. Use a ripsaw at a 60° angle or a crosscut saw at a 45° angle to the workpiece. If the kerf on long pieces begins to pinch and bind the saw, use a kerf wedge to keep the kerf open. When you near the end of the cut, hold the waste piece with your noncutting hand, supporting it through the end of the cut to reduce the chance of splintering and tearing.

Backsaws: Grip the saw handle, extending the forefinger of your gripping hand along the handle for balance and direction. Start your cut with a couple of backward cuts on the far side of the workpiece, holding the saw at a 10° angle. Gradually level out the saw across the piece, starting the kerf across the entire top of the workpiece. Keep the saw parallel to the workpiece while sawing.

Curve-cutting saws: For frame saws (bow saws, coping saws, scrollsaws), hold the saw with both hands, wrapping the supporting hand around the sawing hand and the blade to steady and guide the saw. With feet apart, use the saw at a 90° angle to the workpiece. Clamp the workpiece in a vise and saw close to the vise or clamping spot to minimize vibration. To change direction while sawing, change the position of the workpiece.

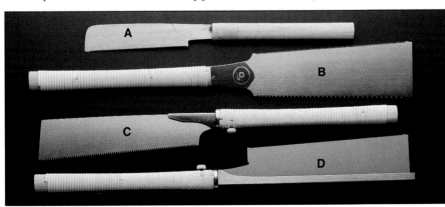

The basic Japanese saws, which have become popular for their clean cuts, are the hugihiki (A), ryoba (B), kataba (C), and dozuki (D).

Hand planes are a highly specialized tool group. Each type of plane is designed for a specific function. Block planes (A) are general-purpose tools. Smoothing planes (B) put a fine finish on a surface. Scrub planes (C) scrape rough wood down to thickness. Jointer planes (D) flatten long, flat surfaces. Shoulder planes (E) shave end grain and trim large joints. Mortising planes (F) clean out and square up mortises. Router planes (G) cut rabbets and dadoes. Combination planes (H) have interchangeable blades for special cuts. Always retract the blade, and store a plane on its side.

Hand Planes

Hand planes are a necessity for fine woodworking.

Available in wood or metal, hand planes are a varied and specialized tool group. Used to smooth wooden surfaces, reduce them to finished dimensions, and carve sophisticated profiles, hand planes remove shavings to precisely controlled depths. From small end-grain trimmers to 2' wooden jointer planes, a plane exists for almost every application.

Block planes
General-purpose block planes are light enough to use with one hand. The wood version has a large depth-adjustment knob for precise settings, but the metal version is more sophisticated. Either fully adjustable or nonadjustable, these planes are ideal for trimming end grain or squaring the edges of short boards, as well as putting a light chamfer on an edge. These may be the handiest of all planes.

Bench planes
Bench planes reduce a wooden surface to finished dimensions by gradually smoothing it. Although wooden bench planes slide easily, metal planes have a cutting edge that is more quickly and precisely adjusted.

Exert pressure primarily on the front, or toe, of the plane at the start of each stroke. Distribute pressure evenly as you push along the surface. Press down slightly on the heel as you finish each stroke.

With their short base, *smoothing planes* follow all surface undulations, skimming along the surface and putting a fine finish on the workpiece.

Scrub planes scrape the wood down to a rough thickness. Their convex cutting edge should be pushed diagonally across the grain.

Jack planes are usually used after the scrub. This general-purpose tool works well in squaring or flattening a surface.

Jointer planes form unusually straight surfaces because of their size. While small planes might follow the contours, jointer planes have a sole (or base) up to 2' long, allowing them to bridge surface undulation and flatten large workpieces.

Mortising planes accurately clean out and form mortises. The mortising plane is often used for creating precise hinge-and-lock mortises on new or rebuilt doors and door frames.

Rabbet planes

Rabbet planes carve recesses along the edges of a workpiece. Little more than a smaller version of the standard jack plane, *bench rabbet planes* have a blade extending over the entire width of the sole.

The *shoulder plane* is capable of shaving end grain, but it is most

Used on its side, the shoulder plane is useful for smoothing mortise-and-tenon joints.

useful in smoothing large mortise-and-tenon joints.

The small, lightweight *bullnose plane* comes in many styles. It resembles a snub-nosed version of the shoulder plane. Because its blade is situated near the front of the toe, the bullnose plane is ideal for planing stopped rabbets and small joints.

Specialized planes

Replaced by power tools in many modern workshops, specialized planes are still a fast, accurate, and relatively inexpensive way to complete many projects.

Fitted with a standard bench plane blade, the *compass plane's* flexible steel sole enables it to trim gradual convex or concave curves,

such as the edges of a round tabletop.

The *router plane* cuts grooves and dadoes with relative efficiency and is a cheap alternative to the electric router. Though easy to make in a workshop, wooden

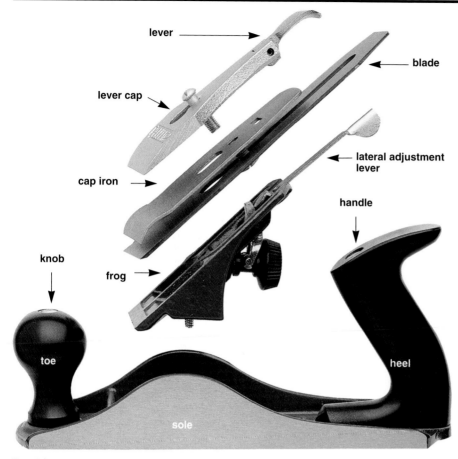

lever

blade

lever cap

cap iron

lateral adjustment lever

handle

knob

frog

toe

heel

sole

Keeping a plane in good working order requires occasional maintenance and adjustment. A finely tuned hand plane is a precision instrument, while a neglected plane can damage a wood surface.

router planes cannot match the accuracy of the store-bought metal versions with their precise depth-gauge and screw adjustments.

Prized by woodworking purists and restoration enthusiasts, *plow* and *combination planes* are ingenious, if expensive, tools. With their interchangeable blades and built-in fences, these highly specialized tools carve grooves, rabbets, tongue and groove joints, moldings, and beads. A combination plane with additional settings, the *multi-plane* will cut ovolo moldings, window sash moldings, flutes, and beads. It is fitted with a slitting knife to slice parallel strips of wood off the edge of a board.

Japanese planes

Simply constructed with expert craftsmanship, Japanese hand planes are very specialized to the Japanese slanted work bench. Japanese planes' rectangular, hardwood bodies make them easy to

identify. Unlike traditional western planes, the Japanese planes cut on the pullstroke.

Adjusting planes

Hand planes, like most tools, require occasional adjustment. To dismantle a metal plane, lift the blade and cap iron out of the housing. Loosen the cap iron locking screw and separate the two parts. Removing the blade assembly exposes the frog, a wedge-shaped piece that slides backward and forward to regulate the extension of the blade. Release the two locking screws and turn the adjusting screw with a screwdriver. Tighten the locking screws when you finish adjusting.

The adjustment of a plane should suit the grain of the wood and the required surface finish. For general use, remember how to adjust the cap iron, mouth opening, blade depth, and lateral adjustment lever.

The cap iron prevents splintering

by fracturing the shavings as soon as they are raised by the blade. For softwood, the cap iron should be set about 1/16" back from the cutting edge. For hardwood or a fine finish on softwood, this space should be reduced. After adjusting the cap iron, tighten the locking screw to prevent wood chips from penetrating the mechanism.

The width of the mouth opening is governed by the position of the frog. For general planing, line up the edge of the frog with the top edge of the mouth. For fine work, the mouth should be narrower. To adjust the size of the mouth opening, remove the blade assembly, slacken the screws that hold the frog, and move the frog using the adjustment screw.

The depth of cut is determined by extending the blade. The blade depth is controlled with an adjustment nut. Check the setting by holding the plane upside down with the sole level with the eye. For extra-fine work, the blade should hardly show above the sole.

The lateral adjustment lever makes sure that the blade protrudes evenly across the width of the sole. Move the lever from side to side. Hold the plane upside down to adjust it. After positioning blade, take up the slack in the adjustment screw to immobilize it.

If a plane is to be used to its maximum potential, it must be tuned up. Your plane sole must be true and smooth, or wooden surfaces will be damaged. For this reason, keep the bottom of your plane clean and free from scratches. Truing up the plane bottom can be done by a professional machinist, but you can easily lap it yourself. Simply sprinkle one-half teaspoon of 400-grit abrasive powder on a piece of perfectly smooth glass. Silicone carbide is a good powder for this application. Place the plane bottom on the glass and lap it by hand in a figure-eight motion, making sure to cover the entire glass surface. The abrasive eventually wears out and must be rinsed off to continue the lapping. Sole

You can lap the sole at home with abrasive powder and a flat piece of glass.

irregularities will show up as shiny spots untouched by the abrasive. Continue the lapping until the entire bottom is uniform gray. Once your plane is flat and true, lap the surface once more with 600-grit powder for a fine finish. You can polish the bottom with jeweler's polishing compound, but remember to rinse away the residue with soap and water.

Friction and impact work together to dull blades. Keeping a sharp edge on the blade is one key to smooth planing. Do not drag a plane backward across the workpiece at the end of a stroke, and sharpen the blades whenever needed (see *Sharpening,* pages 18 to 21).

Brace the end grain with a scrap piece and a clamp to prevent splitting the workpiece.

Planing end grain

Skim end grain with a lightweight block plane. Make sure the blade is very sharp. Putting plenty of pressure on the toe, plane from both ends toward the middle to avoid splitting the wood. If you prefer to plane in one direction, an end block can be clamped to one side of the piece to support the edge and prevent tearout. Planing a small chamfer on the edge will usually reduce the risk of splitting.

Shooting boards are stationary jigs designed to hold the workpiece and guide the plane through repeated controlled movements. Shooting boards help to trim

Before power miter boxes, woodworkers used shooting boards, which can be used to hold stock at any angle desired and are still used extensively in planing end grain.

workpieces without tearout and cut stock down to final dimensions. With a sharp plane and an accurate shooting board, you can remove shavings as small as two-thousandths of an inch.

Mount the workpiece against the stop, along the top of the shooting board. With the plane on its side, push it along the rabbeted edge of the shooting board. With the workpiece barely projecting beyond the stop, plane the end grain with a finely set sharp blade. Miter shooting boards have angled stops to trim miter joints with precision.

Using planes

The blade angle affects the amount of cutting pressure you will need to plane a workpiece surface. Softwoods need a much lower cutting angle than most hardwoods, so purchase your planes accordingly.

When planing off large pieces of stock, always plane diagonally

A jack or jointer plane, pushed diagonally across the grain, is ideal for removing large amounts of wood and smoothing the workpiece surface.

with a jack or jointer plane. Never plane against the grain. Keep the workpiece stationary with a vise, hand screws, or wooden stops. Hold the handle of a metal bench plane with one hand. Press your free hand down on the toe knob at the front of the plane. Stand beside the bench in a comfortable stance and face the direction you're planing. Hand positioning will vary from individual to individual, but always strive for the utmost comfort and control.

Planing should be a push from the lower body, not simply an arm or shoulder movement. At the beginning of each push stroke, apply the pressure on the toe. Then transfer the pressure evenly onto both ends as you move through the cutting motion. Finish the stroke by transferring most of the pressure to the rear, or heel, of the plane. This technique prevents damage and rounding off at the corners of the workpiece.

WORKSHOP TIP

Shallow high or low spots on a flat surface can be difficult to detect and eliminate, even when using long jointer planes. You may not notice them until after staining, and by then it's too late. You can solve this problem by rubbing a small amount of colored line chalk on the surface and planing diagonally with very shallow passes. Chalk remains on depressions, leaving spots clearly visible.

CHAPTER 3

Woodworking Woods

The Raw Material

Oak, maple, redwood, walnut, cherry—these woods are woodworkers' favorites. But each has distinctive characteristics that make it suitable for some applications and less advantageous for others. Here, complete profiles on these five types of wood discuss grain patterns, porosity, color, and degree of hardness. You'll learn which tools, jointing techniques, and finishing products produce the best results.

Pages 80 to 83 take the mystery out of buying hardwoods, softwoods, and plywood. Charts, definitions, and photographs explain the lumber industry's grading system so you know exactly what you're buying.

Red Oak 70
Maple 72
Redwood..74
Walnut...76
Cherry 78
Buying Wood 80

Red oak boards come in the three common cuts: riftsawn (A), with straight grain and short "ribbons" running parallel to the grain; quarter-sawn (B), with straight grain; plain sawn (C), with V-shaped grain. One half of each board is coated with a clear varnish.

Red Oak

Strength, economy, versatility, and availability make red oak
one of the most popular and widely used woods today.

In millions of yards across the country today, red oaks can be found shading the front door or lining the walk. Chances are good that red oak can also be found in beautifully finished hardwood floors inside the front entry that is shaded by these living relatives. Much of the furniture built today is made from red oak, as are many cabinets, cupboards, and door and window frames. Because of its good looks, strength, and durability, it is one of the most popular hardwoods used today. And be-

cause of the abundance of red oak trees, it is readily available and economical to use.

Characteristics

The oak family is comprised of a variety of species. A large number of them, including black, Northern, Canadian, and North American, are considered red oaks. In general, red oaks have a grayish brown, uneven bark and produce a light reddish brown wood. The leaves have sharply pointed lobes which are quite different from the

Red oak leaves are four to nine inches long, with sharply pointed lobes. The caps of the red oak acorn have a hairlike texture inside.

rounded lobes found on white oak leaves. The acorns from a red oak also differ from those of a white oak. The cap of a red oak acorn has a hairlike texture inside; a white oak acorn has a cap that is smooth inside.

Oak trees are one of the richest sources of tannins—chemicals found in the tree's leaves, bark, and seeds. Their primary function is to protect the tree from insect attack by acting as repellents. When working with oak, it is important to know that tannins react with iron to produce a black pigment around the iron. Avoid using steel nails or screws in oak: Brass and stainless steel nails or screws are your best alternatives.

Red oak is a hardwood with a straight grain that is noticeably coarse-textured and open-pored. Because the ring cells, called medullary rays, are quite large and pronounced in red oak, the figure of the wood shows a parallel-line pattern when it is quartersawn (cut parallel to the medullary rays). When red oak is riftsawn (cut at 45° to the medullary rays) the figure will have a ribbonlike pattern. And when it is plain-sawn (cut perpendicular to the rays), red oak produces a figure that has pronounced oval, U-shaped or V-shaped pattern. When working with a wood that has a noticeable figure, like red oak, be aware of the way each particular type of cut used will affect the finished look of the pieces.

Working with red oak

Most woodworkers find that red oak is an excellent wood for jointing, cutting, and turning. It machines well, but carbide blades are recommended because the hardness of red oak will quickly dull plain steel blades.

The open straight grain of red oak makes it easy to get a clean cut when rip-cutting. Use a rip-profile blade with 24 to 32 teeth. Use a 40-tooth blade when cross-cutting oak boards.

When jointing red oak, use sharp blades and feed the wood through

Feed red oak slowly through the jointer, with the rotation of the knives going with the direction of the grain.

the jointer slowly, to prevent splintering and burning.

Rout red oak with sharp, carbide-tipped bits for the best results. To keep red oak from splintering when routing, use shallow passes. When working across the grain, use a backing board clamped to the exit side.

When drilling red oak, use a pilot-point bit. Twist bits are not recommended on red oak because the hardness of the wood causes them to wander.

If you are carving a hard wood like red oak, be sure your gouges are sharp and use a mallet. Use a deeper bevel of 25° to 30° when you rough-in the outline on a relief design, then use a shallow bevel of 15° to 20° for shaving. Try not to stop your cuts when slicing along the straight grain.

Sharp tools are also important when turning red oak on a lathe. And making your cuts shallow will prevent splintering. Because the grain may run on a bias, remove the wood in sections, a little at a time, rather than starting at one end and cutting all the way to the other, to prevent any splintering.

Finishing Facts

An amber color and a reddish tinge give red oak one of the most attractive figures of the oak species. It responds well when bleached, blonded, or stained. The figure varies from a straight, striped, open-pored surface, to a lace-

wood appearance, depending on the way the wood is cut. The prominent grain also makes it a good wood for pickling, but not for painting, because the grain has a tendency to show through paint unless many coats are used.

It is necessary to reduce raised grain of red oak prior to finishing. The water content of water-based stains will cause the grain to swell if it's not sanded off first. One good way to do this is with glue sizing: This product raises the fibers and causes them to stiffen so they can be easily sanded. Use garnet paper for hand sanding and orbital sanders, and oxide-type abrasives for belt sanders.

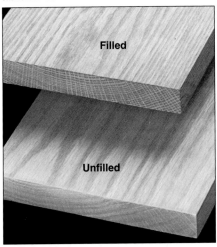
When filled, red oak has noticeable grain contrast. Paste fillers are one option, available in clear or colors.

Because of the open grain, red oak needs to be filled in order to stain or finish well. A paste-type filler is the best way to achieve the smoothest finish. To intensify the grain, use a light stain—a dark stain will hide the grain.

Use Danish oils for a more natural finish. They have a high resin content, which forms a good protective coating.

WOODWORKER'S TIP

Wet-sanding surfaces with Danish oil is an easy way to fill the wood as you finish it. The fiber that has been sanded off will mix with the Danish oil and fill the wood as you wipe it off across the grain.

Maple sold commercially usually fits into one of three categories of grain figure: plain-figured maple (A), which is the most readily available and least expensive; quilted maple (B), and bird's-eye maple (C)—both of which are usually sold as veneer for tabletops and fine cabinetry.

Maple

Brilliant fall foliage hides a wood of subtle color and varied figure.

With its bright autumn reds and yellows, no North American tree is as easily recognized as the maple, and few woods offer as much variety for the woodworker. Maple was the favorite material for colonial American furnituremakers, and it remains popular today, especially for Early American reproduction pieces.

The thirteen species of North American maple are all hardwoods, and are broadly divided into *hard* maples (sometimes called rock maples) and *soft* maples. The hard maples, with wood of similar weight and strength to red oak, include the sugar maple and black maple. The soft maples include red maple, silver maple, and bigleaf maple. Although the soft maples are about as hard as black walnut, they are not as popular as the more dense hard maples. All maples are somewhat unstable, given to substantial shrinkage during the curing process, but the hard maples, because they are heavier, are slightly less susceptible to cracking and splitting.

As a woodworking wood, maple is characterized by a fine-textured, tight grain pattern with a warm cream color, similar to that of birch. Maple, however, frequently has abnormal growth patterns that can create an unusual, distinctive appearance. Even in plain-figured wood, subtle irregularities in the pattern of the wood fibers can create a marblelike appearance that gives the wood quiet drama. When the irregularities are more pronounced, the maple grain pattern tends to fall into one of several dramatic "figures" that are highly prized by woodworkers.

Quilted maple is caused by growth layers that form in blisterlike bulges. Because of variation in the way the fibers reflect light, quilted maple has a very unusual three-dimensional look. Because it is quite expensive, quilted maple is usually applied as a veneer in tabletops and inlay projects.

Bird's-eye maple, one of the most highly prized of all woodworking woods, is the result of growth fibers that form in tight swirls. An expensive, premium material, bird's-eye maple may be available in solid stock, but is more commonly sold as veneer for fine cabinetry.

Fiddleback maple, sometimes called "tiger" maple, is a hard-to-find form characterized by a striped appearance that results from the wavy pattern of the growth fibers. Fiddleback maple is often used in stringed instruments and in decorative boxes.

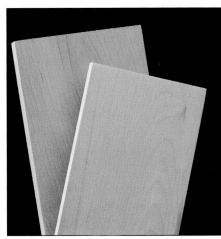

Maple is often confused with birch because the woods have similar color, density, and strength. But close examination shows that maple (left) has brownish growth fibers mixed through the paler wood, while birch (right) has lighter, grayish growth fibers. The grain pattern of maple is likely to be wavy or twisted, unlike birch, which has relatively straight grain.

Woodworking characteristics

Although the more usual maple figures (including bird's-eye and quilted), can be difficult to work with because of the twisted, interlocking grain, plain-figured maple is generally easy to cut and shape.

Maple is quite dense, making it ideal for heavy-wear surfaces, like tabletops and floors. As with any dense, heavy wood, you'll need sharp blades to work with maple. Maple does not bond with glue quite as well as do more porous woods, so it's wise to reinforce all major joints with biscuits, dowels, or screws.

Unless it is carefully air-dried, maple is somewhat unstable and is prone to shrinking and cracking. As a result, table legs and spindles made of maple may loosen over time. Maple has little natural resistance to decay, so it is a poor choice for outdoor projects.

Sawing: Because the grain pattern is closed and finely textured, maple does not splinter and chip out as easily as open-grained hardwoods, such as red oak.

Shaping: Because of its high density, maple can be burned by router and shaper bits. Using a fast feed speed can minimize this problem.

Turning: Maple, because it is dense, gives very predictable, consistent results when shaped on a lathe, making it a favorite material for many lathe projects, from kitchen utensils to bowling pins.

Carving: Because the wood fibers are rarely straight, maple is a difficult wood to carve, although it does hold detail very well. Maple is better suited for smooth wood sculpting than for intricate relief carving.

Finishing: Maple finishes as well as any hardwood. It is just porous enough to accept stains readily, yet its close grain and fine texture make it possible to achieve a very smooth, glossy finished surface without using wood fillers or sealers. In traditional Early American furniture, maple was stained to a reddish brown color, although lighter yellowish browns are more popular now.

Maple (like birch, which is less expensive) makes an excellent base for painted finishes, because there is little chance of the grain pattern showing through.

WOODWORKER'S TIP

You can minimize problems with shrinkage by choosing maple that has been air-dried to a moisture content of 10 percent or less, and by sealing the wood completely with a top-coat finish, like tung oil or varnish. Don't use porous finishes, like linseed oil, because uneven absorption and dehydration may cause the wood to crack.

Differences between rift-sawn (A), plain-sawn (B), and quarter-sawn (C) maple are more subtle than in coarse-grained hardwoods, like oak. Maple's tendency to form wavy grain patterns is most evident in plain-sawn wood.

The sugar maple is the source of most hard maple used in woodworking. It is easily identified by its brilliant blend of red, orange, and yellow autumn colors. (By contrast, the soft maples display either yellow or red-orange autumn colors, but do not mix both shades.)

Redwood

Nature's giant produces the wood of choice for outdoor woodworking projects.

Redwood's fine woodworking characteristics and resistance to decay make it an ideal choice for small outdoor projects like this planter.

For outdoor projects, no wood is in greater demand than redwood. Easy workability, surprising strength, attractive color, and natural resistance to decay make redwood one of the most popular choices for top-quality outdoor projects.

Redwood's enormous popularity was at one time its main enemy. A member of the sequoia family (*Sequoia sempervirens*), which also includes the giant sierra redwood, the coastal redwood was logged so heavily during the 1950s and 1960s that extensive old-growth forests that once blanketed the coastal regions of Oregon and northern California were reduced to a handful of groves.

Fortunately, most of the existing old-growth stands of coastal redwood are now protected by law, and the logging industry has practiced commercial reseeding operations for several decades. Because redwood grows quickly, it is no longer regarded as an endangered species. However, redwood lumber can be hard to find in many parts of the country. Use it only for small projects and be prepared to pay—redwood is among the most expensive of all softwoods.

Redwood is a nonresinous softwood ranging in color from dark reddish brown heartwood (bottom) to cream-colored sapwood (center). Less expensive grades may mix heartwood and sapwood and may include knots (top). The natural chemicals that give redwood its resistance to decay are most heavily concentrated in the heartwood, making this grade the most desired and most expensive. However, sapwood-grade redwood works well for indoor projects, and even for outdoor projects when properly sealed.

solution of water and baking soda. Rinse the project well and wipe the wood dry before applying a top-coat finish.

If you apply a top-coat finish of varnish or polyurethane, choose a product with UV sunlight inhibitors designed for outdoor use.

Redwood boards can be cut and sold *surfaced* (A), with smooth-planed faces, or *rough-sawn* (B) with a natural rustic look. Surfaced wood is more expensive and is often used indoors. Saw-textured wood is commonly used for outdoor projects. Redwood can be purchased with *vertical grain* (C) or *flat grain* (D).

WOODWORKER'S TIP

Old weathered redwood can be restored to its original color using a commercial wood brightener you mix with water. Wood brightener helps you salvage old redwood for new projects.

Woodworking characteristics

Though redwood is slightly brittle, its straight grain can be cut and shaped easily. To minimize the tendency to splinter, use backer boards to support the edge grain and fine-tooth blades when cutting.

Always select kiln-dried lumber for outdoor projects, because air-dried redwood is not stable and eventually splits and cracks. Kiln-dried redwood also has a better general appearance and stability. Apply a fresh coat of sealer, varnish, or polyurethane once a year to any outdoor project.

Redwood joints secured with nails or screws may loosen over time, especially on large projects. Use brass or galvanized nuts and bolts for best durability. Drill pilot holes before driving screws.

Planing: Run redwood through the planer in shallow passes of no more than 1/16" to prevent tearout.

Turning: When turning redwood on the lathe, use sharp gouges to reduce tearout, especially when turning end grain. To further minimize tearout, sand down to the final turned profile.

Carving: Redwood, soft enough to carve easily, works best for large-scale relief work. Redwood splits and chips when used for intricate carving designs. Sharp tools help reduce splitting.

Finishing: Redwood is usually finished with clear sealers or top-coat finishes. It is rarely stained, except when evening out the differences between heartwood and sapwood. To retain the original reddish color of the wood, finish the redwood immediately after completing the project using an exterior wood sealer designed to protect the original wood color.

All redwood used outdoors eventually turns a silver gray if left unfinished, a look some people prefer. To achieve this weathered look, leave your project exposed to the weather for a few months. Then coat it with clear exterior-grade wood sealer containing mildew inhibitors. On indoor projects, simulate the weathered look by treating redwood with a

CONSERVING REDWOOD

Although redwood is no longer regarded as an endangered species, only responsible use will guarantee its future availability.

• *Limit your use of redwood to small, decorative projects. For large outdoor projects like picnic tables and benches, use cedar or pressure-treated pine.*

• *Settle for lesser grades of redwood. Sapwood grades are much more plentiful (and more affordable) than heartwood and work just as well for many projects.*

• *Build projects to last. Unless protected with a sealing finish, even the best redwood will eventually decay if left outdoors.*

• *Consider recycling old redwood. Salvaged wood from old decks and fences often can provide ample wood for woodworking projects.*

• *If possible, determine how the redwood you buy is harvested. Look for certifications that identify lumber companies that harvest from renewable forests.*

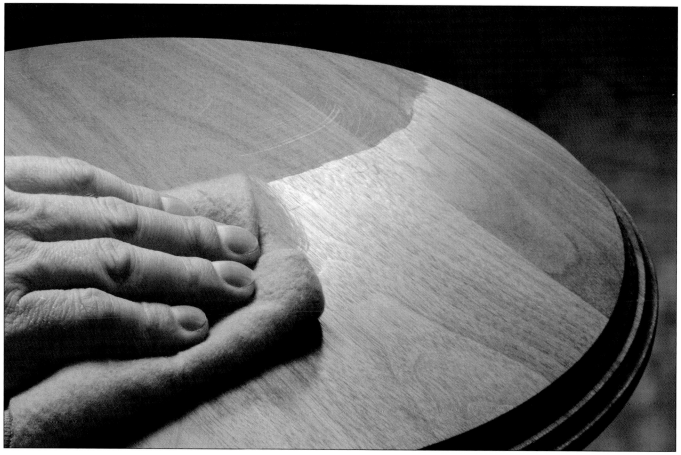

Clear finishes such as waxes or oils highlight the natural color and grain of walnut.

Walnut

A premier wood because of its beauty and durability, walnut is a woodworker's favorite.

Walnut has long been considered one of America's most valued domestic hardwoods, and for good reason. Both strong and durable, walnut works easily. Its rich, chocolate-brown color does not require a stain to enhance it. Walnut's attractive grain finishes beautifully, soaking up oil finishes and holding a hard shine from a wax coat. Walnut trees also are prized for the walnuts themselves, which contain oils and meats used to produce medicines, soaps, paints, and food items.

The name "walnut" has been attributed to the old English word *wahl*, which means "foreign." The English probably gave the trees this name because walnut trees were introduced to England by the Romans, who brought them from Asia.

Usually straight-grained, walnut sometimes contains wavy patterns, or figures, which are created when the wood grows into crotches or around obstructions. Veneers made from figured walnut are highly prized. Walnut grain also can be enhanced by the angle at which it is sawn.

Walnut often has a uniform texture. It is an oily wood, dense, hard, and highly resistant to decay.

Black walnut, also called American black walnut, is the native species

Black walnut sapwood can be a creamy white (bottom). To blend the lighter colors in with the darker brown and purple-toned heartwood, black walnut lumber often is steamed before reaching retail centers (top).

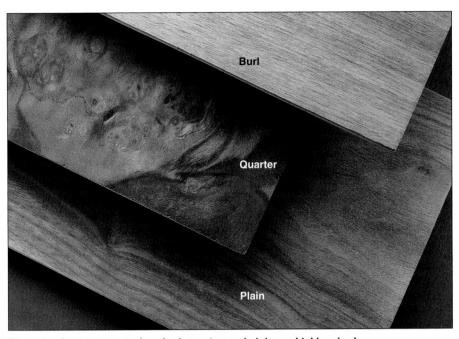

Figured walnut veneers such as burl, quarter, and plain are highly prized.

of the United States and Canada. The botanical name for black walnut is *Juglans nigra*. American black walnut lumber's color varies from cream-colored sapwood to dark brown or purplish black heartwood.

Early Colonial cabinetmakers found American black walnut to be a superior wood for making furniture, interior joinery, and musical instruments. Its popularity today has produced a demand for walnut veneer plywood. Its exceptional strength and resistance to rot have also made it the preferred wood for gun stocks.

Another species of walnut trees that shares the genus of *Juglans* is European walnut (*Juglans regia*). Also known as English, French, or Italian walnut, European walnut grows not only in Europe but also in Asia Minor and southwest Asia. Its lumber is lighter colored than American black walnut, usually gray-brown with darker streaks throughout. European walnut is harder to find in this country than American black walnut and is used less frequently in woodworking projects.

Other American species of the black walnut family are butternut and southern and northern California walnut. But American

black walnut has remained the most popular species. When a wood supplier refers to a wood as walnut, the wood is usually of the American black walnut species.

Working with walnut

Walnut responds easily to various woodworking techniques. Worked equally well with sharp hand or power tools, walnut is suitable for a wide range of projects.

Sawing: Although a hard, fairly dense wood, walnut cuts easily with standard sawing techniques. Properly dried (less than 8 percent moisture content), walnut rip-cuts without chatter, tearout, or burning with common ripping blades or planer blades. For crosscutting, 40-tpi crosscut blades or planer blades work well. Slightly softer than oak, walnut can be worked successfully with high-grade steel blades. Carbide blades are required only when cutting large amounts of material.

Because of its usually straight grain, walnut can be bandsawn and scrollsawn without much blade wandering. This makes it an ideal wood for cutting intricate shapes for furniture, jewelry, and decorative items.

Shaping: Walnut steam-bends and retains its new shape well.

Steaming also reduces color and shade differences in the wood, making it darker.

Turning: Wood turners often choose walnut for a variety of projects. Colorful grain patterns and figures are revealed as layers of wood are cut away. Turning at medium speeds (800 rpm on 4" stock) produces smooth cuts without burning tools or wood. High speeds (over 1000 rpm on 4" stock) can cause the oils in the wood to heat up and promote burning. Sharp, clean tools are required at any speed.

Faceplate turning exposes considerable end grain, which is subject to tearout. Avoid tearout by sanding the turned blank to its final shape.

Carving: Walnut works well for whittling, relief carving, and sculpting shapes and simple designs. Carving intricate designs in hard walnut requires firm pressure and sharp tools, but the grain cuts cleanly and sands or polishes to a high luster.

Veneers: Figured walnut is created by the wood's growth pattern or the direction in which it is sawn. Popular in marquetry and other veneering projects, figured walnut contrasts well when inlaid against background woods like maple, ash, or oak.

Finishing: Prized for its color and grain, walnut is usually finished clear. It responds beautifully to a wide range of penetrating oils, including Danish oil and tung oil, and holds a hard, glossy finish with paste wax. Clear top-coats protect oil finishes.

BUYER'S TIP

Walnut has a high percentage of waste wood per board. Not many big walnut trees remain, so most available walnut lumber has been harvested from smaller trees. Walnut from smaller trees has many knots, checks, and cracks. To adjust for the increased waste percentage, buy 30 percent more wood for a walnut project than the cutting list specifies.

Cherry

Cherry's beauty makes it among the finest of the world's furniture woods.

Cherry, an extremely photo-sensitive wood, darkens dramatically with age. The lightly colored tones react with sunlight to season the wood to its popular deep burgundy. This process can be accelerated with lye treatments or staining. Special sealers keep the color light.

American cherry, or black cherry, is considered one of the classic furniture woods. Early American woodworkers, noticing a resemblance to Honduran mahogany, used it as a replacement for the expensive import. Its deep reddish tones and above-average hardness soon earned it the name "New England Mahogany." Turn-of-the-century loggers helped to make cherry plentiful when they cleared vast stands of white pine and hemlock from the Allegheny Plateau forest, allowing cherry, ash, and other hardwoods to flourish.

Characteristics

Black cherry (*prunus serotina*), a native of North America, grows from the Atlantic Ocean to the Dakotas. The finest stands exist in the Appalachian Mountains of New York, Pennsylvania, and West Virginia. The price and availability elsewhere varies greatly.

Another species of cherry known as European cherry (*prunus avium*), or wild cherry, is native to the European continent but extends as far south as the mountains of north Africa. Used mostly for veneering, European cherry trees are smaller than the American variety and produce heavy, lightly colored wood.

Both species have a straight, fine grain and an even texture. A dark red-brown wood, black cherry often contains irregularities such as pin knots and gum pockets. Many woodworkers believe pin knots add character to the even texture of the wood. Gum pockets, on the other hand, make woodworking difficult by heating up drills, dulling blades, and smearing the wood with pitch.

A moderately heavy material, cherry dries rapidly after cutting and has a strong tendency to warp and shrink. When buying rough cherry wood, make sure to purchase more than your cutting list calls for, because the waste per-

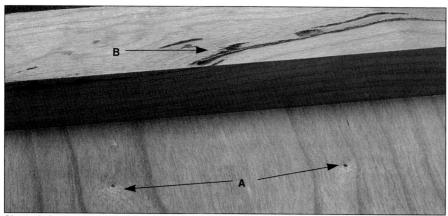

Cherry is known for surface irregularities such as pin knots (A) and gum pockets (B). Pin knots may add character to a project, while gum pockets can burn, smear, and mark your project as you work.

centage is fairly high (12 to 21 percent). Because of this waste percentage, cherry is a fairly expensive wood.

Working with cherry

Black cherry weighs less than maple, but is nearly as strong. Its workable composition makes it popular in the furniture industry, particularly in the construction of bookcases, desks, panel doors, cabinets, carvings, and sculpture.

Though cherry works well with hand and machine tools, the wood has a moderate blunting effect on cutting edges. It does not chip or tear easily, but it burns very quickly during cutting or routing. Avoid burning by using steel blades instead of carbide-tipped. Quick cutting passes with minimal hesitation also reduce burn damage.

Cherry turns well on lathes. Well suited to detail work despite its hardness, cherry turns easily with sharp cutting tools. Any type of drill does fine, except for the common twist drill. Slower drilling speeds prove more effective, but a long pause or hesitation may burn the wood.

Extremely durable and versatile, cherry holds screws and nails well and glues easily. It also works well for steam-bending and is of-

Cherry is ideally suited for working with sharp hand tools such as cabinet scrapers, which leave a smooth finish faster than sandpaper.

ten used for decorative veneers.

Cherry works well with most hand tools. Planes and cabinet

WORKSHOP TIP

For good results with cherry, remember these rules:
- *Avoid pieces with dark spots or gum pockets.*
- *Use a rip-profile blade with 24 to 32 teeth for clean ripping cuts.*
- *Drill pilot holes for all screws.*
- *Do not use externally unless treated.*
- *Avoid cross-grain sanding; cherry scratches easily.*
- *Coat the end grain with paraffin to avoid overdrying when storing.*

---

scrapers generally create a smooth finish with an absolute minimum of effort. Cross-grain sanding, especially on joints, can scratch cherry wood terribly. If you must sand, do not overlap the strokes where joints bring the grain together at right angles, such as the corner of a face frame. For best results, use a long, thin cabinet scraper to work the tight-grained cherry, and use hand planes on the end grain.

Finishing cherry

Generally a good finishing wood, cherry looks great with oil finishes or clear lacquers. Cherry's natural color is almost always attractive, but many people associate the wood with the sleek, paintlike finish found in store-bought cherry furniture. Factory staining, with its sophisticated bleaching and staining techniques, is impossible to achieve in the average home workshop.

Do not be disappointed with your light-toned home projects. Remember that cherry wood is extremely photosensitive and darkens dramatically with age and exposure to direct sunlight. Special sealers with UV protection are available if you want to stop the seasoning process and maintain the original light-toned color of your cherry project.

Staining cherry is a tricky process that involves a lot of experimentation and time. Some of the more expensive store-bought furniture is given a dark, almost black fin-

ish. If you desire this type of finish, simply purchase the piece in a furniture store. Staining cherry should generally be avoided on home projects.

As an alternative to staining, you can mix 1 to 2 ounces of lye with 1 gallon of water to darken your cherry projects. Red-colored woods such as cherry contain high concentrations of tannic acid, which reacts with lye and darkens to a deep burgundy color. Always experiment on a piece of scrap cherry wood sanded to exactly the same smoothness as your finished workpiece. Brush on the water/lye mixture, being careful not to overlap your strokes. Any overlapping strokes will produce dark, uneven lines on the finished workpiece. Allow the workpiece to sit for a short time, then wipe away the excess liquid. Neutralize the project with fresh water. If the color is still too light for your tastes, increase the lye/water concentration and repeat the darkening process.

The water/lye mixture has an almost immediate effect on cherry wood. You should see a change in as little as 15 minutes.

WOODWORKER'S TIP

To get a smooth finish when using high-quality oil finishes or shellac on fine-grained cherry, thin the first coat to act as a sealer. Then sand the wood with 400-grit sandpaper or 0000 steel wool when it's dry, and recoat.

Buying Wood

Understanding how lumber is graded helps you select the best boards for your projects.

Choosing hardwood, softwood, and plywood products at the lumber yard can be a little bewildering. Why are the hardwoods from the stack labeled "FAS" so much more expensive than wood labeled "Select"? What's the difference between ponderosa pine labeled "B & BRT" and that labeled "D Select?" Understanding the designations of lumber will help you buy the wood best suited to your projects.

Lumber basics

Lumber yards categorize the wood they sell according to the inspection criteria set forth by industry grading organizations. The National Hardwood Lumber Association (NHLA) and the Western Wood Products Association (WWPA) are two such grading organizations. Lumber is graded according to the amount of "clear" perfect wood and according to the number of checks, knots, and other faults in the board.

Grading for softwoods is different than for hardwoods. In some cases (especially with softwoods and plywood), the lumber is graded and stamped at the mill

Moisture meters gauge moisture by measuring electrical current passing between the meter's two sharp prongs. To get the most accurate reading, drive the prongs into the center of the board where the moisture content is highest.

before it gets to your local lumber yard. In other cases, and more frequently with hardwoods, personnel at your local lumber yard evaluate the wood and categorize it for sale.

Hardwoods

The grading guidelines established by the NHLA govern most of the hardwoods sold in North America. Most hardwood used in woodworking falls into one of the top three grading categories. Lower grades of hardwood (2A, 2B, 3A, 3B) are not generally available. These grades are used

by manufacturers to make flooring, pallets, and other wood products.

FAS (Firsts and Seconds): Boards in this category have the largest percentage of clear wood but may have small faults on up to 20 percent of the wood. Clear portions of FAS boards will be defect-free on both faces.

Select: Hardwood boards in this grouping have the same amount of clear wood as FAS boards on one face, but the back face may have small defects.

No. 1 Common: More economical than FAS or Select, this grade's boards have smaller areas of clear,

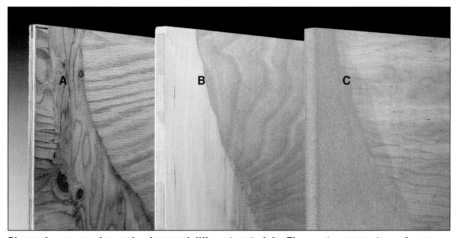

Plywood cores can be made of several different materials. The most common type of core consists of several veneers of softwood glued together so grain patterns are arranged at right angles for stability (A). A solid lumber core (B) is used for better grades of hardwood-faced plywood, and is heavier and more stable than veneer core. Composite material, like fiberboard, also is used as core material to make economical cabinet-grade hardwood plywood (C).

defect-free wood. Waste wood may account for up to 30 percent of the total.

Softwoods

Grading categories for pine and other softwoods vary according to the species and the grading organization used by the timber producers in your region. WWPA uses the following grading categories for classifying most of the western pines, including ponderosa pine:

Select: This top-of-the-line grade includes three subcategories: B & BTR, C Select, and D Select. The first two subcategories are nearly free of defects, while D Select contains small knots.

Finish: This grade includes three subgrades—Superior, Prime, and E. The first two subgrades are clear of knots and are suitable for fine woodworking applications.

Common: This grade, which includes five subgrades (1 Common to 5 Common) always has visible knots and other defects. The top three subgrades are of value to the woodworker for use in knotty paneling and other such applications. The lower two subgrades are suitable only for framing and hidden structural elements.

Plywood

"Plywood" refers to any of a number of sheet materials that are made by bonding surface plies of thin wood to a core layer made of cheaper material. The core layer can be solid wood, a composite material like particleboard or fiberboard, or several plies of softwood glued together.

Hardwood plywood: Consisting of thin layers of hardwood surface veneer bonded to a softwood or composite core layer, hardwood plywood is sold in five grades. *Premium plywood* (Grade 1) has surface veneers which are matched for consistent grain and are virtually clear, except for very small burls and pin knots. *Good plywood* (Grade 2) has virtually clear surface veneers but no grain matching. *Sound plywood* (Grade 3) has surface veneers with knots and other defects that are filled to provide a smooth surface adequate for painting. *Utility* and *Backing*

plywood (Grades 4 and 5) are structural grades that should be used only in hidden applications.

When buying hardwood plywood, look for the Hardwood Plywood and Veneer Association (HPVA) designation on the edge stamp. The species and dimensions will usually follow these markings.

Softwood plywood: The American Plywood Association (APA) grades softwood plywood alphabetically according to the quality of the surface veneers. Each sheet of plywood carries two grades, one for each face. A-C grade plywood, for example, has one face graded A, the other graded C.

N grade is the premium surface for natural finishes, with veneer pieces carefully matched for grain consistency. It is usually only available by special order. *A* grade is the top painting grade. It contains no knots or pitch pockets but may have small patched areas. *B* grade contains small defects but no large open flaws. If it is filled and sanded by hand, it makes an excellent painting surface. *C* grade and *D* grade have many open flaws and are normally used on hidden applications.

Lumber selection

The grading systems that categorize hardwoods, softwoods, and plywood can help you narrow your selection. Remember that the quality of wood varies substantially within each category. Unless you need very large quantities of wood, hand-select each board you

BUYER'S TIP		
Rough Thickness	Quarter Designation	Surfaced Thickness
⅝"	⅝"*	⁷⁄₁₆"
¾"	¾"*	⁹⁄₁₆"
1"	4⁄4	¹³⁄₁₆"
1¼"	5⁄4	1¹⁄₁₆"
1½"	6⁄4	1⁵⁄₁₆"
2"	8⁄4	1¾"

*Rough lumber less than 1" is expressed in inches.

need. Select your boards according to the elements listed below.

Moisture content: Of all the variables, the moisture content of the boards you use most dramatically influences the success of your woodworking projects. Too damp or too dry wood is unstable; unpredictable shrinkage and expansion can ruin your project.

In general, use hardwoods with a moisture content of no more than 9 percent. Because air-drying outdoors generally cures hardwood only to about 15 percent, buy kiln-dried lumber unless you are willing to let your wood cure indoors for several months.

To determine the moisture content of boards, use a moisture meter. Battery-operated moisture meters work by measuring electrical resistance through the wood fibers: Wet wood conducts more current. Most lumber dealers let you use their moisture meters to check boards you may buy.

Surfaces: The "S" in lumber grading refers to the number of surfaces cut or planed. "S4S" lumber has been surfaced on both faces and straight ripped on both edges. Almost all soft lumber sold at building centers has been surfaced on all four sides.

Grain pattern: Two boards of the same species can look and handle quite differently, depending on how they were cut relative to the growth ring in the log. The three most common grain patterns are quartersawn, riftsawn, and flatsawn (see *photos,* below).

Lumber storage

Before it is used, all wood should be stored for a set time in

> ## WORKSHOP TIP
>
> *When air-drying damp wood indoors, coat the end grain of each board with beeswax or latex paint to prevent it from drying out too quickly. End grain loses moisture much faster than face grain; this can result in small cracks, called "checks," which can widen later.*

an environment similar to that of the finished project, regardless of the moisture content at purchase. This allows the wood to achieve equilibrium moisture content (EMC), minimizing the likelihood of shrinkage or expansion in the finished project. Many woodworkers use a humidifier or dehumidifier to control the humidity of the

Quartersawn boards are cut at a 60° angle to the growth rings. They are expensive, very stable boards. The faces of quartersawn boards have closely spaced parallel grain lines.

Riftsawn boards are cut at a 30° to 60° angle to the growth rings. The faces of riftsawn boards have parallel grain lines spaced more widely than quartersawn boards.

Flatsawn boards are cut at a 30° or less angle to the growth rings. Flatsawn boards are the least expensive boards, but they are also the most unstable in terms of shrinkage. The faces of flatsawn boards often show dramatic V- or U-shaped grain patterns.

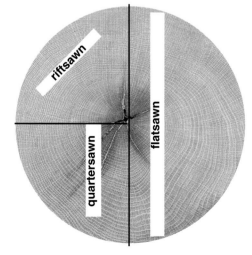

workshop—especially in basement workshops, where moisture levels can fluctuate a great deal.

Kiln-dried lumber, whose moisture content is from 6 to 9 percent, should be stored for two or three weeks in your workshop before you use it in projects. Depending on the relative humidity of your workshop, the lumber may continue to dry out during this time, or it may actually gain moisture to match the ambient humidity of your workshop.

Lumber that has not been kiln-dried, with a moisture content above 9 percent, requires several months of storage before it reaches EMC. Slow drying is key to producing good lumber for woodworking projects. In very dry surroundings, wet lumber loses moisture too quickly, which can result in cracking and warping.

Store wood correctly to prevent warping and to promote even drying. Lumber is usually best stored horizontally in layers separated by 1 × 1" wood strips of scrapwood (also known as "stickers") that allow air to circulate freely between the boards. Heavy weights placed on top of the stack of lumber can help prevent twisting. Plywood sheets should be stored upright. Make sure that all wood is stored off the floor so that air can circulate freely all around the lumber.

Imported woods

Today's woodworker can choose from dozens of imported woods from around the world—from Agba wood native to Nigeria to Zebrano wood indigenous to Cameroon. But with this wide choice comes greater responsibility. Much of the world's imported hardwood grows only in tropical rain forests which are being destroyed at the rate of 27 million acres each year. The responsible woodworker must consider how the use of imported lumber affects this threatened environment.

It is hard to overstate the importance of preserving endangered forests. Tropical forests, for example, produce enormous amounts of oxygen, reducing global carbon dioxide levels that cause the greenhouse effect. These forests are also home to thousands of species of plants and animals, many of which are indispensible ingredients for important pharmaceutical products.

When rain forest preservation first gained prominence as a political cause, a blanket boycott of all rain forest timber was widely regarded as the best way to save the forests. Today it has become apparent that boycotting all rain forest timber is not the answer; in fact, indiscriminate boycotts may actually speed the destruction.

Observers have discovered that nearly two-thirds of tropical deforestation comes not at the hands of the logging industry, but at the hands of landowners and tenants who practice slash-and-burn clearing to make room for agriculture. Not only does this practice waste valuable hardwood, but the smoke from the burn-off contributes almost 20 percent to the yearly increase in harmful carbon dioxide levels.

On the other hand, by contributing to the economic development of a region, a conservative, well-controlled logging industry can reinforce the value of timber and encourage the conservation of old-growth forest land and the replanting of clear-cut forests. In tropical regions that have undergone a shift from an agricultural to an industrial economic base, forest areas have actually increased over the last 20 years.

Wherever possible, determine where imported woods offered at your retailer came from and avoid any woods harvested from endangered forests. For example, South American and African hardwood forests have suffered less devastation than Central American forests. A number of environmental organizations monitor rain forest logging and identify timber companies that practice sustainable, environmentally responsible harvesting techniques. Addresses for two of these important organizations are listed below.

Use imported hardwoods only for smaller projects. When larger stock is needed, glue up smaller boards rather than demanding large solid boards that must be cut from old-growth timber. Use veneers rather than solid wood wherever possible.

Don't use any hardwood species identified as endangered, no matter where it came from. Brazilian rosewood, for example, takes almost 200 years to mature and is currently so rare as to be in danger of virtual extinction. The list of endangered species changes constantly, however, so check regularly with environmental organizations to learn the most current status of endangered hardwoods.

THE RAINFOREST ALLIANCE

The Rainforest Alliance Tropical Timber Project sponsors Smart Wood certification, a grading procedure that judges tropical lumber producers according to environmental responsibility, sustained yield production, and community impact. For updates to the Smart Wood list of approved, non-endangered hardwoods, contact:
The Rainforest Alliance
65 Bleecker Street
New York, NY 10012-2420
212/677-1900

WOODWORKERS' ALLIANCE FOR RAINFOREST PROTECTION

The Woodworkers' Alliance for Rainforest Protection (WARP) publishes a list of tropical wood producers who practice environmentally responsible logging techniques and retailers who sell these "good wood" products.
WARP
1 Cottage Street
East Hampton, MA 01027
413/527-0284

Note: Membership in WARP costs $25 a year.

CHAPTER 4

Hardware and Materials

Hardware Know-How

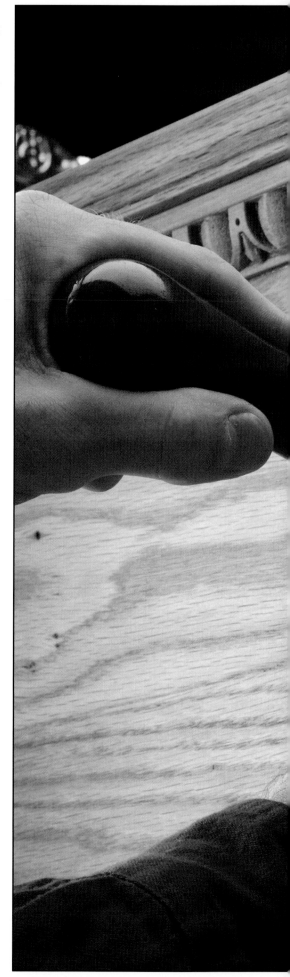

Do you know the difference between a soss hinge and a single-pivot hinge? Do you know which type of caster works best on carpeting or on hard-wood floors?

Do you know that there are three types of drawer glides, and the type you select will affect your drawer measurements?

The information provided in this chapter is invaluable. Concise explanations, precise definitions, and handy charts tell you what kind of hardware is available, where it should be used, and how to install it. You will never again be confused at the hardware store.

This chapter will help you finish your woodworking project in a professional manner, with a polished appearance and a smooth, efficient function. Whether you're constructing a kitchen drawer cabinet or a jewelry box, a fancy curio cabinet or a simple shelf, a drop-leaf table or a television stand—the correct hardware ensures durability, safety, and performance.

Drawer Hardware...86
Hardware Guide...88
Hinges...90

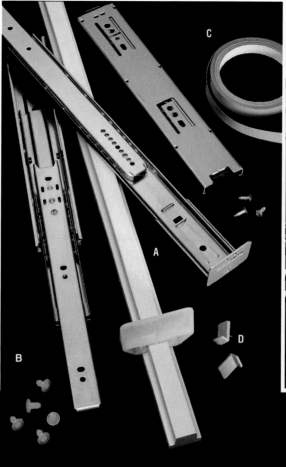

Carefully chosen drawer knobs and pulls will enhance any project. Styles range from traditional to contemporary and include materials like brass, chrome, porcelain, and wood.

Add a lock, either simple or elaborate in design, to provide attractive security and safety for any drawer.

Drawer installation accessories *(above, center)* include metal or wood glides (A), plastic bumpers (B), nylon tape (C), and plastic stops (D).

Drawer Hardware

Choose the right hardware to make a well-built drawer even better.

Drawer hardware, including knobs, pulls, handles, and glides, comes in a dizzying array of styles and materials. Choosing these items can be a challenge, but knowing what to look for will help you select the best hardware for the project.

You can make or purchase drawer hardware, but if you're buying the hardware, remember you usually get what you pay for, so it's worthwhile to spend a little more for better quality. This is particularly true when you're shopping for drawer glides because they need to be sturdy enough to hold the weight of the drawer and its contents, and they can be time-consuming to replace later. If you're making the glides or knobs yourself, choose wood that is as warp-free and evenly grained as possible to avoid swelling and shrinking. Paying extra attention to detail will give you a chance to show off the project to its best advantage.

Choose hardware that matches the style of the project. This seems obvious when selecting knobs and pulls, but remember that even the drawer glides will be visible when the drawer is opened. Save the high-tech metal glides for contemporary projects, and use simpler wooden glides for more traditional designs.

Also keep scale in mind when choosing drawer hardware. Large drawer handles or knobs may complement a full-sized dresser, but they'll overpower a small nightstand.

Be sure to select hardware that is sturdy enough to hold up to its intended use. Handles may be a better choice than pulls or knobs, depending upon how much use the drawer will get.

You'll find numerous pages in woodworking catalogs devoted to drawer hardware, making it easier to find the perfect items for whatever project you're building.

Knobs & pulls

You can find knobs or pulls to match almost any style of furniture. Porcelain, wood, and metal are the most common materials used. Some knobs have screws built in, but most knobs are attached by drilling a hole in the drawer face and then fitting a machine screw through the back of the face to the threaded hole in the knob. If the screw is too short to go through the thickness of the drawer face, drill a countersunk hole through the back of the drawer face so the screw will reach through to the knob.

Make sure to mark the location of the knobs or pulls so they're centered (or spaced evenly apart if there are more than one) and appear in alignment on the drawer face. They'll look best if they're installed just above the halfway mark on the drawer face.

A jig makes it easier to drill the holes for drawer pulls in the right location.

If you're building several drawers at once, you can save time by making a jig to drill the holes for the knobs or pulls. Attach a strip of wood to one edge of a board to create a lip that fits over the top of the drawer. Measure, mark, and drill holes in the board at the planned spacing for the drawer pulls, then use the jig to drill the holes for the drawer pulls on all of the drawer faces.

Recessed pulls appear to be sculpted into the drawer front when installed and are often used for contemporary designs. They're easy to install in a recess cut into the drawer face.

Drawer glides

Installing drawer glides is usually one of the last steps in a project, but should be the first consideration in the planning stage.

Glides come in three styles; all three types can be made or purchased. They are bottom-mounted (also called center-mounted), side-mounted, and corner-mounted. It's important to choose a style before you begin building the drawer, because you'll need to adjust the drawer dimensions accordingly (see *Making Drawers, pages 126 to 129*). Most commercial glides come with detailed measurement information to help you make the adjustments, and manufacturers even make jigs to help you install their glides.

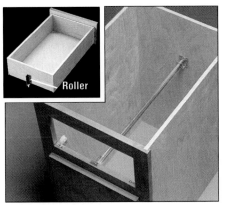

This bottom-mounted glide has a track to hold the roller that is attached to the back of the drawer.

Bottom-mounted glides have a track that's attached either to the face frame and the back of the cabinet, or to a cabinet shelf, if there is one in the opening.

Side-mounted glides consist of a runner that is attached to the drawer and a matching track that attaches to the cabinet walls.

One of the simplest ways to make side-mounted glides is to cut dadoes in strips of wood and attach the strips to the sides of the cabinet. Then, attach mating runner strips to the drawer sides

sized to fit the dadoes in the strips. Apply a light coat of paraffin to help the runners slide freely.

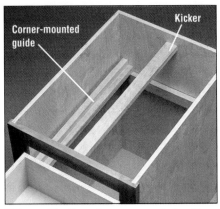

This combination of corner-mounted guides and a kicker creates an effective guide system, holding the drawer on all sides.

Corner-mounted guides can be made by rabbeting along one edge of a strip of wood to create an L-shaped track for the drawer. Attach the strips to the inside of the cabinet at the sides, and apply a light coat of paraffin to help the drawer slide over the strips.

Locks

Desks, cabinets, or workshop cupboards are just a few of the places where adding a lock can increase safety and security. Many locks come with decorative plates, called escutcheons, that are mounted behind the lock.

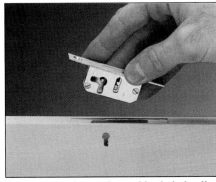

Cutting a simple mortise and keyhole is all that's needed to install a drawer lock.

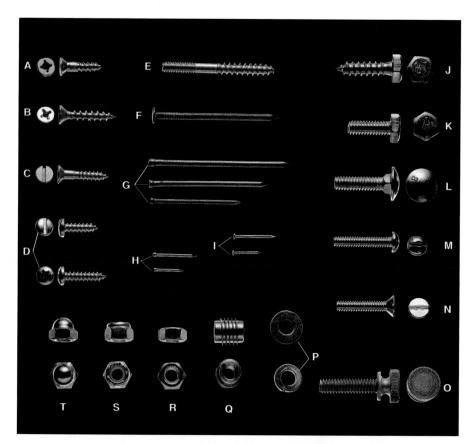

Fasteners

A) Flathead wood screw with a square-X head is driven by a square driver or a Phillips driver.
B) Flathead wood screw with a Phillips head is the standard for use with power screwdrivers.
C) Flathead wood screw with a slotted head is still a traditional favorite in woodworking.
D) Pan-head screw is made for use with a washer and can be removed easily.
E) Hanger bolt is driven by threading a nut onto the bolt end, then turning nut with a wrench.
F) Common nail is driven flush with surface.
G) Finish nails are very easy to set.
H) Brads are small finish nails, often of brass.
I) Wire nails, or box nails, are light-duty nails often used to attach thin panels.
J) Lag screw has very high holding power. Hex or square head is driven with a wrench.
K) Hex bolt is used with washers and a nut.
L) Carriage bolt has a square shoulder that holds fast in a pilot hole. Needs no washer.
M) Machine screw with slotted, pan head.
N) Machine screw with slotted, flat head.
O) Knurled knob is made for hand-tightening.
P) Washers: plain (above), locking (below).
Q) Threaded insert is set into wood for bolts.
R) Hex nut used with all types of bolts.
S) Lock nut has an insert that compresses and grips the shaft of the bolt.
T) Acorn nut, or cap nut, is very decorative.

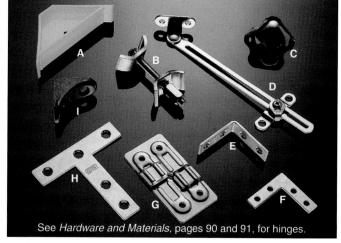

See *Hardware and Materials*, pages 90 and 91, for hinges.

Catches & hasps

A) Magnetic catch draws against a steel strike plate to hold cabinet doors shut. Model shown is spring-loaded for touch-activated release.
B) Magnetic touch catch will release a door with a slight push. Special clip-on strike plates (not shown) allow use with glass doors.
C) Draw catch, like those found on suitcases or briefcases, is used most frequently in woodworking to secure lids.
D) Hasp is used with lids and doors. Can be fitted with a padlock.
E) Cupboard catch: Doors won't pop open accidentally, but catch must be mounted on the face of the cabinet doors.
F) Adjustable ball catch can be set for a range of holding powers by adjusting the screws on the release.
G) Surface bolt holds double doors together when closed.
H) Bullet catches have very low profiles. Pins mount in the top edge of the face frame, and receivers mount on the bottom edge of the door.
I) Double roller catch is an economical choice for cabinet doors.

Brackets & braces

A) Plastic corner brace reinforces corners and helps keep them square, while providing a surface for mounting tabletops.
B) Joint connector has braces at ends to fit into mortises on adjoining sections of a countertop. Connecting bolt draws sections together.
C) Chest corner adds a decorative touch to chests and boxes, while protecting the corners from damage.
D) Lid support keeps box and chest lids under control.
E) L-brace can be used to attach tabletops or to reinforce corners.
F) Flat corner brace can be used to reinforce mitered corners.
G) Table alignment clips are mounted on the undersides of adjoining leaves of a tabletop. The clips slide together to lock leaves in place.
H) T-plate can be used to strengthen a weak butt joint or to join a vertical panel with horizontal panels.
I) Chair brace is a form of corner brace that's used to attach seats to chairs and benches, as well as to attach tabletops and countertops.

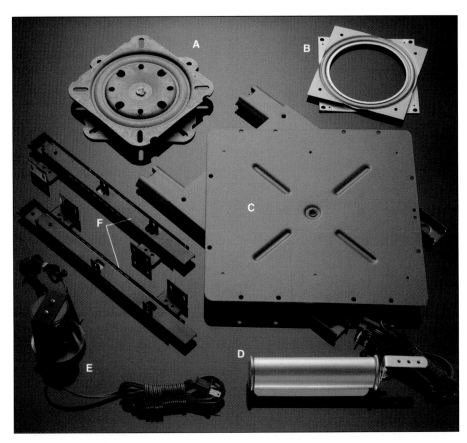

Specialty hardware

A) Swivels come in many sizes and load ratings. Use them for any seating project with a pivoting seat, or even to create rotating shelves in cabinets and cupboards. Most swivels have a limited pivot range, but they're spring-loaded to return to their original position. Some have a built-in tilt for use with stools and chairs.

B) Lazy Susan bearing gives full 360° rotation for shelves and tabletops. Standard sizes are from 3" to 12" in diameter.

C) Television pullout slide screws down to any solid, flat surface. Set your television directly on the rotating pullout or attach a tray to the pullout first. Before you purchase a television pullout, weigh your television set to find your required load capacity.

D) Cabinet light mounts flush onto any surface inside a cabinet, illuminating the display area. Most have a reflector to shield the mounting surface from heat generated by the 25-watt light bulb.

E) Canister light recesses into the top panel of a cabinet. Canister lights take bulbs of 40 watts and more, and the light can be directed if you select a swiveling model.

F) Keyboard slide has two retractable tracks that mount to the underside of a desktop, supporting a tray for your computer keyboard.

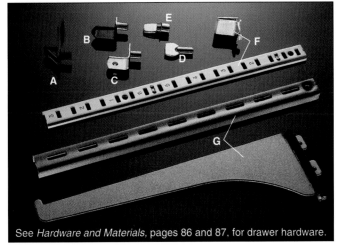

See *Hardware and Materials*, pages 86 and 87, for drawer hardware.

Casters & wheel

A) Locking caster is a heavy-duty wheel that can be locked in place. Used often on workshop tables, benches, and stationary tools.

B) Ball casters have a heavy-duty steel ball that rolls and pivots in a steel housing that's mounted with a mounting plate (left), or a stem that fits into a pilot hole or sleeve. Good for hard-surface floors.

C) Twin wheel caster has two wheels per caster, which makes them a good choice for carpeting and other soft surfaces. Stem and locking styles are available. Relatively lightweight duty.

D) Wooden hobby wheel and axle are available in a wide variety of sizes and styles for toys and other woodworking projects.

E) Caster with Philly stem has a ridged stem, much like a joining dowel, that helps the stem fit securely into a pilot hole. This eliminates the need for a sleeve to hold the stem.

F) Swivel casters are the most basic (and economical) casters used in furnituremaking. Wheels are usually nylon, plastic, or porcelain.

Shelf hardware

A) Locking shelf pin has a beveled flange above the support, creating a recess that holds shelves securely in place.

B) Coated shelf pins have a rubbery coating that cushions and grips the shelves. Designed mostly for use with glass shelving.

C) Bracket-style shelf pin has a convenient hole in the support that lets you secure the shelf with a screw or install rubber shelf cushions.

D) Spoon-style shelf pin is a basic pin that's barely visible from below.

E) Library-style shelf pin and socket give strong support, while maintaining a low profile. The socket fits into the pin hole, ensuring that downward pressure on the shelf doesn't make the pin loosen.

F) Pilaster-and-clip shelf support system eliminates the chore of drilling pin holes in perfect alignment, but still provides adjustability for clips. The pilasters usually are mortised into shelf sides.

G) Standard-and-bracket shelf support system is very strong and fully adjustable, but its bulky appearance limits its use in fine woodworking.

Hinges

The right hinge enhances your project's appearance, effectiveness, and strength.

Joining the moving parts of your woodworking pieces with the right hinges gives them stability and longevity. Good hinges can be expensive, but they are worth the investment. High-quality hinges reduce the risk of hinge failure, a problem that can damage your project and compromise safety, especially on doors, chests, and cabinets.

It seems that a specific hinge has been manufactured for almost every type of moving joint. Learning about the different types of hinged joints will enable you to choose wisely from the wide variety of beautiful, functional hinges.

Flush hinges

Flush hinges are used to attach items that are in the same plane, or flush, at the attachment point when the door is closed.

Butt hinges: The traditional flush hinges used for cabinets and doors, butt hinges usually are recessed into a mortise. They can also be used on overlay doors, where the hinge shows at the side, or on inset doors, where the hinge shows in front. Butt hinges come in loose- or fixed-pin types. The pin is removable in loose-pin butt hinges, making it possible to remove the door without removing the hinge.

Flush hinges: These hinges serve the same purpose as butt hinges except that they are used for light doors only. These hinges do not have to be mortised.

Knowing which hinges work for which jobs makes it easier to select from the wide array available: piano hinges (A), concealed cabinet hinges (B), soss hinges (C), cylinder hinges (D), glass door hinges (E), inset hinges (F), knife hinges (G), loose-pin butt hinges (H), fixed-pin butt hinges (I), backflap hinges (J), overlay hinges (K), flush hinges (L), drop-leaf hinges (M), and pivot hinges (N).

Continuous (piano) hinges: Very long versions of butt hinges, piano hinges are used for chest lids or other applications where a normal butt hinge could be pulled loose by heavy use. Piano hinges normally run the entire length of the joint and are usually recessed into a mortise. Piano hinges are commonly sold in 3' or 6' lengths. Cut them to fit your joint by using a metal-cutting hacksaw.

Backflap hinges: Used to attach a fall flap to a bureau or table, backflap hinges create a horizontal surface when the fall flap is opened. Backflap hinges are recessed into a mortise.

Drop-leaf hinges: Also called table hinges, drop-leaf hinges have one flange that is longer than the other. The longer flange is attached to the drop leaf of a table while the shorter flange is attached to the center of the table. Drop-leaf hinge flanges may or may not be recessed into mortises, but the barrel of the hinge must be recessed into a groove on the table center.

Overlay hinges

Overlay hinges attach doors that are not in the same plane at the attachment point, such as when doors overlay, or overlap, the door opening on a cabinet or doorway.

Wraparound hinges: The overlay equivalent of a butt hinge, a wraparound hinge has an L-shaped back leaf that attaches to the inside of the door opening and a front leaf that attaches directly to the back of the overlay door.

Lipped hinges: Always offset, lipped hinges are used for doors that are partially recessed and partially overlaid at the same time. The back of the hinge attaches to either the front or the inside of the door opening. The front of the hinge attaches to the back of the recessed door.

Flush glass hinges: These hinges slide over the corner of a glass door without any glass cutting. They are tightened against the glass with screws. The pivot for the hinge is installed against the inside of the door opening.

When choosing concealed cabinet hinges, know whether your application is an inset (A), partial overlay (B), or full overlay (C). Each application has its own kind of hinge.

Concealed hinges

Concealed hinges are partially or completely hidden when the door is closed. These hinges are available in a variety of types and opening widths.

Soss hinges: Mortised into an inset door and the inside edge of the door opening, soss hinges require exact mortising and boring installation. These hinges, although more difficult to install than most hinges, are very effective and completely hidden.

Single-pivot hinges: Used on inset doors, single-pivot hinges have two parts: a pivot pin on a metal attachment plate that attaches to the top and back of the door, and a nylon bearing that is placed in a hole drilled into the top of the door opening. The pin turns within the bearing.

Cylinder hinges: Also called hidden barrel hinges, cylinder hinges are inserted in holes bored into the door and door opening and attached within the holes with screws. These hinges have 180° movement and are excellent for bi-fold doors.

Knife hinges: Mortised and bored into the top of the door and the door opening, knife hinges are available for inset, partial overlay, or full overlay doors. Knife hinges reveal only the pivot when the door is closed on overlay doors. They are invisible on inset doors when the door is closed.

Concealed cabinet hinges: Adjustable three ways after installation for ease in lining up cabinet doors, concealed cabinet hinges can be used on overlay, partial overlay, or inset doors. No mortise is needed for the portion of the hinge that attaches to the door opening, but the part that attaches to the door requires a round mortise that must be cut with a drill bit or jig. Concealed cabinet hinges are usually spring-loaded so the door will stay closed. Concealed cabinet hinges come in a variety of opening widths, such as 95°, 110°, 165°, or 176°.

Hinge installation

Hinges should be fastened with screws, using a self-centering drill bit. Some hinges can be attached to the project's surface without a mortise. But most hinges must be recessed into the project's surface to function effectively.

Mortised butt hinges: Lay the hinge on the wood at the attachment point, parallel to the joint. Scribe around the hinge flap with a pencil. Remove the hinge from the worksurface, and score the scribed lines with a sharp knife and a straightedge. Then chisel out sections of the waste. For a piano hinge mortise, you may use a router with a mortising bit. Adjust the depth of the cut to match the thickness of the hinge flange, and

Use a chisel to make small horizontal cuts in the scored space. Then cut out each small section with the chisel.

square out the rounded corners of the mortise. Sometimes butt hinges also require the barrel pin groove described below.

Cut with the grain when using a chisel to cut out the waste from the barrel pin groove.

Barrel pin groove: Lay the hinge on the surface in which the pin groove will be cut. Scribe around the hinge leaf and pin with a pencil. Mark the width as well as the length of the barrel pin. Use a chisel to remove gently and gradually the wood in the groove. Or use a router with an appropriately sized roundnose bit to cut the groove, adjusting the cut depth to match the drop of the hinge pin. Square the corners as needed, using a chisel.

Concealed cabinet hinge mortises: Cut the round mortise in the back of the door, using a 35-mm. multispur drill bit, Forstner bit, or a modified 1⅜"-wide spade bit. Modify the spade bit by grinding down the spur on the bit to prevent it from breaking through the door's front while drilling. Control the depth of the hole with all bits so that you don't break through the wood. Perfect the hang of the door by using the adjustment screws on the hinges.

Cylinder and soss hinges: Cut the mortises into both the door and door opening surfaces. Use a Forstner bit to create cylinder hinge mortises. Cut soss hinge mortises by using a specialty jig or by boring and chiseling carefully around a template for soss hinge mortises. Soss hinges do not work well if the mortise is even slightly inaccurate, so use extreme care measuring, fitting, and mounting soss hinges to your doors.

CHAPTER 5

Shaping Wood

Creative Satisfaction

You'll have a burst of creative satisfaction each time you shape a formless chunk of wood into a graceful work of art, be it useful or purely decorative. Whether your interest leans toward turning bowls on a lathe, carving figurines with a bench knife, or contouring table legs, there is immense pleasure in the creation.

This chapter discusses several methods of shaping wood. Each section teaches the tools and the materials as well as the techniques. Easy-to-follow directions and photographs will inspire beginners to practice their skills. Even experts may learn something new.

Basic Bowl-Turning Techniques 94
Cutting Tapers 96
Basic Carving 98
Cutting Multiple Workpieces 102
Resawing Techniques...............................104

Basic Bowl-Turning Techniques

Use our shop-tested tips and a faceplate to turn your favorite woods into bowls.

To make a bowl, you simply need to mount a large-enough piece of wood, called a blank, on your lathe and turn the shape you want. Because the wooden blank is only supported at one end, some special tools and techniques are needed to help you turn your blank into a bowl you can be proud of. So, take a look at these ideas, find yourself a faceplate, and you'll be turning a bowl by lunchtime.

Wood for bowls

Any wood can become a beautiful bowl. Hardwood, softwood, spalted wood, burl—even the wood you trim from trees in your yard—makes suitable wood for turning. Look for appealing colors, grain patterns, figure—even scents—when you choose wood for your blank.

For your first projects, use seasoned, dry wood that's free from cracks or large or loose knots. Advanced bowl turners will sometimes use cracked or diseased wood for special bowls, but turning those pieces safely takes practice. You can build a blank by laminating layers of wood to create dramatic effects or build up thickness, but the glue joints must be solid for both safety and for a good appearance.

Bowl design

Once you've picked the wood for your blank, consider shape, size, and proportion when you design a bowl to turn. First, measure the swing of your lathe. Plan your bowl so the diameter of the blank is smaller than the swing.

Next, think about shape. To sit steadily, a bowl needs an adequate base. Start with a base that is two-thirds the widest diameter of your bowl. After you've made a few bowls, you'll find other proportions that provide good bases as well. Also, avoid very thin sides until you've gained some turning experience. Sides that are ½" thick work well for most bowls. After that, let your sense of proportion take over, and have fun designing your bowls.

WOODWORKER'S TIP

If your workshop is not humidity controlled, cure your blank before turning by leaving it in your shop for several months. Or bring it inside and put it in an out-of-the-way place. This curing prevents splitting and warping later.

Tools for turning

While some of the gouges, scrapers, and tool rests used for spindle turning can be used for bowls, there are some different tools you should know about. Dif-

ferences come from the stress put on tools when turning large diameters, and the need to turn the insides of bowls.

The gouge is the main tool of the bowl turner. Deep-fluted gouges are strong and have long cutting edges. They cut fast to make roughing your bowls a breeze. Shallow-fluted gouges are easier to maneuver, but, because they

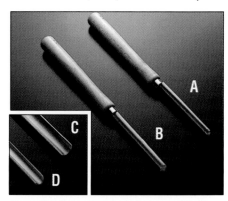

Deep-fluted square-ground gouges (A, C) are the fastest cutters, while shallow-fluted taper-ground gouges (B, D) are easier to maneuver for cutting details.

have less blade edge, they need to be sharpened more often.

The fastest-cutting gouges are square-ground. These gouges have flat, even bevels, ground at 45° to 65°. The flat design cuts evenly without leaving ridges in the wood. Taper- or fingernail-ground gouges, ground to 25°, leave more ridges to even out, but they're great for detail work.

Scrapers make finishing and adding details easier. Choose a round nose tool for finishing the inside of your bowl. When it's time to even out a flat bottom, you can't beat the square-nose scraper. Reach into deep bowls with small openings with offset scrapers and bottom-edge scrapers. Regrind files or chisels to make scrapers with custom profiles.

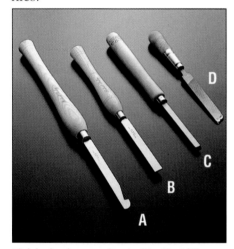

Finish shaping your bowl with offset (A), square-nose (B), roundnose (C), or customized molding-head scrapers (D).

Reach difficult areas with a special rest. The bowl-turning tool rest (see *photo, right*) is made to support your tools as you work around the inside and outside of your bowl. Its curved shape keeps your cutters close to the wood.

Preparing to turn

Hold your work with a faceplate. A faceplate attaches to the blank with screws through holes or slots in its face, and threads onto the headstock shaft of your lathe. Mount the blank so the grain is *not* perpendicular to the plane of the faceplate—screws would pull out of end grain.

Centering your faceplate precisely makes roughing faster and safer. If your blank is rectangular, draw diagonal lines, corner to corner, to locate your center and give you guide lines for faceplate

mounting. Mark the center on your blank with an awl and use dividers to scribe the largest diameter of your bowl on the bottom. Use a saw to cut around the outside of this circle to remove the excess wood, so you'll spend less time removing waste on the lathe.

Center the faceplate, then trim your blank to the outside diameter.

Bowl blanks are fairly large chunks of wood turning at high speeds. Roughing takes place at 400 to 800 rpm, final cuts at 800 to 1200 rpm, and sanding at up to 2000 rpm. This puts quite a lot of stress on the faceplate. To help minimize the chance your blank will go flying off into your workshop, pick the largest faceplate you can get that will still allow you to shape the bottom of your bowl. Center the faceplate, and fasten it to the blank with the largest and longest screws you can use. Stop the screw tips at least ¼" below the planned bowl bottom to avoid hitting them as you turn.

Wear a faceshield and dust mask to protect yourself. Thread the mounted blank onto the shaft, then, *before turning the lathe on,* adjust your tool rest so the blank clears by ⅛". Turn the blank by hand, to be sure. Step out of the way as you first start the lathe. If the blank isn't securely mounted, it could fly off as you start.

Roughing the bowl

Turning your bowl to its basic shape is called *roughing*. There's a lot of pressure against your gouge during roughing, so use a

1 to 1¼" gouge held firmly against the rest. The rest should be positioned so you're cutting a little above the center of the diameter. Work from the rim toward the base of the blank to create the outside profile, repositioning the tool rest as you go. Take care not to strike the faceplate with your gouge.

When the profile is cut to shape, move to the face. Cut in the upper left quadrant of the face (9:00 to 11:00 on a clock face) with a sharp ½" gouge. Start the cut with the shoulders of your gouge taking smooth, even strokes across the tool rest. Take care as you near the center of the bowl—if you cross the center, the turning of the bowl will lift your gouge from the tool rest.

Work the face of your bowl with a ½" gouge held firmly against the bowl-turning rest.

Smooth out all your cuts and bring your bowl to finished shape with a freshly sharpened gouge or your favorite scraper. Details, such as beads or grooves, may be added at this stage.

Fast sanding

Sanding goes quickly on the lathe. If your bowl is less than 8" in diameter, move up to high speed for sanding. (On bowls larger than 8", stay under 1200 rpm.) Sand inside and out with 100- to 220-grit papers. Keep your paper moving to avoid sanding streaks and burns. Use the non-abrasive side of the paper to burnish the bowl.

After sanding, remove your bowl from the faceplate. Finish with your favorite salad-bowl oil.

Cutting Tapers

A taper adds elegance and style to furniture legs and other project pieces.

Cutting tapers is one of the fastest ways to dress up a furniture project. Tapered legs are more slender and graceful than square stock. Whether you use the tablesaw or the jointer to make them, the result will be an eye-pleasing marriage of practicality and beauty.

A taper is a sloped cut often used to shape table or chair legs. Full-length tapers run from the bottom to the top edge of a piece; stopped tapers start and end at points in between. Furniture legs may be tapered on all four sides or just the outer faces, depending upon the project.

Making an adjustable taper jig

The jig shown here can be used to make tapers on either a tablesaw or bandsaw, and will work for pieces up to 36" long.
1 Cut two pieces of straight hardwood, ¾ × 3¼ × 36", to serve as the arms (A, B) of the jig.
2 Clamp the pieces together, then

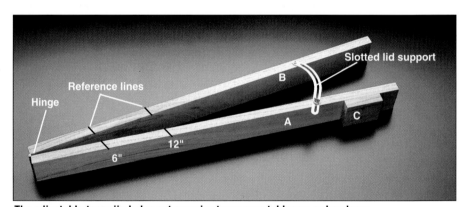

The adjustable taper jig helps cut any-size taper on a tablesaw or bandsaw.

use a ¾ × 2½" butt hinge to join them at one end.
3 Screw a ¾ × 3¼ × 4" stopblock (C), to the outside of one leg, 2" in from the end opposite the hinge.
4 Fasten a slotted lid support between the arms, just below the stopblock, using flat washers, a lock washer, and a wing nut.
5 Close the jig and tighten the wing nut. Use a combination square and marker to measure and draw permanent reference

lines across both arms of the jig, 6" and 12" from the hinge.

Cutting tapers with a tablesaw

The following steps show you how to taper a workpiece on all four sides. You'll need to reset the jig after cutting the first two tapers, to keep the correct spacing for the next cut. If you're only tapering one side or tapering two sides that are adjacent, you won't need to reset the jig.

1 Use a pencil and straightedge to lay out the tapers on your stock.
2 To determine the jig setting, measure 12" up from the beginning of the taper (or 6" if the top point of the taper will be less than 12" from the bottom edge). Draw a perpendicular line across the stock at this point and measure the distance from the taper line to the edge of the stock.
3 Adjust the jig so the distance between the arms at the 12" reference line (or the 6" line if your taper is less than 12") on the jig equals the measurement you just made. Tighten the wing nut to lock the jig setting.
4 Set your tablesaw blade for a straight cut. Position the taper jig against the fence with the stopblock facing out. Place the workpiece against the jig with the bottom edge braced against the stopblock. Slide the fence closer to the blade, and then move the jig and workpiece forward until the line for the top point of the taper touches the saw blade. Lock the fence in this position.
5 Start the saw, and use the jig and a pushstick to guide the workpiece as you cut the first taper.
6 Turn the workpiece 90° so that an uncut adjacent side is against the fence. Cut a second taper.
7 Before cutting the other tapers, you'll need to double the spacing of the jig arms to compensate for the amount of material that has already been removed. Increase the jig arm spacing to double the current setting and place a tapered side against the jig. Position the jig and the workpiece so the top point of the taper touches the blade, and cut the tapers on the remaining sides.

Cutting stopped tapers

You can make stopped tapers using a tablesaw by clamping a stopblock to an auxiliary fence on the far end of the cutting table.
1 Clamp a 50"-long auxiliary fence to your rip fence.
2 Mark the top and bottom points of the stopped taper on your workpiece and then draw a

connecting line between them.
3 Measure the distance from the bottom point of the taper to the edge of the stock. Make stop cuts equal in depth to this measurement at the bottom point, on all four sides of your workpiece.

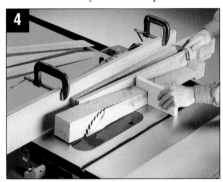

4 Raise the tablesaw blade to its fullest height, and set up the jig and workpiece for the first taper cut. Cut the taper until you almost reach the stop cut, then stop your saw blade. Before you continue, butt a small block of wood against the workpiece, on the end opposite the stop cut, and clamp it to the auxiliary fence.
5 Carefully back the workpiece out of the cut, and finish cutting the wood away to the stop cut with a handsaw or bandsaw. This block will serve as a stopping guide when you go to cut the tapers on the other sides.
6 Cut stopped tapers on the remaining sides of the workpiece, using the block as a guide.

Cutting tapers on a jointer

You can use a jointer to cut tapers following these easy steps.
1 After marking the taper lines on your workpiece, position it on the jointer so the starting point of the taper rests directly above the cutter. (For safety reasons, the stock must extend at least 1" past the cutter on the outfeed bed. For full-length tapers, leave extra stock above the top taper point and cut it off later.)
2 Set the infeed table for a ⅛"-deep cut. Set a scrap block against the workpiece on the infeed end and clamp it to the table. Remove the workpiece from the table.

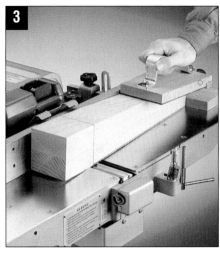

3 With cutter guard removed, turn on the jointer and set the end of the workpiece that was against the scrap block back in place, while holding the other end up. Carefully lower the other end of the workpiece down onto the cutter.
4 Use a pushblock (very important for safety) to guide the workpiece through the jointer. Make several passes, checking after each cut to see how much material still needs to be cut away. You may need to change the infeed table height for the last cut, to trim away just enough to reach the taper line.

Cutting stopped tapers on a jointer

To make stopped tapers on a jointer, you can use the same setup as for regular tapers, but you'll need to add another block on the outfeed side of the jointer. This block will stop the piece before the cutter reaches the end. You may need an auxiliary fence, if the fence or bed on your jointer is not long enough to allow for both blocks.

Instead of cutting a taper on one side and then doing the other sides, make an initial pass on all of the sides to be tapered. Then, lower the infeed table by ¹⁄₁₆" and make another pass on all the sides. Lower the infeed table by ¹⁄₁₆" before each additional pass, and repeat until you've cut the stopped tapers on all sides.

Finish the stock below the stopped taper using decorative carving or shaping techniques.

Basic Carving

Carving is Woodworking's most expressive art form.

Relief carving

For hundreds of years, amateur and professional woodworkers have practiced the craft of transforming ordinary pieces of wood into unique masterpieces of function or decoration. With patience and the very simplest of hand tools—knives and chisels—anyone with a love of wood can enjoy this beautiful craft.

The craft known as wood carving can range from simple recreational whittling to very elaborate three-dimensional sculpting. In between these extremes are other common woodworker's activities: chip carving and relief carving.

Whittling, the simplest form of carving, requires nothing more than a good knife and some wood. It is an excellent introduction to carving, because it helps the beginner develop the delicate touch and coordination that is essential for the more demanding forms of carving.

Chip carving is a simple technique and one of the oldest. It is used primarily for decoration and is often seen in furniture, plaques, and boxes. Though it looks quite intricate, chip carving is essentially based on geometric shapes—usually 3-cut or 6-cut triangles. Chip carving can be done with nothing more than a single carving knife, although for more detailed work you can buy a small set of three or four knives. Chip carving can quickly and easily transform a plain wooden project into a handsome piece of artwork.

Relief carving, the most common form of wood carving, is the technique of raising a three-dimensional image or design out of a two-

Whittled carving

Chip carving

Sculpture

dimensional wood background. Because relief carvings can range from very simple designs made with one or two chisels and gouges to elaborate and ornate projects requiring dozens of specialty gouges, the craft is one that can be pursued by both beginners and experienced woodworkers. Relief carving will help you gain

an appreciation of light and shadow and the dramatic effects they bring to a carving.

Sculpting is wood carving that is fully three-dimensional, the most difficult form of the craft. Though sculpting presents the greatest challenge, carving in the round also gives the greatest freedom of design and expression.

Buying a packaged set of carving tools is much less expensive than buying chisels, gouges, and accessories individually. The selection shown *above* is adequate for the beginner and intermediate carver, and includes: a wood mallet (A), assorted gouges (B), a skew chisel (C), a V-parting tool (D), spoon gouges (E), a fishtail gouge (F), a basic carving (bench) knife (G), and coarse and fine sharpening stones (H, I).

Tools

There are literally hundreds of specialized carving tools, each designed to make a unique type of carving cut. Although these specialized tools can make your work easier, the beginner and intermediate carver really needs only a dozen or so basic tools to learn the craft.

The cutting tools for wood carving are categorized as *knives, gouges,* or *chisels.*

Knives: The first woodcarver's tool is also the simplest—the knife. A basic pocketknife or fixed-blade bench knife works well for whittling, chip carving, highlighting details in relief carvings, and sculpting.

When choosing a woodcarving knife, look for one that feels comfortable in your hand, with a blade no longer than 1½". The blade should be made of good-quality, high-carbon steel, which will stay sharp longer than stainless steel.

Gouges: These tools, resembling ordinary carpenter's chisels with curved or rounded cutting edges, are the mainstays of the carver's tool kit. Standard gouges are identified by the shape of the curved sweep, and by the measurement between the edges of the blade.

Specialty gouges, identified by their unique blade shapes, include veiners, V-parting tools, spoon gouges, and fish-tail gouges.

Most gouges are categorized by a number which identifies the angle of the cutting edge, and by a measurement of the distance between the edges of the blade, given in inches or millimeters.

Chisels: These wood-carving tools have flat blades that are beveled on both sides (unlike standard carpenter's chisels). Chisels with angled blades are known as skew chisels.

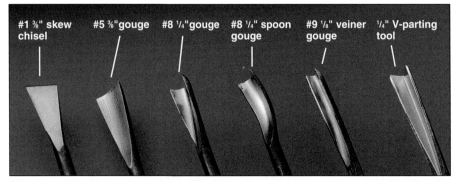

Chisels are identified by basic shape of the blade, by a cataloging number which identifies the sweep of the blade, and by a measurement of the distance between the edges of the cutting blade. A sample selection of gouges and chisels is shown *above*, with identifying labels.

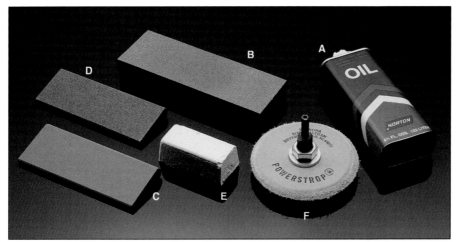

A basic sharpening kit should include lubricating oil (A), a coarse bench stone (B), a fine slip stone for honing (C), and an extremely fine black slip stone (2000-grit) for final polishing (D). Final polishing can also be done with a buffing compound (E) and a leather strop attachment for your drill (F).

Sharpening your tools

Sharpening is an intense process that, in the beginning, may take more time than the actual carving. Although sharpening is time-consuming, there is great reward in carving with razor-sharp tools. A finely honed cutting edge will cut through the wood and leave it with a polished look that brings out its beauty. We'll show you how to sharpen a gouge, but the techniques are similar for sharpening flat chisels and carving knives.

1 Clamp a coarse bench stone to your worksurface and wet it with a few drops of lubricating oil.

2 Hold the gouge with both hands so the outer beveled surface is flat on the stone. Stroke the tip back and forth, rolling the tool to shape the entire outer bevel of the blade. Make sure to grind away any nicks or gouges in the cutting edge. (For flat chisels, shape both sides on the coarse stone.)

3 Whet the outer beveled edge by moistening it with oil and sharpening it on a medium-grit stone until a fine burr forms on the inside edge.

4 Place a few drops of oil on the rounded edge of a slip stone, then sharpen the inside beveled edge of the gouge, removing the burr.
5 Use the leather strop or a black slip stone (extremely fine) to polish both sides of the bevel to a razor-sharp edge.
6 Test the sharpness by carving across the end grain of a piece of soft pine. If the gouge cuts a smooth chip without tearing, the blade is sharp enough.

WOODWORKER'S TIP

Sharpen your tools before every use, and resharpen them frequently during long carving sessions. Even brand-new gouges need to be sharpened, because the manufacturer rarely hones them to a razor-sharp edge. Sharp tools improve results and make the job easier.

WORKSHOP TIP

Cabinetry shops run by professional woodworkers and vocational schools generate hundreds of small wood scraps that are useless for cabinet making, but are ideal for the creative woodcarver. Making friends with the shop manager is an easy way to establish a ready supply of inexpensive material for carving.

Choosing wood for carving

Nearly any kind of wood can be used for carving, so long as you consider the following factors.

Grain: As a general rule, the best wood for carving has fine- to medium-textured, straight grain. Poplar, soft maple, basswood, and butternut have good grain for carving. Woods with coarse, inter-locked grain, such as hickory and elm, are apt to split or crumble when carved. Avoid any wood with distorted grain, like that found around knots.

Softwood or hardwood: Soft-woods with consistent grain, like white pine, are a good choice for beginning woodcarvers because they cut easily. Cedar, fir, and red-wood are softwoods with inconsistent grain; they are best avoided by woodcarvers. Hardwoods require a little more skill to carve because of their density. Fine-grained hard-woods, like aspen, basswood, and soft maple, are easier to carve than coarse-grained woods, such as oak, mohagony, and elm.

Color: The color of wood can be an important consideration, de-pending on the type of project. If you are going to paint a carved project, use a less expensive, less attractive wood that is easy to shape.

Moisture content: Because all woods have a tendency to split as they dry out, make sure to choose wood that is completely seasoned for your carving proj-ects. Use wood that has been air-dried for one to two years, and avoid kiln-dried wood, because it often has hidden splits and checks you may not notice until you've already invested hours in your project.

BASIC CARVING TECHNIQUE

The key to successful carving is careful control of your tools. To do this, you'll need sharp cutting edges, and simple practice at reading the wood grain and carving with, not against, the wood grain (see *photos, below*). Before you start your first project, it's a good idea to practice on scrapwood.

In the following example, you'll see how to make a simple relief carving in red oak, a coarse-grained wood that displays a rough-hewn, rustic look when carved.

Carve "uphill" with the direction of the wood grain (top) so the wood fibers shear off in smooth curls. Carving "downhill" against the wood grain (bottom) will likely cause the gouge to dig in and splinter the wood fibers.

Layout the design

1 If you are using a printed pattern, use a photocopier capable of variable enlargement to make a copy scaled to fit your project.
2 Lay a sheet of carbon paper, ink side down, on your workpiece, then tape the pattern in place.
3 Use a ball-point pen or sharp pencil to outline the pattern, transferring it to the workpiece.

Outline the design

1 Clamp the workpiece securely to your bench.
2 Use a ¼" V-tool to carve an outline for the raised portion of the design, holding the tool with one hand and lightly tapping the butt with a mallet (on softwoods, you can cut by simply pushing the V-tool). Make the outline cuts about ⅛" to the waste side of the marked lines.

3 "Set-in" the design using a gouge with a curve (sweep) that matches the curve of the design. Hold the blade vertically and lightly tap the butt of the gouge to trim the walls of the outline cuts and enlarge them.

WOODWORKER'S TIP

If your design requires removal of large amounts of wood, you can save time by using a router, held freehand, to do rough removal of background material.

Cutting the background

1 Remove the recessed background material by holding a gouge at an angle and driving the tool toward the outline cuts. Do the rough cutting using a gouge with a steep sweep (#8 or #9).

2 Finish cutting the background using a shallow gouge (#3 or #5), driven with a scooping motion.

Model the design

1 Shape and smooth (model) the design using a series of vertical depth cuts to remove the waste material. Choose gouges and chisels with sizes and shapes appropriate to the design, and drive the tools by hand to avoid cutting too deep.
2 Shape the rounded edges of the design using a skew chisel.

3 Clean up any rough edges on the pattern with a carving knife.
4 Use a flat chisel to smooth out any ridge marks left by gouges.

Finishing

Proper application of a finish helps seal your carving project and prevents uneven drying from cracking the wood. The finish also brings out texture, details, even tool marks that all enhance the beauty of the carving.

DESIGN TIP

To simulate the look of shadows and enhance the feeling of depth in your carvings, dab a darker oil finish in the recessed areas of the design.

As with any woodworking project, there are a variety of finishes to choose from. In general, avoid high-gloss varnishes or polyurethanes, because the shininess makes it hard to see fine details in the carving. Dark finishes also hide detail, so if you stain your carving, use dark stains only to accent recessed areas. Oil-based finishes work best, because water-based stains and top-coat finishes may raise the wood grain, leaving a slightly fuzzy appearance that reduces the clarity of your carving.

Penetrating oil is a good all-around finish for woodcarving projects. Simply soak the surfaces with oil, let it sink in for 10 minutes, then wipe away all excess oil.

WOODWORKER'S TIP

Whatever finish you choose for your carving, apply it to all sides, including surfaces that are not carved. This seals the wood to prevent cracking.

Cutting Multiple Workpieces

Save time and get uniform results by cutting several identical workpieces at the same time.

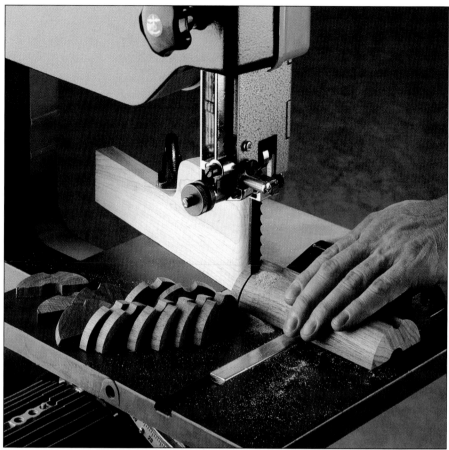

Use a resaw fence or a stopblock as a guide when cutting stock into many identical pieces. The bandsaw is especially useful in producing small identical parts.

Building projects faster and with less waste influences just about every decision made in the workshop, from shop organization to tool selection to cutting order. If a project involves a large number of identical parts, you can speed up production and ensure uniform work by learning a few basic techniques for cutting multiple workpieces.

Techniques for cutting multiple workpieces fall into three categories: *gang-cutting,* which means cutting many workpieces at one time; *making repeated cuts* using a stopblock or auxiliary fence as a guide; and *using a template* to mark identical patterns or to guide your router as it makes cuts.

Stationary power saws make excellent tools for cutting multiple workpieces. These saws have the power to handle many pieces at once and are easily fitted with guides and stopblocks. Routers, especially when mounted in a router table, work well for making repeated cuts and for shaping stock that can be sliced into identical pieces with a bandsaw (see *photo, above*). They are also the best tool to use with a template.

Gang-cutting

Done properly, gang-cutting ensures that workpieces are uniformly machined and shaped in a single cutting setup. Radial-arm saws, tablesaws, bandsaws, and routers all work effectively for gang-cutting.

Make sure the ganged workpieces

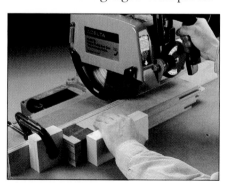

Because the saw moves instead of the wood, the radial-arm saw is ideal for gang-cutting stacked workpieces.

are aligned properly and fixed together securely before cutting. Errors in alignment transfer from

piece to piece, and if the bundle slips even slightly, all the cuts will be ruined.

To prepare workpieces for gang-cutting, bind them together securely so that the pieces can be sawn as if they were one solid piece. The method of binding ganged workpieces depends on the size and number of workpieces and the tool being used.

You can bind the workpieces by driving drywall screws through

To gang-cut multiple pieces, you can attach the pieces by driving screws through waste portions. Do not use nails, which may slip.

waste areas, or by securely clamping along the edges of the workpieces. Hot glue fastens the pieces securely and needs only be heated for quick removal. Avoid finish nails, which are difficult to remove and do not fasten the workpieces securely. A few light workpieces can be fastened to each other with masking tape or double-faced carpet tape. Tape gums up cutting blades, however, and should only be used in areas that will not be sawn. Do not use tape as the only fastener on cuts involving significant side pressure, such as cross-cutting with a radial-arm saw.

Making repeated cuts

Stopblocks and auxiliary fences allow you to use your stationary power saws to make repeated cuts that produce identical workpieces. Simply secure a stopblock

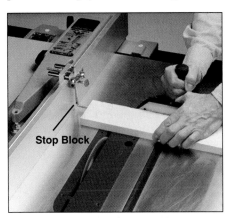

Stop Block

Clamping a stopblock to your rip fence on the infeed side of a tablesaw blade lets you make fast cuts that produce identical workpieces. This technique is very useful for cutting multiple pieces from one piece of stock.

with a C-clamp to your rip fence. Make sure the stopblock is well ahead of the blade. Use the stopblock as a guide for positioning a piece of stock against the miter gauge, then feed the stock past the blade. Use stopblocks this way for any power saw that has a table.

Using a solid block of wood as a stopblock can be dangerous on a miter saw or radial-arm saw. Small pieces of wood can jam between the blade and block, causing kickbacks. Avoid this hazard by using

Attach an auxiliary fence with a stopblock to the tablesaw miter gauge to make repeated cuts on larger workpieces.

a spacer block between the stopblock and workpiece.

A custom-crafted auxiliary fence attached to a miter gauge also helps you cut identical pieces. Attach a stopblock to the end of the auxiliary fence so the workpiece is the proper distance away from the saw blade when the miter gauge is in its slot.

Cut several similar pieces from one shaped workpiece. A radial-arm saw or tablesaw works best for multiple cuts on long stock, but a bandsaw equipped with a resawing guide works best when cutting short pieces. Most bandsaws have a large enough throat to cut up to eight pieces of ¾"-thick stock at one time. Whenever you resaw on a bandsaw, tighten the blade one size tighter to keep it from wandering. For multiple cuts on longer stock, use a tablesaw or a radial-arm saw.

Using a template

Perhaps the simplest cutting technique is to use another workpiece as a template. Normally, templates are used to mark many pieces of stock for cutting, but in some

---

TOOL TIP

The rip fence on a tablesaw is valuable for guiding a workpiece through when ripping, but never attempt to use it as a stopblock for making repeated cuts. The workpiece can easily wedge between the blade and the fence, causing a jam or kickback.

---

cases they can be used as guides for making actual cuts. Use the same template for each successive cut. Always clamp templates securely to the workpiece.

Make a template out of ¼" masonite or plywood. Either trace around the template or use it to control the movement of the router. Freehand routing around a traced pattern can be a risky proposition, with the quality of the product determined by the operator's skill. Routing against a solid template simplifies repeated cuts and increases your level of accuracy (see *Woodworking Tools, pages 44 to 47*).

Pattern-following bits are fitted with a small bearing that allows them to follow a template exactly. These bits are exclusively straight bits. For other kinds of router bits, such as dovetail bits or core box bits, use template guides, small collars that fit over the bit and attach to the router baseplate. Template guides protect the template from the bit and guide the

Use a template to make multiple-shaped pieces with a router. A special pattern-following bit has a bearing that follows the edge of a clamped-on template.

router as it moves along the template. When routing along the *outside* edge of a template with a template guide, you must allow for the distance between the outside edge of the collar and the cutting edge. As a result, the template must be smaller than the desired finished workpiece. On the other hand, when routing along the *inside* edge of a template, the template must be larger than the desired finished workpiece.

The bandsaw can resaw wide stock (up to 8" wide, on some models), and its thin blade wastes little wood. Before resawing, use a jointer/planer to joint one edge and one face of the wood—the edge to rest against the table and the face to rest against the fence.

Resawing Techniques

Don't special-order uncommon-sized lumber. Save time and money by cutting it yourself on the bandsaw or tablesaw.

If your woodworking projects call for lumber in unusual thicknesses, such as ⅜" or ⅝", you could special-order the stock from a dealer or woodworkers' store. A cheaper, faster option is to resaw thicker stock down to size on the bandsaw or tablesaw.

Resawing also can turn rough-surfaced lumber into faced boards. Many woodworkers buy rough stock in bulk and resaw nearly all the wood for their projects.

Bandsaw blades and tablesaw blades do not leave a very smooth surface. Resaw your wood ⅛" larger than desired size. Plane the cut faces to final size.

Making a resawing guide and fence for the bandsaw

Use this resawing guide and fence to guide stock on the bandsaw when resawing. Adjust the guide and fence size to match your bandsaw's proportions.

We made the wood parts of the guide and fence from oak, for its strength and durability. The pressure plate is made from ⅛"-thick acrylic sheeting for flexibility.

1 Cut the fence, fence base, fence braces, guide arm, and guide base from ¾"-thick oak.

2 Cut a notch in the fence for the upper blade guide of the bandsaw, allowing it to move to within

CUTTING LIST

Key	Qty.	Description & Size
A	1	**Fence,** ¾ × 5½ × 10"
B	1	**Fence base,** ¾ × 4½ × 10"
C	2	**Fence braces,** ¾ × 4 × 4"
D	1	**Guide arm,** ¾ × 4 × 5½"
E	1	**Guide base,** ¾ × 4 × 12"
F	1	**Pressure plate,** ⅛ × 4 × 8" acrylic sheeting

Note: All parts are made of ¾" oak, except the pressure plate, which is acrylic sheeting.

Misc.: #8 × 1¼" wood screws and #8 × ¾" wood screws.

2" of the bandsaw table. Measure the width of the upper blade

The resawing guide and fence for the bandsaw lasts longer when constructed of oak and acrylic sheeting.

guide. Then cut a notch 3½" deep and as wide as the blade guide.

3 Joint one edge and one face of the fence base. The jointed edge fits against the back of the fence, and the planed face rests against the bandsaw table when in use.

4 Joint the bottom edge and one face of the fence. Then plane the second face of the fence parallel to the jointed face of the fence.

5 Make a 45° miter cut on one end of guide base (see *photo, above*).

6 Make a diagonal cut on a ¾ × 4⅛ × 4⅛" piece of oak to form the fence support brace triangles.

7 Cut the pressure plate from ⅛"-thick acrylic sheeting.

8 Drill and countersink all screw holes (see *photo, above*).

9 Screw the guide arm to the guide base using #8 × 1½" wood screws. Align the edge of the

Bandsaw blades do not cut a perfectly smooth surface (left). Use your planer to smooth the cut faces to final size (right).

guide arm with the long edge of the base.

10 Screw the pressure plate to the guide arm using #8 × ¾" wood screws. Align the edge of the pressure plate with the edge of the guide arm (see *photo, left*).

11 Screw the fence to the fence base using #8 × 1½" wood screws.

12 Place fence braces on the fence base centered 2" from each edge. Screw fence braces in using #8 × 1½" wood screws.

Resawing on the bandsaw

The bandsaw is the most effective tool for resawing. It resaws wide stock in a single pass and wastes little wood.

Resawing on the bandsaw takes some practice to master. The blade wanders slightly as knots and irregular grain patterns deflect it. The resawing guide and fence help minimize the difficulties of resawing on the bandsaw, but guide the lumber carefully.

For best results, use a new, sharp blade, the widest one that your bandsaw will accept (½-¾").

1 Mark cutting lines, using a marking gauge. To allow for final surfacing on the planer, lay out the stock ⅛" thicker than final size.

2 Clamp the resawing fence to the bandsaw table. Set the fence at the same distance from the blade as the desired width of the stock.

3 Clamp the resawing guide to the bandsaw table. Position the guide so that the pressure plate bends slightly as it presses firmly against the stock being resawn. The pressure plate should contact the stock several inches before the blade (see *photo, opposite*).

4 Turn the bandsaw on and feed the stock across the blade, holding the planed face tightly against the fence. Use a moderate feed speed and watch the blade for twisting. Use a pushstick to finish the cut.

5 Plane the cut face to final size.

Resawing on the tablesaw

By cutting in two passes on your tablesaw, you can resaw stock almost twice as wide as the maximum cutting depth of your

tablesaw and blade.

When resawing on the tablesaw, use an auxiliary rip fence for better stability when feeding stock. The auxiliary rip fence should be as long as your tablesaw fence and taller than the stock's width.

Use a planer blade in your tablesaw with teeth angled at a minimal set. To allow for final smoothing on the planer, cut stock ⅛" thicker than final size.

1 Joint one edge and an adjacent face of the stock. For wide stock that will require two passes through the saw, joint one edge and an adjacent face, and cut the other edge parallel to the jointed edge. The edge(s) and face that rest against the table and the fence must be straight, and the edges on wide stock must be parallel to each other.

2 Adjust the tablesaw fence for the correct thickness, allowing an extra ⅛" for final surfacing.

3 Set the blade so the teeth emerge at least ⅛" above the wood. If cutting wide stock in two passes, set the blade depth for just slightly more than half the width of the stock.

4 Use a featherboard to press the jointed face of the stock against the fence. Then feed the stock across the blade. Use a slow but steady feed speed, especially when cutting in two passes, to prevent the blade from overheating and burning the wood.

5 For wide stock, turn stock over and make a second cut, keeping the jointed face against the fence.

6 Plane the cut face to final size.

CHAPTER 6

Joining Wood

Putting It Together

Joining two or more pieces of wood is a fundamental workshop skill. Almost every project calls for some kind of jointing technique—sometimes it's a simple gluing and clamping procedure; other designs require a more complicated joint. Often, the design itself dictates the jointing technique. Cabinet doors, for example, may call for frame-and-panel construction. A picture frame requires mitered joints. In other projects, the decision is dependent upon the need for strength and stability, or a decorative appearance.

Become familiar with the many jointing options. As your knowledge and skill improves, your workshop flexibility increases. Acquiring an expertise in jointing techniques will propel you from the ranks of amateur woodworker to master woodworker.

Box Joints 108
Dadoes and Rabbets 110
Miter Joint Techniques and Jigs 114
Gluing and Clamping 118
Frame and Panel Technique 122
Biscuit Joinery 124
Making Drawers...126
Basic Dowel Joints.....................................130
Veneer Basics 132
Dovetail Joints 136
Mortises and Tenons 140

Box Joints

Add a decorative touch to your projects with these simple, sturdy joints.

Apply contrasting stains or finishes, or use contrasting woods, to showcase the simple beauty of box joints. Apply contrasting finishes before cutting the fingers and notches.

Box joints, also known as finger joints, are often used to join drawer parts and make corner joints. The interlocking fingers and notches make it an especially attractive joint that is worth showing off. Unlike other joints, box joints give you the chance to be creative with joint design without sacrificing strength. You have many choices when it comes to planning a box joint—wide or narrow fingers, similar or contrasting wood grains and finishes.

Consider the overall size of your finished project when you are mapping out the width of the fingers. On a smaller box, for example, narrow fingers may be a better choice, to give the finished project a more delicate look. But larger projects, like cabinets, may look better with wide fingers that create a more substantial-looking box joint.

The length of the fingers in a box joint should equal, or slightly exceed, the thickness of the pieces you are joining. If you are joining two pieces of ¾" wood, for example, the fingers should be at least ¾" long. It's better to make them just a little bit too long, ¹⁄₁₆" for example, than too short. You can always trim off any slight excess by sanding the assembled joint. If the fingers are too short, however, you'll be left with no choice but to start over.

Most box joints are made using two pieces of wood with matching thicknesses. It's possible to make them using woods of different thicknesses, but it requires special jigs and can be more trouble than it's worth.

When you use the handmade jig shown here, along with your tablesaw, you'll find it's fairly easy to make box joints quickly and accurately. The trickiest part of planning box joints is getting the top edges of the joints to match.

When you look at a completed box, it usually looks better if both ends of each part are cut the same, so they both begin with a finger or both begin with a notch. The easiest way to accomplish this is to set up the pieces you're joining in advance and mark each one as starting with a finger or a notch. This way, you'll be sure of the results.

After you've got the jig board attached to your tablesaw miter gauge, you can clamp your workpiece in place and slide the whole assembly forward to cut the first notch.

Making the jig

This jig is made by taking a board and installing a small extending guide pin that is the same height and width as the planned box-joint fingers. The jig board is lined up one finger-width away from the cutting blades of your dado set and attached to the tablesaw miter gauge. Then, each piece is set against the guide pin for the initial cut. After each cut, the piece is shifted over so that the most recent cut fits over the guide pin, preparing the piece for the next cut.

1 Cut a piece of ¾" plywood to 4 × 36" to make the jig board. Center and attach it to the miter gauge of your table saw with 1¼" screws.

2 Install a dado-blade set equal to the planned width of the box joints. Adjust the height of the blade to equal the thickness of the boards you will be joining, plus an additional ¹⁄₁₆". If, for instance, you are joining two ¾" boards, adjust the blade set height to ¹³⁄₁₆".

3 Cut a notch (equal to the width and height of the planned fingers) for the guide pin in the jig board.

4 Cut a 5" guide pin from a strip of hardwood to fit in the notch in the jig board. The guide pin should fill the notch and have perfectly square edges.

5 Cut off a 2" piece of the guide pin and insert it into the notch so one end fits flush against the back edge of the jig board. Set aside the remaining cut-off piece to use as a spacer.

6 Unscrew the jig board from the miter gauge, remove the guide pin, and apply wood glue inside the notch. Re-install the pin.

Making box joints

1 Use the cut-off portion of the guide pin as a spacer to position the jig board for the first cut. Place the spacer against the dado-blade set and position the jig so that the guide pin rests against the other side of the spacer. Attach the jig to the miter gauge with screws and take away the spacer.

2 Take a board that is marked to start with a finger and clamp it to the jig board, with one side against the guide pin. Cut the first notch— you will be cutting a notch in the jig board at the same time.

3 Shift the workpiece over so the notch you just cut fits over the guide pin. Cut another notch.

4 Shift the workpiece over after each cut, using the guide pin as a reference, until you have cut notches across the full width of the board. Flip the board over on end, and then cut notches in the other end.

5 Take a workpiece that's been marked to start with a notch. Slide the spacer between the dado-blade set and the guide pin. *Leave the spacer in place* and butt the workpiece against it. Clamp the workpiece to the jig board, then *remove the spacer.*

6 Make the first cut, which notches the top edge of the workpiece.

7 Shift the workpiece over so the first cut fits over the guide pin, then clamp it to the jig and cut another notch. Continue shifting and cutting notches across the remainder of the workpiece. Flip the workpiece over on end and cut notches in the other end.

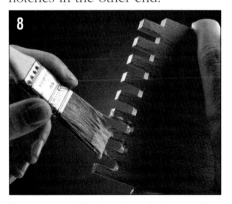

8 Use a small paintbrush to apply glue to the fingers and notches. Apply glue sparingly to reduce the mess and keep a clean look.

9 Assemble the parts to form a box, then fit pipe clamps, with wood scraps under the ends, over the assembly. Make sure to run the clamps across the assembly in both directions and measure the diagonals to check for square.

10 Let the joints dry, then remove any excess glue. Sand and finish to your taste.

Dadoes and Rabbets

Versatile, strong and easy to make, dadoes and rabbets are the meat-and-potatoes of wood joinery.

Learning to make dadoes and rabbets is one stepping-off point that marks a beginner's passage from rough carpenter to woodworker. But even a master woodworker with a shopful of jigs for making biscuit, dowel, dovetail, and box joints will be drawn back, time and again, to the simple elegance of a dado or rabbet joint.

A *dado* is a square channel cut across the grain of a workpiece. A dado cut that runs with the grain pattern and lengthwise along the workpiece is called a *groove* or sometimes a *plough*. A *rabbet* resembles a dado or groove, but it's cut along the edge of a workpiece and is open on one side.

Just about any tool that can cut wood can cut a dado, groove, or rabbet. The question of which tool works best has spurred a lot of debate among woodworkers.

If you value speed, you'd be likely to favor using a stackable dado-blade set mounted on a tablesaw—especially if you have several similar cuts to make. If you're more interested in short setup time, you'd probably choose a portable router with a carbide-tipped router bit and a jig. And if you like working with hand tools, you'd appreciate the fine control and precision you get when using a backsaw to cut the edges of the channels, then removing waste wood with a sharp chisel.

But whichever method suits you best for making dado and rabbet joints, do not overlook the importance of proper preparation and careful measuring.

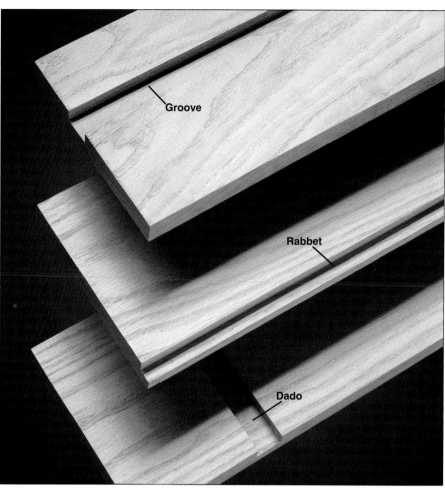

Dadoes, grooves, and rabbets are considerably stronger than plain butt joints, although they're not much harder to make. In addition to the structural support provided when a board is inserted, dadoes, grooves, and rabbets also increase the surface area in the joint, creating much stronger glue bonds.

Guidelines for dadoes & rabbets

For most dadoes, rabbets, and grooves, the depth of the cut should not exceed one-half the thickness of the workpiece. The width of the cut should be about 1/32" wider than the thickness of the insert-board, to allow for expansion and contraction of the joint. Make rabbets slightly wider than the insert-board so you can create a perfectly smooth joint by sanding the workpiece flush with the insert-board.

To widen a dado or groove, make a custom sanding block by wrapping a piece of fine sandpaper around a scrap of lumber the same thickness as the insert-board. Scrape the sanding block back and forth in the channel. When the cut is the right size, an insert-board should slide back and forth easily, but not loosely, in the cut. If the cut is a little too wide, you can fill the gap above the insert-board with wood putty.

For a stopped (blind) dado or rabbet, leave at least 1/2" of wood between each end of the cut and the edges of the workpiece.

WOODWORKER'S TIP

Use the insert-board to mark dadoes and rabbets on the workpiece. **For dadoes,** *mark one edge of the cut with a rule, then set the insert-board next to the line and mark the other edge with a sharp pencil.* **For rabbets,** *set an insert-board about 1/32" inside the edge of the workpiece, making sure the outside edge of the insert-board is parallel to the edge of the workpiece. Mark the workpiece along the inside edge of the insert-board.*

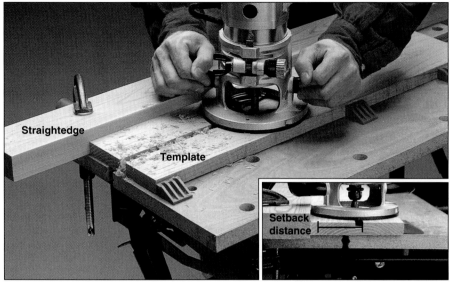

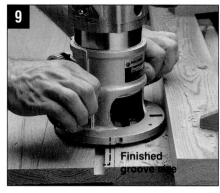

A straightedge guide is a must for making accurate dadoes with a router. Making a test-cut on a piece of scrap wood butted against the straightedge creates a template you can use to check the actual width of the router bit and to measure the setback distance from the straightedge to the inside shoulder of the cut.

Cutting dadoes with a router

Short setup time and clean cuts are two of the advantages to using a router for making dadoes and grooves. A portable router is an especially good choice for making dadoes or grooves in sheet goods or wide cabinet panels, which are very difficult to maneuver through a tablesaw.

1 Select a straight router bit the same size or slightly smaller than the width of the dado. Mount the bit in your router.

2 Secure a piece of scrapwood to your workbench, then butt a straightedge (at least ½" thicker than the scrapwood) next to the scrapwood. Use the straightedge as a guide for making a test cut in the scrapwood, then use the scrapwood as a template for your actual cut (see *photo, above*).

3 To make the dado cut, begin by securing the workpiece to your workbench and marking the dado or groove on the workpiece with a sharp pencil.

4 Set your scrapwood template (step 2) on the workpiece, with the test cut aligned directly over the marks for the dado. Draw a line along the outside edge of the template. Remove the template.

5 Position a straightedge on the template line, check to make sure it's parallel to the dado lines, then secure it to the worksurface.

6 Set the router bit to a depth of about ¼", then make the first pass for your dado or groove, using the straightedge guide to steer the router. Cut evenly, moving the router against bit rotation (see *Router Basics, pages 44 to 47*).

7 Extend the bit depth no more than ¼", then make a second cutting pass. Continue deepening the bit and cutting until the dado or groove is the desired depth. Attempting to remove more than ¼" of wood in a single pass can cause burning and tearout.

8 For cuts that are wider than the router bit, move the straightedge to the other side of the workpiece. Align the guide as you did for the first section of the cut, maintaining the setback between the shoulder of the cut and the straightedge.

9 Make the first pass, then finish the dado or groove cut by gradually deepening the passes. Make sure both sides of the cut are equal in depth.

10 Test-fit the insert-board in the dado or groove. If it sticks, then smooth out the cut with fine sandpaper and a piece of scrapwood used as a sanding block.

Cutting rabbets with a router

Special rabbet bits with a ball-bearing pilot, like the one *above*, make it easy to cut fast, accurate rabbets.

Most rabbet bits have a pilot that guides the bit along the edge of the board. The pilot does away with the need for a straightedge or jig, making rabbets one of the easiest cuts to form with a router. To make an accurate cut, however, you must have a straight, smooth edge on the workpiece. A quick run through the jointer helps ensure a clean rabbet cut.

1 Select a rabbet bit the same size as the planned width of the cut, and mount the bit in your router. Bits that match most standard board thicknesses can be found at any hardware store (for nonstandard rabbets, you may have to resort to a straight bit (see *Cutting dadoes with a router, left*).

2 Run the edge of your workpiece through a jointer or over a stationary sander to create a smooth surface for the pilot to follow. Check for chipping or tearout.

3 Set the workpiece on the workbench, then set a piece of scrapwood the same thickness as the workpiece on each side. Align the scraps so they are even with the edge of the workpiece, then clamp the workpiece and the scraps in place. The scraps will keep the router bit from rounding off the cut at the start and finish.
4 Set the rabbet bit to a depth of about ¼" and make the first pass of the cut, moving the router against the rotation of the bit.
5 Extend the bit no more than ¼" and make the second pass, deepening the cut. Continue deepening the cut until the rabbet is the desired depth.

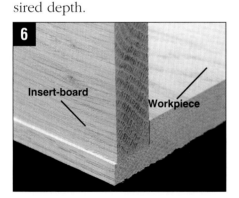

6 Smooth away any rough spots on the side or bottom of the rabbet with sandpaper, then test-fit the insert-board in the rabbet. The edge of the workpiece should extend just past the outside surface of the insert-board. Then, after the joint is reinforced, the edge of the workpiece should be sanded down so it is exactly flush with the insert-board.

Cutting dadoes with a tablesaw

Tablesaws and radial-arm saws are used frequently for cutting dadoes, grooves, and rabbets, but to be an effective tool for the job, a special blade or blade set is required. The best are stackable dado-blade sets, which have a cutting blade on each side of the stack to cut the shoulders, and chipper blades in between to remove the waste wood. The cutters are used with some or all of the chippers, and paper or plastic spacers to create any cutting width between ¼" and ¹³⁄₁₆". Good stackable sets, usually costing at least $100, can cut smooth, flat-bottomed dadoes in a single pass.

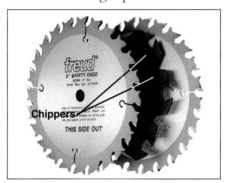

Stackable dado-blade set.

A cheaper cousin of the stacked dado set, called a "wobble blade," also can be used to cut dadoes and rabbets. A wobble blade is a single blade that tilts on its hub, causing it to wobble from side to side as it spins. The wobbling increases the width of the cutting path, allowing you to cut wider dadoes by increasing the tilt. Most wobble blades cost only $40 or so, but they are serviceable for rough work only, since the cut they make is rough-edged and rounded on the bottom.

Using a stackable dado-blade set

1 Calculate how many chippers and spacers are needed to cut a channel the desired width. The manufacturer of the set usually provides guides for this purpose.
2 With your tablesaw unplugged, replace the saw blade with the dado set, making sure the teeth of the blades and chippers will rotate in the proper direction.

3 Secure the blade set, plug your saw back in, and set up the saw for the cut. For grooves and long dadoes, use the saw fence as a guide. For dadoes that will be cross-cut in the workpiece, use the miter gauge to guide your cut.
4 Make a test cut on scrapwood, using a pushstick.
5 Check the dimensions of the cut by measuring and by placing the insert piece into the cut. Make any necessary adjustments to the blade height and width, or to the fence or miter-gauge position.
6 Feed the workpiece through the saw, using the miter gauge or a pushstick, and a featherboard. For cuts deeper than ¾" or in very hard stock, make several passes, deepening the cut after each pass.

Cutting rabbets with a tablesaw

The easiest way to cut a rabbet on a tablesaw or radial-arm saw is with a stackable blade set using dado-cutting techniques.

Make a fence attachment for your tablesaw, using a straight 2 × 4, if you plan to make a lot of rabbet cuts. Notch the 2 × 4 to fit over the entire width of the dado-blade set, then clamp it to the fence, directly over the blades. Adjust the width of the rabbet by moving the fence and attachment to expose as much of the blade set as needed to make your cut.

If you don't own a dado set or you would rather not install the set for just a few cuts, you can cut rabbets on a tablesaw with just two cuts, using a standard blade. Simply set the saw height to the depth of the rabbet and set the fence distance to the width. Feed the workpiece through the saw facedown, then reverse the depth and width settings and feed the workpiece through on its edge.

Cutting stopped dadoes

Stopped dadoes, sometimes called "blind" dadoes, create invisible joints that have all the strength of a standard dado or groove. They're commonly used for shelves in cabinetmaking.

For cuts that are stopped at both ends, use a plunge router or tilt a straight bit mounted in a fixed base router into the cut on one end and make the cut (see *Cutting dadoes with a router, page 111*).

For dadoes or grooves that are stopped on one end only, a table-saw with a stackable dado-blade set works very well. Mark the stopped dado on the workpiece, at least ½" from the ends of the

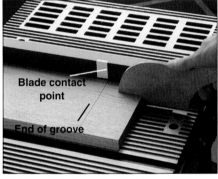

To cut a stopped dado, mark the workpiece and the contact point of the saw blade. Stop cutting when the marks meet.

board, then measure and transfer the end marks to the back side of the board. Find the point where the workpiece will contact the blades by feeding scrapwood up to the blades until contact is made. Mark the point on the fence, then clamp a featherboard to the fence just outside the contact point to keep the workpiece stable. Set the fence the proper distance from the blades, then feed the workpiece under the featherboard and into the saw blades until the mark on the back of the workpiece meets the mark on the fence.

Most tools used to cut a stopped dado make cuts that aren't square at the ends. A stackable blade set leaves a channel that slopes up from the bottom of the cut because of the curvature of the blades. A straight router bit leaves a stopped cut that is full depth, but rounded on the end.

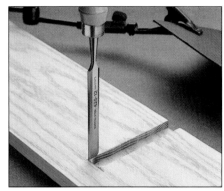

Use a sharp wood chisel to square off the ends of stopped dadoes.

To square off the end of a stopped dado or groove, set a sharp wood chisel on the line marking the end of the stopped dado, with the beveled edge of the chisel facing away from the line. Give the chisel one or two sharp raps with a mallet to score the wood at the end and sides of the cut (don't try to remove all the wood in one chunk).

Next, begin chiseling out the waste wood a little at a time. Remove the last of the waste wood with the chisel blade resting in the bottom of the cut, bevel side down.

Gluing & reinforcing joints

Because they create a supportive ledge for insert-boards, not all dadoes and grooves require gluing or reinforcement—especially those cut to hold shelving. A loose dado or rabbet joint is great for resisting expansion and contraction stress, but it doesn't contribute to the overall strength of the project.

Rabbet joints usually require gluing, reinforcement, or both.

To glue a dado, groove, or rabbet joint, apply carpenter's glue to the insert-board and the bottom of the cut. Set the insert-board into the cut, and slide it back and forth

WOODWORKER'S TIP

When making stopped dadoes, turn off the saw and wait for the blade to stop before you remove the workpiece. Removing a board while the cutting tool is still running is a safety hazard, and it can also cause a kickback that may scar your workpiece.

to spread the glue around. Clamp as you would any other joint.

Practically any kind of fastener can be used to reinforce a dado or rabbet joint. Countersunk finish nails are used very frequently for general-purpose joints. Blind dowel and biscuit joints provide a little more strength, and they don't need filling or plugging.

Hiding dado & rabbet joints

Dado and rabbet joints are simple and strong, but a lot of woodworkers prefer to keep them out of sight. Designing cabinets, shelves, and other projects to include a face frame is one common way of hiding joints and fasteners. Attaching thin hardwood strips or wood tape to the exposed edges of the lumber also hides joints, but a lot of woodworkers consider the practice to be something of a "band-aid" approach.

One old trick for hiding dado joints is to cut the edges of the insert-board with a protecting lip

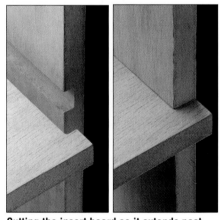

Cutting the insert board so it extends past the dado joint and wraps around the exposed edge of the workpiece is one way to hide a dado joint.

that overlaps and covers the dado. This technique, however, creates a slight shelf overhang.

A variation of a rabbet joint is sometimes used to hide plywood edges. Instead of a standard rabbet, cut a rabbet that goes all the way to the bottom veneer layer. Then, when the joint is formed, only a very thin layer (about ⅛") of plywood edge will be exposed. This kind of rabbet joint isn't much stronger than a butt joint.

Miter-Joint Techniques and Jigs

Easy-to-make workshop aids help you cut and assemble perfect miter joints.

Miter joints should always be reinforced for maximum strength. Wooden dowels (left) or biscuits (right) inserted at right angles to the cut make a mitered joint very durable.

Miter-cut corners make attractive woodworking joints because they hide end grain and create smooth, continuous grainlines.

Good miter joints are demanding, however, because they require the utmost precision for layout, cutting, and clamping. Fortunately, there are several helpful workshop accessories you can build or buy that make it easy to create miter joints.

Miter-cuts can be made on any number of handsaws and power saws, but whatever method you use—hand miter saw, power miter box, circular saw, tablesaw or radial-arm saw—it is crucial that your workpieces are cut to the correct angles. Never trust the angle markings on your saw; use a protractor and sliding T-bevel to mark workpieces and to set the angle on your saw. Make test cuts on scrapwood before each work session.

Layout

Determining the angles for the miter-cut pieces is relatively easy for projects that have equal-size pieces and straight sides: The ends of the adjoining pieces are miter-cut to an angle that is one-half that of the joint.

Layout is more complicated when adjoining pieces are made from different-sized stock, because the pieces must be miter-cut to different angles.

Mark workpieces for miter-cutting using a sliding T-bevel. Adjust the T-bevel to the desired angle using a simple protractor.

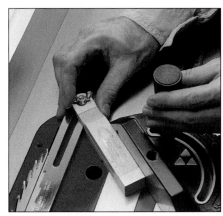

Set the miter gauge on a tablesaw to the chosen angle, using the T-bevel. Make sure to position the arm of the T-bevel between the teeth of the saw blade, so the cutting tips do not affect the angle.

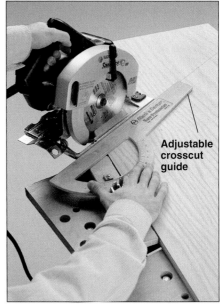

Adjustable crosscut guide

To mark miter-cuts on pieces that have different widths, align the pieces one over the other and mark the inside corner where the pieces intersect. Draw cutting lines on each piece from the outside corner to the intersection mark.

Projects with sloping sides, like those often used in outdoor planters or wooden buckets, will require that the segments be both mitered and beveled. This type of cut, called a *compound miter,* can require irregular angles measured by fractions of degrees. If your project requires compound miters, make sure to lay out the angles carefully with a precise protractor.

Miter shooting box

A homemade miter shooting box lets you shave a precise edge on 45° miter-cut workpieces, using a block plane. It is especially useful for workpieces that are rough-mitered with a circular saw, saber-saw, or handsaw. The miter shooting box is made of three parts: a ¾ × 10 × 24" plywood base (A), a ¾ × 5½ × 24" hardwood ledge (B), and a ¾"-thick, 90° tri-angular stopblock (C) with 7¾" short sides and an 11" long side. Join the three pieces with glue and counterbored wood screws, so the back edges are exactly aligned.

To use the miter shooting block, position the miter-cut workpiece across the ledge, tight against the stopblock, so it just slightly over-hangs the ledge. Turn a block plane on its side and position it so the blade just touches the workpiece. Push firmly on the plane to shave a thin layer of wood from the workpiece.

> **DESIGN TIP**
>
> *Not all miters are cut to 45°. To find the correct cut angle for any circular workpiece, divide 180° by the number of segments in the project. For example, for a planter with six sides, each piece will be mitered at 30° (180 divided by 6).*

Adjustable crosscut guide

This purchased jig *(shown above)* is helpful for making rough miters or compound miters with a circu-lar saw or sabersaw. When ad-justed and locked to the desired angle, the crosscut guide forms a fence to steer the base of the saw.

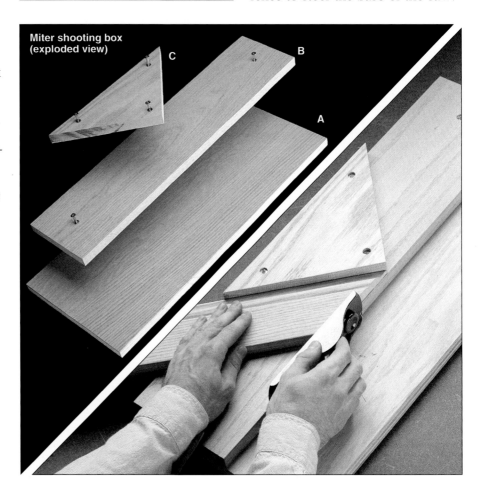

Miter shooting box (exploded view)

C   B   A

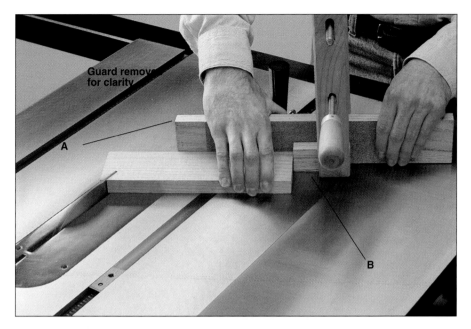

Miter-gauge extension

When miter-cutting on the table-saw, the motion of the saw blade tends to slide the workpiece along the miter gauge, causing inaccurate cuts. By extending the miter gauge with the jig shown here, you'll cut more accurate miters.

The miter-gauge extension is simply a 1×3 hardwood fence (A) attached to your miter gauge with wood screws driven through the back. Sandpaper glued to the face of the extension helps grip workpieces as they are fed into the blade. When cutting several pieces to the same length, clamp a small wood block to the extension to make a stopblock (B).

Crosscut fence with angle guides

For greater precision when cutting miters on the tablesaw, make a double-runner crosscut fence and triangular angle guides.

The crosscut fence is made from a 30"-long fence made from a maple 2 × 4 (A), attached with glue and wood screws to a 5 × 30" brace made from ¾" plywood (B). Hardwood runners (C), sized to fit the dimensions of the miter-gauge slots in your tablesaw, are attached to the bottom of the fence with glue and counterbored wood screws.

Make angle guides by cutting triangular pieces of ¾" plywood to the desired miter angles. Attach the triangle (D) to a 1 × 4 cleat (E) with one end beveled to the same angle, using glue and counterbored wood screws.

To use the crosscut fence and angle guide, clamp the cleat of the angle guide to the front of the crosscut fence so the point just touches the path of the blade. Butt the workpiece against the edge of the angle guide when feeding the crosscut fence into the saw blade.

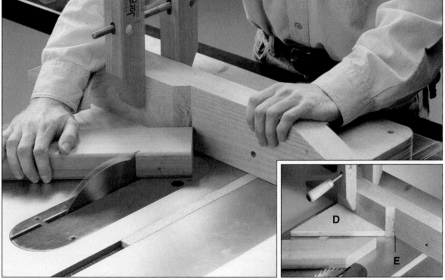

Taper jig

This accessory is useful for cutting shallow angles on long workpieces, like the tapered edges often used on table and chair legs. (*see Cutting Tapers, pages 96 and 97*). This taper jig is made from two 30"-long pieces of 1 × 3 oak (A, B) joined at one end with a small butt hinge. A wing nut and curved lid support mounted 7" from the opposite end let you adjust the jig to the desired angle. A 1 × 3" piece of ¾" wood (C) screwed to the back of one board serves as a cleat.

To use the taper jig, set the arms to the desired angle, then place the jig next to the rip fence and use it to feed the workpiece into the saw blade.

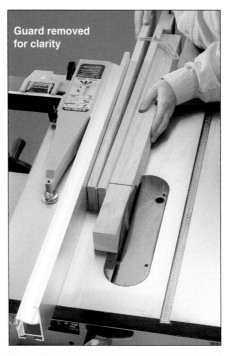

Guard removed for clarity

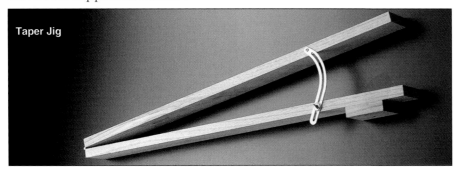

Taper Jig

Reinforcing with dowels

Miter joints reinforced with dowels are quite strong, but making them requires careful techniques. Dowel holes drilled in the miter-cut ends of workpieces must be exactly perpendicular to the cut. If you do not have a doweling jig that works with mitered edges, drill the holes with a drill press. Where possible, use at least two dowels in each joint. After drilling holes in the first workpiece, use dowel centers to align the holes in the adjoining workpiece. Glue and clamp all the joints at the same time, using band clamps or miter clamps.

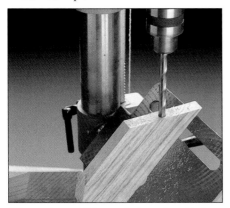

When using a drill press to bore dowel holes, tilt the table to the angle of the miter cut and clamp the workpiece on edge to the table.

Reinforcing with biscuits

If you have a biscuit joiner, reinforcing miter joints is very easy. The biscuit joiner is basically a miniature plunge saw, specially designed to cut grooves for pre-milled, compressed wooden discs, called biscuits. When coated with glue and inserted into the grooves, the biscuits swell to create tight, strong joints. The smallest biscuits available are about 1½" long, so if you are mitering small stock, you'll need to use other reinforcement methods. When using a biscuit joiner, make sure that the grooves on adjoining workpieces are aligned correctly.

When using a biscuit joiner to cut slots for biscuits, clamp the workpiece so it overhangs your workbench and hold the joiner flat against the surface of the miter cut.

Reinforcing with splines

A spline is a thin piece of wood glued into matching grooves in adjoining workpieces to bridge and strengthen a joint. Spline grooves usually are cut with a tablesaw and dado blade, but they can also be cut with a biscuit joiner or a router.

Splines usually are installed so they are visible at the ends of a joint, so many woodworkers make them from an attractive, contrasting wood. For greatest strength, make sure the splines are inserted so the wood grain does not run parallel to the wood grain in the mitered workpieces.

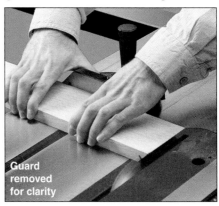

Guard removed for clarity

When cutting spline grooves on miter-cut edges, set the blade on your tablesaw at 45° and feed the workpieces with the miter gauge.

Edge-gluing with alternating growth-ring patterns and top and bottom clamps helps keep tabletops and other wide stock flat.

Gluing and Clamping

The right gluing and clamping techniques give your projects the durability they deserve.

A good glue joint becomes stronger than the wood it- self. When performed cor- rectly, gluing adds strength and durability to your work without detracting from its appearance. Knowing how to use wood glue, epoxy glue, and plastic resin glue in combination with a selection of woodworker's clamps will help you build lasting beauty into all your wood projects.

Glues for your shop

Three basic kinds of glue will be all a woodworker needs for most jobs. For interior use, wood glue, known also as aliphatic resin glue, is the standard for most common woods. High-acid woods and some waterproof applications are better glued with epoxy glue. For outdoor projects, moisture- resistant plastic resin glue makes a sensible choice.

Wood glue is the most often- used glue in woodworking. Sometimes referred to as yellow glue, it is the least expensive woodworking glue. It offers dura- bility and strength without toxic fumes or solvent cleanup and has a working time, before clamping, of about ten minutes at 70°. De- pending on humidity and mois- ture content, you can remove your clamps from the project

25 to 90 minutes after clamping, as long as you don't put stress on the glued parts for several hours. Wood glue sands easily when dry, and, best of all, the glue lines are nearly invisible.

Epoxy glue is the best choice for boat building, kitchenware, and gluing high-acid woods. Epoxy is a two-part glue that be- gins to harden as soon as the parts are mixed together. Some epoxies are made for fast setting—as little as five minutes curing time hardens the glue to working strength. Other epoxies cure more slowly, so several glu- ing operations can be completed before the glue sets.

Some very dense imported woods, like rosewood, and com- mon woods, like red oak, contain high amounts of acid. Although these woods can be joined with wood glue, high-stress applications, like bentwood construction, are better served with epoxy. Epoxy resins are waterproof, so they resist the weakening properties of the water-soluble acids contained in the wood and provide a much longer-lasting bond.

Because epoxy depends on a chemical reaction to harden, always mix the glue according to the manufacturer's instructions. Be aware that epoxies emit toxic fumes while mixing and curing, so be sure your gluing area has plenty of ventilation. A respirator will help prevent harmful exposure to epoxy fumes.

Wearing rubber gloves and a respirator, use a cloth dampened with acetone to remove excess epoxy glue from the joint, clamps, your clothes, or your skin. Unlike water, acetone won't raise wood grain, so use it freely to clean up excess epoxy before it hardens.

Plastic resin glue has a high resistance to water. Birdhouses, sports equipment, lawn and garden furnishings, and exterior doors need long-lasting joints that will stand up to moisture. Plastic resin glue provides the strength and moisture resistance these types of projects require. Plastic resin glue is not totally waterproof, but it is less expensive and easier to mix than epoxy. Because this glue leaves visible glue lines, it is often used for projects where visible glue lines don't matter or are incorporated into the design. Its color blends well with cedar or redwood, so it is widely used for building lawn furniture.

Plastic resin glue usually comes as a powder that you mix with water. While it's wet, it cleans up easily with a cloth and water, but, like wood glue, it will penetrate the pores of the wood and leave glue spots. When it's dry it's almost indestructible, so be sure to apply plastic resin glue only to the areas you wish to bond.

Clamps for woodworking

You'll need several types of clamps to choose from to hold

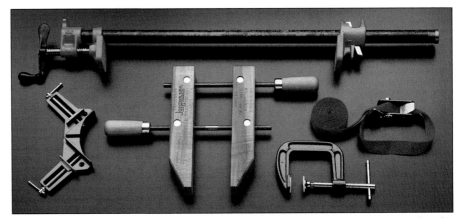

Pipe clamps, handscrews, C-clamps, band clamps, and corner clamps all deserve a place in the woodworking shop.

glue joints together for edge-gluing, laminating, and making joints. While everyone has favorites, no shop is complete without the pipe clamp, handscrew clamp, C-clamp, corner clamp, and band clamp.

Pipe clamps are a variation of the more expensive bar clamp. Unlike bar clamps, they have removable heads that can be fitted to any length of pipe. Keep a few sets of clamp heads and pipe lengths on hand, and you'll have clamps ready for fast and efficient edge-gluing of tabletops, laminating posts or legs, and holding work. Their sturdy metal jaws will cut into your work as you tighten, so you'll need to use pads to protect your workpiece.

Handscrew clamps deserve a prominent place in your shop. They're fairly expensive, but they earn their keep. Because the jaws are wood, they can be used to hold down work near saw blades without fear of damage to expensive blades, and the wooden jaws don't need pads to keep from leaving marks in your work. They adjust quickly and can apply plenty of pressure when you need it. Their widely adjustable jaws can be maneuvered to fit odd shapes when holding workpieces, jigs, or tools.

C-clamps are used all over the workshop, but they're versatile glue clamps as well. C-clamps are used for laminating blanks, holding corner dogs in place, or squeezing cauls together.

Corner clamps are the quickest clamps to use when you're gluing miter joints in picture frames. Some even have miter slots built in for cutting the miter. Their shape also allows them to hold butt joints, often found in face frames. The design of the corner clamp lets you slide the pieces to be glued past one another easily so aligning the parts is a breeze.

Use band clamps to tighten multijointed or difficult-to-clamp shapes.

Band clamps are the best choice for holding odd-shaped or multiangled projects, such as chairs or octagonal shapes, but they hold picture frames and other regular shapes securely, too. Band clamps consist of a strap or web made of strong, flexible fabric attached to a catch designed for applying pressure as it reels in the strap. You could make blocks to use with other clamps to hold these shapes, but the band clamp does it simply. The straps are usually at least 6' long, making band clamps perfect for large, hard-to-clamp items.

Edge-gluing

Use this technique to make table-tops, cabinet sides, and other wide-stock pieces. We'll demonstrate by using wood glue and pipe clamps to edge-glue a cedar tabletop.

As with any gluing technique, the wood surfaces must be clean and dry for bonding. Freshly cut, planed, or sanded surfaces will readily soak glue into their open pores, making the deepest possible bond. Accurate jointing and planing are important for strong glue joints. If joining surfaces aren't smooth and even, gaps will form between the boards and the glue joint will be weak.

You can joint the boards with a tablesaw, router, hand planer, or jointer. Dry-fit them on a flat surface, and alternate the end grain by placing a board with growth rings arching up next to a board with growth rings arching down. This pattern equalizes the effects of warping. Place everything for your glue-up within easy reach. Assemble the glue-up in a practice run, using everything but the glue. Slide half of your clamps under the boards. Use the clamps to squeeze glue from the entire length of the glue-up. (usually one every 12 to 18".)

Hold boards vertically to prevent dripping as you apply glue to the second side.

Tighten the clamp at one end of the glue-up, applying enough pressure to hold the boards together. Adjust the boards so they are just above the pipes. Continue adjusting clamps along the length of the glue-up, aligning boards so they are flat across the width of the glue-up. When the bottom clamps are adjusted, alternate the

clamps, placing one top clamp between each two bottom clamps. Use a straightedge to check for flatness. Tighten the top clamps to arch the surface in the middle. To lower the middle, tighten the bottom clamps. If the boards are correctly jointed, unclamp them just enough to remove them, leaving the bottom clamps in place.

Slightly round the corners on a chisel blade and use it to remove glue.

Turn all the pieces up on edge to apply the glue. Work on one pair of boards at a time. Use a glue bottle to lay a moderate bead of glue down the middle of ¾" boards or one bead along each edge of wider boards. With light pressure on a glue roller, roll the glue into a smooth, thin film that completely covers the edge. The glue roller is a flat-wheeled roller of wood or plastic that can also be used in wallpaper installation. Turn the inside board over and apply glue to the other edge. Roll the glue as quickly as possible to prevent drips. Place this edge against the glued edge of its mate, and lay both boards down on the clamps. Move along the glue-up, repeating this process. Work quickly, so the first boards don't set before you finish the glue-up.

When all the boards are glued, raise them off the pipe and clamp them lightly in position, working quickly. Raising the wood off the pipes prevents black glue marks from forming on the wood and gives you some room to adjust the boards. Add the top clamps, and use the straightedge as you check for flatness. Maintain a flat surface by using a rubber mallet to tap boards into position.

Tighten the clamps along the glue-up so squeeze-out appears. Continue to use the straightedge to check for flatness and correct, if necessary, to make a flat glue-up. Store the clamped glue-up in a verticle position so squeeze-out glue will run along the joint lines, not across the face of the glue-up.

When the glue-up has dried for an hour, use a chisel or stiff putty knife to remove the beads of drying glue. Setting time for glue depends on temperature, humidity, and moisture content, among other things, so an hour is just an approximate time. When you time removal right, the beads will come easily without tearing the wood or smearing the glue.

Unclamp after an hour, if you need to reuse the clamps right away for something else. Otherwise, overnight drying can't hurt. Don't plan on sanding or planing the glue-up until the wood on both sides of the glue joints has had a chance to absorb the moisture from the glue evenly. This will take about a week. Resurfacing before this point will leave very visible shrink lines in your glue-up once the wood is completely dry.

Cauls spread the pressure from clamps evenly across the glue-up.

Face-gluing

Face-gluing, also called laminating, is a technique used to make thick stock from thinner boards or to create stock that has a special appearance, such as the "striped" effect. This process usually bonds larger surface areas of wood than edge-gluing, so it requires some different techniques.

Because you'll be using lots of glue, wood glue is an economical adhesive for face-gluing. Freshly jointed and planed lumber is essential for a good bond, but hard, dense woods like maple, birch, and red oak will benefit from an additional sanding with 60-grit paper to provide a rougher surface for the glue to bond to. Dry-fit the boards to determine clamp size, and check for a tight fit. Gaps cause tools to catch and voids to appear when cutting or shaping.

Placing the boards tightly together speeds up glue application and controls the mess.

Handscrews and C-clamps provide the pressure you'll need for face-gluing. When the boards are so wide that the clamps are unable to reach across the whole face, you need to use cauls. Cauls help spread the clamping pressure evenly across the glue-up.

To make cauls, take straight sections of 2 × 4s long enough to reach across the glue-up. Cut slight tapers, no more than ⅛", from each end of the bottom edge to the middle. This gives the clamp room to pull down on the caul and force it to bend slightly, applying pressure evenly along its length. Label your cauls on their tops so you can easily tell which edge to place on the lamination. Make enough cauls to place one every 12 to 18" along the glue-up.

Lay out your boards for gluing by turning over the faces of all but the bottom board. Place them tightly against one another to make applying the glue easier. Lay a moderate bead on all exposed faces, and roll the beads out to a thin film. Place your bottom board on the cauls. Flip your next board over

on top of the bottom board to mate the glued surfaces. Apply glue to the top surface and mate the next board, continuing until the lamination is complete.

Square up your lamination and place the cauls on top. Start placing your clamps at one end, tightening only slightly, and work your way to the other end. Keep the lamination squared. Tighten the clamps gradually, working from end to end, until a bead of glue squeezes out between the layers along the entire lamination.

Store the glue-up vertically to dry. Scrape the beads of glue from the edges and ends of the lamination after about an hour; then unclamp, if you wish. Let your blank cure for one week before any additional machining.

Corner clamps, pipe clamps with miter blocks, or corner bench dogs will hold miter joints in place.

Gluing reinforced joints

Gluing joints takes some special care to make them strong and invisible. Splines, biscuits, and dowels are used to give joints additional strength without being seen. Even with reinforcement, however, glue has to coat the faces of the joint, as well as the reinforcing materials.

Butt joints and miter joints are the most common joints in woodworking. Similar techniques and tools are used with both, but miter joints are a little trickier. Miter joints must be cut carefully. Undercutting or overcutting the angle will tend to force the joint apart during expansion and contraction. Splines, biscuits, and dowels help hold miters together,

even under stress, and are treated in much the same way. We'll join a picture frame with biscuits to show how the job is done.

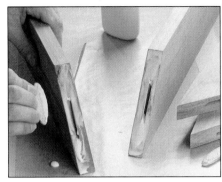

All the parts being joined need to be coated with glue before assembly.

Start by dry-fitting the miter joints on a flat surface. Use all the clamps and pads you'll use in the actual glue-up, and be sure the joints are snug, especially when using epoxy. (Because epoxy will fill gaps, the glue line will be visible in any place the joint doesn't fit perfectly.) When you're satisfied with the fit, take the joint apart and clean all the pieces to be sure there is no dust or oil on them. Lay all the parts out in their approximate locations, so they'll be easy to reassemble as you glue the pieces together.

Spread a thin, even layer of glue on the miter-cuts of both parts of the joint. Coat the inside of the biscuit grooves, then coat the biscuit and insert it in the groove. Repeat the process until all the pieces you're joining have been glued. Leave the parts on edge with the glue-side up to keep the glue from flowing away.

Assemble the joints quickly. The biscuits will have begun to swell a little, so the joints will be tight. Clamp the joints with corner clamps, bar clamps and corner blocks, or bench dogs and shims—any of these clamps will do the job. Adjust the clamps to bring the pieces firmly together with some squeeze-out, and then clean away the excess glue. It's a good idea to leave the joints clamped until the glue is completely set, since there is always some stress on a miter joint.

Frame-and-Panel Technique

Durability and classic good looks make frame-and-panel construction a technique worth mastering.

Frame-and-panel construction has long been favored by fine furnituremakers as one of the most visually appealing techniques for making long-lasting cabinet carcasses and doors. This is a technique you'll put to good use for a variety of projects.

Basic frame-and-panel construction consists of cutting a groove centered along the inside edge of the frame stiles and rails. These parts are then assembled, in stages, to make a frame that is fitted around a panel.

Making frame-and-panel doors is not difficult, and it also presents many creative possibilities. The frames and panels can be shaped using a router with specialty bits. These bits are available in a variety of styles to create different-shaped profiles.

Solid wood is the most common material used to make the frames and is also a good choice for the panels, unless they will be more than 10" wide. In this case, plywood is preferable because it does not expand and contract as much as hardwood. But other materials, like glass, tin, and even fabric, may be used to create unique-looking panels.

Frame-and-panel techniques can be used to create a wide variety of styles and effects. Varying the angles and shapes of the raised panels, and adding decorative shapes to the frames are two common methods of achieving a unique frame-and-panel look.

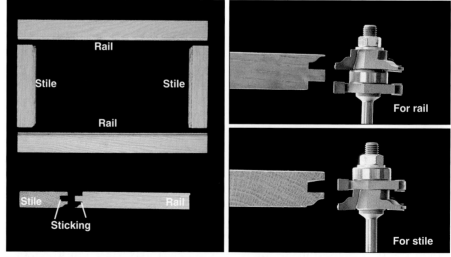

The frame *(above, left)* consists of vertical *stiles*, and horizontal *rails*, which are shaped to form grooves (called the *sticking)* that hold the panel. With most frame-and-panel joinery techniques, the ends of the rails are shaped and glued, then inserted into the sticking on the inside edges of the stiles. Stile-and-rail router bits *(above, right)* cut both profiles for the mating edges of the stiles and rails in a frame, simply by reversing the position of the cutters in the bit. The bit shown *above* is used to cut both profiles for an ogee shape.

Making the frames

For our frame, we used a 1½ hp. router, mounted in a router table, with a ¼"-shank carbide-tipped ogee rail-and-stile bit to make the sticking (the shaped profile on the inside edge of the frame). There are many other shaped bits available, and you can use the following steps to work with all of them.

1 Use your tablesaw to cut the rails and stiles out of stock that is at least ⅝" thick.

2 Set up your router with a rail-and-stile bit in a router table. Position the cutters on the bit to shape one of the sides of the stiles and rails first. Move the fence just close enough to make a shallow cut in the stock during the initial pass past the bit.

3 Make a light pass over the bit to rough-cut the sticking profile. Use a hold-down to keep the stock flat against the table. Avoid pausing during the cut to prevent chipping or burning. Make several passes, moving the fence out farther from the bit after each pass, until you've completed the profile.

Scrap piece

4 Remove the holding nut at the base of the router bit, then switch and secure the cutters. Cut the profile for the ends of the rails using the miter gauge to feed the rail over the cutter. To ensure a clean cut at the end of the rail, set up a scrap block behind the piece you're cutting. To prevent strain on the router and the workpiece, make the cut in several passes until the profile is complete.

Making the panels

There are many different methods you can use to dress up a flat panel. Covering the surface with veneer or laminates, or applying decorative molding are just a few of the possibilities.

You can also shape the panel using a panel-raising router bit. These specialty router bits make cutting raised panels easy, and they come in a range of styles for creating different profiles. After making the cut, the bit will leave a collar on the panel that will slide into the grooves in the frame. Make a test-cut on a scrap piece first, to make sure the collar is narrow enough to slide freely inside the sticking of the frame.

1 Install a panel-raising bit in your router and adjust it so the cutter extends ¼" above the router table. Clamp the router table fence in place and shape all four sides of the panel.

2 Use a featherboard to hold down the panel. Raise the router bit ¼" each pass until you've reached the desired profile.

Assembling the frame & panel

Although the parts of a frame-and-panel door appear to fit together tightly, only the frame portion is glued up, while the panel floats freely in the surrounding grooves without being glued. The frame has to be put together in stages so that you can glue and square it up but still can insert the panel. It's important to avoid letting glue get in the frame sticking so that the panel will be able to

float as it expands and contracts, without putting stress on the joints of the frame.

1 Beginning with one rail and two stile pieces, lightly brush glue on the ends and fit them together. Wipe away any excess glue from the groove inside the sticking.

2 Add the remaining rail to the assembly, without any glue, and clamp the four sides together—not too tightly. Check the frame for square, adjust the clamps as necessary, and let the glue dry.

3 After one hour, remove the clamps and carefully remove the unglued rail from the assembly. Check the inside edges of the frame for dried glue and remove it with a ⅛" chisel.

4 Slide the panel into the three-sided frame. Spread glue sparingly on the remaining rail and the corresponding ends of the stiles. Re-clamp the rail to the assembly and check the frame for square. Let the assembly dry.

The tablesaw option

In addition to using a router, you can use a tablesaw to do frame-and-panel construction. There are special molding cutterhead sets that make it possible to cut a wide range of stile, rail, and panel profiles on your tablesaw.

Even without these cutting sets, it's possible to make a simple frame-and-panel assembly with your tablesaw. Cut a dado along the inside edges of the stiles and rails, then cut your panel and assemble the parts following the assembly steps presented earlier.

A biscuit joint is a basic butt joint reinforced with beech biscuits glued into slots that are cut with a specialty saw called a biscuit joiner.

Biscuit Joinery

For many woodworking projects, this newest of joinery techniques is also the best.

Biscuit joinery, sometimes called plate joinery, is a relatively new technique in the world of woodworking. But since the introduction of portable power biscuit joiners in the mid 1980s, the popularity of the technique has grown enormously.

Much simpler to make than a dowel joint, a biscuit joint is basically a flush butt joint with its joined surfaces slotted to hold a flat, elliptical "biscuit" made of compressed beech wood.

Biscuit joinery is an excellent option for reinforcing most butt joints—including edge-to-edge joints, corners, right-angle joints, and miters—which account for most woodworking joinery. The beauty of the technique lies in its speed and its strength. A biscuit joint can be completed in mere moments using any one of the inexpensive biscuit joiners now available. Tests show that joints reinforced with biscuits are considerably stronger than those reinforced with dowels or wood screws.

There are limits to the strength of a biscuit joint, however. Where maximum strength is crucial, such as for large furniture projects, it's usually best to stick with mortise-and-tenons or dovetails for the critical leg joints.

The tool that makes this magic possible—the biscuit joiner—is nothing more than a small, specialized saw with an adjustable base and a 4" circular blade that cuts slots to fit the exact thickness of standard biscuits.

Beech biscuits are commonly available in three sizes: #0 ($\%_{16} \times 1^{13}\!/_{16}"$), #10 ($\frac{3}{4} \times 2\frac{1}{8}"$), and #20 ($1^{5}\!/_{16} \times 2\frac{3}{8}"$). The standard blade on the biscuit joiner will cut slots for each of these biscuit sizes, but because #0 biscuits are the smallest size that is widely available, you won't be able to use biscuits on thin, narrow workpieces, like small picture frames.

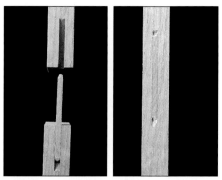

Slots for biscuit joints (shown cutaway, *above*) are cut so they are slightly wider and longer than the biscuit, allowing you to slide the joint into alignment after inserting the biscuit. As the compressed beech biscuit absorbs glue, it swells to hold the joint securely.

Recipe for basic biscuit joints

Biscuit joiners differ considerably, depending on the manufacturer, but all of them can be adjusted to provide precise control of the position and depth of the biscuit slots.

For maximum strength, use the largest biscuits that will fit your workpiece.

1 Dry-fit the workpieces as they will look when joined, then make alignment marks on both workpieces to indicate where the center of the biscuit slots will be located. On joints less than 4" wide, you'll use one biscuit centered in the joint; for longer joints, space the biscuits so their centers are 4" to 8" apart.

2 Adjust the fence on the biscuit joiner so the biscuit slot will be centered between the faces of the workpiece. (When joining workpieces more than 1½" thick, install two biscuits at each point.)

3 Adjust the plunge depth on the blade so the depth of each slot will be just slightly more than one-half the width of the biscuit. For example, with #10 biscuits, which are ¾" wide, the slots should be about ¹³⁄₃₂" deep. It's a good idea to make test cuts on scrap material to make sure the slots are deep enough.

4 Clamp the workpiece to your workbench, then hold the biscuit joiner tightly against the surface to be slotted. The faceplate should be flush against the workpiece, so the index mark lines up with the pencil mark on the workpiece.

5 Holding the joiner securely, turn on the motor and smoothly plunge the blade into the workpiece. (With some biscuit joiners, you plunge the motor assembly straight forward, bayonet-style, while with others you pivot the motor assembly lever-style to extend the blade.) Be sure to hold the tool firmly, because the motion of the spinning blade can cause the tool to creep. Release the pressure to retract the blade, then turn off the motor.

6 Cut the remaining biscuit slots in both workpieces.

7 Test-fit the biscuit and workpieces to make sure the slots are aligned correctly.

8 Brush glue onto the biscuits and surfaces to be joined, and into the slots. Insert the biscuits in the slots, then join the workpieces and clamp them together. (Work quickly; the biscuits will begin to swell immediately.) Don't sand the joints until the glue dries completely. Because the biscuits swell as they absorb glue, sanding too soon can leave you with depressions in the wood when the glue dries and contracts.

WOODWORKER'S TIPS

These photos show common biscuit joinery applications.

Flat miters

Clamp the pieces to a flat surface against adjacent sides of a square spacing block, so the mitered edges are facing out. Hold the faceplate of the joiner flat against the worksurface when cutting the biscuit slots.

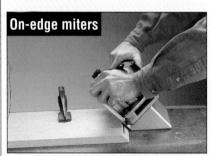

On-edge miters

Attach the biscuit joiner's miter attachment to set the blade at the correct 45° angle. This ensures that the slots will be cut perpendicular to the miter edges.

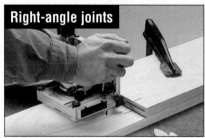

Right-angle joints

After marking the joint, lay the horizontal workpiece on the vertical piece so the edge just touches the outline. To cut the slots into the horizontal workpiece, hold the biscuit joiner flat on the vertical workpiece. To cut the slots in the vertical workpiece, turn the joiner on end so the bottom is flush against the horizontal workpiece.

Simple wooden drawer glides can be made by attaching hardwood strips to the sides of a drawer. The strips will fit into grooved wooden tracks attached inside the drawer opening.

Making Drawers

Review the basics to build a drawer that stands up to the test of time.

A well-constructed drawer operates smoothly and holds up over time. Building one requires a combination of careful planning and solid assembly techniques.

Drawers can be made using either four- or five-piece construction (the bottom panel is not included in the count). Four-piece drawers are made up of two sides, a back, and front. Five-piece drawers are made up of these parts, plus another piece called a false front, which is shaped or decorated separately and then attached to the front with screws.

A false front gives you the option of changing the look of the drawer later by simply removing the false front and replacing it. This can be a quick and inexpensive way to transform the look of a piece of furniture.

The drawer sides and front usually have a dado, slightly above the bottom edge, to hold the bottom panel. The back is cut shorter than the other parts so the bottom panel can slide underneath it into the dadoed sides and front. Then, with the drawer set upside down, the bottom panel is tacked to the bottom edge of the back to hold it in place. In finer cabinetry, the back is the same height as the other parts and is also dadoed. All of the drawer parts are assembled around the bottom panel, so it is sandwiched in place on all sides.

Choosing materials

Sturdy drawers can be built inexpensively using ½"-thick plywood for the sides, front, and back, and ¼" plywood or hardboard for the bottom panel. If the drawer will be getting heavy use, you may want to use ¾"-thick wood for the front, back, and sides, but still use ¼" plywood for the bottom panel.

For best results, use hardwoods, like maple or birch, or a top-grade plywood, like Baltic birch (also known as solid birch veneer), for the drawer parts. This plywood is made up of several layers of tightly bonded wood. The bonding makes it particularly stable and strong, and the contrasting layers, revealed when the plywood is cut, make for an attractive edge. This eliminates the need for adding veneer or edging to hide the end grain. The raw edge accepts oil readily, making it easy to apply finish.

For other projects, you can save money by using less expensive woods like plywood, pine, or poplar for the drawer sides, front, and back. Also consider inexpensive materials like particleboard with a melamine laminate covering or regular plywood with a veneer covering.

WOODWORKER'S TIP

Woodworking stores carry precut drawer parts in standard sizes that cost a bit more than preparing them yourself but make it possible to build drawers quickly and easily.

False fronts are usually made from ¾"-thick hardwood that is shaped or decoratively routed. Other possibilities include building a front using frame-and-panel construction, or applying laminate or veneer to a plywood or particle-board core.

Drawer-front styles

There are three basic styles of drawer fronts: flush, lipped, and overlay. If you're installing a drawer in a cabinet that also has a door, choose a matching style for both.

Flush drawer fronts are smooth panels that fit inside the drawer opening and line up evenly with the front edges of the cabinet face frame. Because they require a precise fit, they are the trickiest type of drawer front to build and install.

Lipped drawer fronts are rabbeted (typically a ⅜"-deep rabbet) so that part of the front overlaps the surface of the face frame, while the rest fits inside the opening. When the drawer is closed, a lipped front appears to be made

Each of the drawer front styles shown here—flush, lipped, and overlay (top to bottom)—has a unique appearance when the drawer is closed (see *inset photo*).

of thinner material than it is because part of it is recessed.

Overlay drawer fronts are attached so the entire front fits over the front surface of the face frame. This drawer-front style has the most substantial appearance when the drawer is closed.

Drawer layout

Before you can map out the dimensions of a drawer, you need to consider how it will be installed. There are several methods for mounting drawers, which can be made or purchased, and each one affects the sizing of the drawer differently. You may also

Apply paraffin along the wood strips attached to the drawer and the bottom edges of the grooved strip on the cabinet sides so the drawer will open and close easily.

Rabbets (A), sliding dovetails (B), double dadoes (C), dovetails (D), and box joints (E) are just some of the joints you may use when building a drawer, and they vary not only in appearance but in strength. Rabbets are the most common choice for building a basic drawer with ½"-thick sides, but other joints, like double dadoes or dovetails, give the strength needed for heavy-duty construction with thicker material.

want to consider how visible a mounting system will be once it is installed.

Side-mounted glides brace the drawer on both sides and make it extremely stable, so they are also a good choice when installing larger drawers. Make side-mounted drawer glides by cutting a ¾" groove in two strips of 1 × 2 hardwood and attaching the strips to the insides of the cabinet. Cut ¾" strips to fit in the grooves and attach the strips to the sides of the drawer. Slide the drawer into the grooved strips. This method uses up some of the width of the drawer opening, but it is simple and inexpensive. It was popular in the past, and the appearance makes it a good choice for reproduction pieces.

Bottom-mounted glides allow you to build the drawer to almost the full width of the opening, and they are well hidden when the drawer is open or closed.

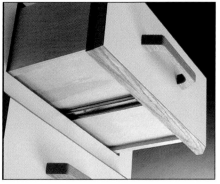

Bottom-mounted glides are generally hidden from view and take up little space.

Corner-mounted glides combine the best features of the other two, because they are almost hidden from view and do not take up too much room. But they may not be as durable as the other styles, particularly when compared to purchased metal glides. Consider the choices available, keeping in mind how the glide system will affect the drawer dimensions (see *Drawer Hardware,*

page 86 and 87).

Regardless of the installation method you choose, plan the drawer at least 1" shallower than the depth of the opening, so the drawer does not hit the back cabinet wall when it's closed. You'll also need to allow for the drawer-front style, so take this into account when measuring the depth of the drawer opening.

Drawer joinery

Familiar joints like rabbet and dado joints work well for connecting drawer parts, but you can also use more elaborate joinery techniques on finer projects. Box joints, multiple dovetails, sliding dovetails, or locked joints are just a few of the possibilities. The front and side joints will be most visible, so use decorative joints there. Save the simpler joints for attaching the drawer sides to the back piece.

Commercially made jigs are

available to help you make some of these joints quickly and easily. Dovetails, for example, are time-consuming when cut with a handsaw, but there are jigs that allow you to cut them with a tablesaw or a router. These jigs can be especially helpful if you're making several drawers, and will save time and prevent headaches.

Always test-cut and fit the joints using scrap first, to avoid wasting expensive wood.

Building a basic drawer

Use the following steps to build a basic five-piece drawer. Remember to choose your drawer glides and drawer-front style before you begin measuring for the sizes of the parts. Also, work carefully when it comes time to square up the assembled drawer. Checking for square takes just a few extra seconds but is worth doing with care, because a drawer that is square will be easier to install, will open and close smoothly, and will be more durable.

1 Cut the sides, front, and back pieces out of ½"-thick material. Cut the bottom panel out of ¼"-thick material.

2 Trim off ⅝" from the bottom edge of the back piece so it will be shorter than the other pieces.

3 Cut a ½ × ¼"-deep rabbet on both ends of each side piece, to hold the drawer front and back.

4 Cut a ¼ × ¼"-deep groove in the sides and front piece, at least ⅜" up from the bottom edges, to

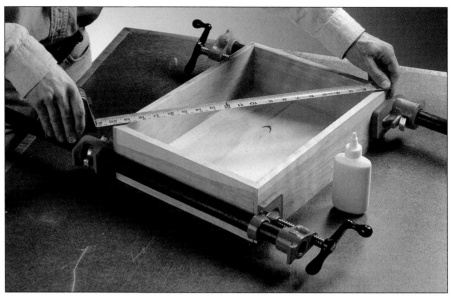

Check to see if the assembled drawer is square by measuring the length of each diagonal—they should be equal. If not, adjust the parts and clamps until the assembly is squared.

hold the bottom panel. This groove has to be slightly above the bottom edge of the pieces to prevent the bottom edge of the drawer from chipping or breaking off—for purchased glides, check the manufacturer's information that comes with the drawer glides for the correct distance.

5 Glue and clamp the front and back into the rabbeted sides. Reinforce with nails.

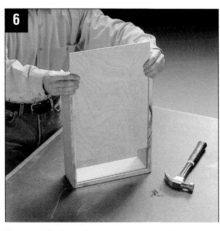

6 Stand the drawer up on its front, and slide the bottom panel into the groove.

7 Tack the bottom panel in place by driving 1" nails up through it into the bottom of the back.

8 Check the drawer for square and adjust as needed. Let the drawer assembly dry.

9 Measure and cut the false front

piece. Shape or decorate the false front if desired.

10 Attach the false front to the assembled drawer with 1½" countersunk screws driven from inside the front of the drawer.

11 Install the drawer glides and fit the drawer into the opening.

Other options

Fine furniture pieces, particularly clothing dressers, often have dust panels (simple frame-and-panel-construction shelves) to keep clothes from falling between the drawers and getting caught. These panels can also serve as drawer glides if you add nylon tape to them at the side edges. The tape will allow the drawer to slide smoothly over the dust panels.

Adding dividers inside a drawer makes it more useful for storing silverware, stationery, or other small items. Cut slots in thin plywood to make an interlocking framework that can be assembled separately and inserted in the completed drawer. Or, plan ahead, and cut vertical dadoes inside of the drawer sides, back, and front to hold dividers made of thicker material. Glue and install the dividers as you are building the drawer. Woodworking stores also carry specialty tapes with precut grooves for installing dividers in drawers.

Basic Dowel Joints

This classic wood joinery technique still stands the test of time.

A dowel joint is basically a butt joint or miter joint that is reinforced with wooden pegs (dowels) that span the seam. The dowels are often hidden, but sometimes are left exposed ("through-dowels") for decoration. Dowel joints are often used for edge-to-edge glue-ups, and for corner joints in cabinet face frames or carcass construction.

Dowel joints are considerably easier to make than mortise-and-tenon joints, but they do require you to drill straight, precisely positioned holes for the dowels. To ensure accuracy, it is a good idea to use a drill press, or a hand power drill and one of the many commercial dowel jigs that are available at woodworking stores.

There are few set guidelines for sizing and spacing of dowels in a joint, but because the strength of any joint is directly related to the size of the gluing surface, you'll want to use the largest dowels that are practical for your workpiece. In general, use dowels with diameters that are about half the thickness of the workpiece. Precut dowels are sold in ¼"-, ⁵⁄₁₆"-, and ⅜"-diameters, and in lengths ranging from 1½" to 2½". If you need other sizes, you can cut your own dowels from hardwood dowel rods (see *opposite*).

A wooden mallet helps you tap dowel joints together without marring the surfaces.

Dowel joint basics

First, we'll show you an easy way to lay out and complete a dowel joint from scratch, without the benefit of commercial doweling jigs. Our example shows a corner joint like that you'd see in a cabinet face frame, but the same techniques work for other types of joints. When gluing up a face frame, remember that you'll need to join two opposite corner joints first, then complete the last two corners at the same time.

1 After cutting the workpieces to size, joint the edges that will be mated to provide a smooth, square surface. Use a marking gauge to draw a centerline along the edges.

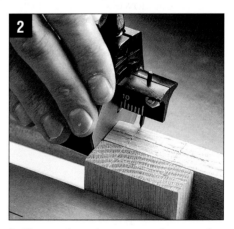

2 Clamp the pieces together so the edges to be joined are facing up and are flush. Use the marking gauge to draw intersecting lines where dowels will be located.

3 In your drill press, mount a brad-point bit equal in diameter to the dowels you'll be using. Attach a bit stop, setting it so the depth of the holes will be 1/16" more than half the length of your dowels. To drill each dowel hole, clamp the workpiece to the table of your drill press, carefully positioning it so the tip of the bit will bore into the center of the dowel location.
4 Counterbore each dowel hole about 1/8" deep with a slightly larger drill bit. The counterbores will provide space for excess glue to seep into when the joint is clamped together.
5 Dry-fit the dowels and join the pieces together to test the fit. If you've made a mistake, you can glue plugs into the holes and redrill them after the glue has fully dried.
6 Apply glue to the surfaces to be joined and in the dowel holes. Tap the dowels into the holes in one workpiece, then position the adjoining piece and tap it into place until the joint is tight.
7 Clamp the workpieces together until the glue is dry. Remove any dried glue that has oozed out of the joint, using a scraper or chisel.

Using a doweling jig

Dowel jigs come in many styles—some are best suited for drilling holes for edge-gluing, others are designed for making corners or T-joints. Most doweling jigs feature some type of clamping device and guide bushings to help you drill straight holes, and the best models let you automatically center your dowel holes across the thickness of the workpiece.
1 Hold the workpieces together as they will look when finished, then make reference lines across both pieces to help you align the doweling jig.
2 Clamp the dowel jig to the first workpiece, aligning the top of the jig with the top of the joint. Mount a drill bit that matches the size of your dowels, and attach a bit stop, setting it so the depth of the holes will be 1/16" more than half the length of the dowels you'll be using.

3 Drill dowel holes through the guide bushing that matches the size of your dowels.
4 Move the doweling jig to the other workpiece, aligning it with the reference lines. Drill matching dowel holes and assemble the joint (see *Dowel joint basics, opposite*, steps 4 to 7).

Using dowel centers

Metal dowel centers are most useful in any location that is not well suited to using a doweling jig, such as for T-shaped joints, where the end grain of one piece is joined to the face of the other piece. Dowel centers are available in sizes to match all common dowel diameters.

1 Drill dowel holes in the first workpiece, using the same technique shown in *Dowel joint basics, opposite*, or *Using a doweling jig (left)*.

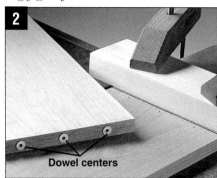

Dowel centers

2 Insert dowel centers in the dowel holes, then align the adjoining workpiece against the first piece, and force the pieces together so the sharp points of the dowel centers leave reference marks in the butted workpiece. (A clamped straightedge will help you align the pieces precisely.)
3 Separate pieces, then drill dowel holes at reference marks left by dowel centers. Complete dowel joint (see *Dowel joint basics, opposite*, steps 4 to 7).

Making your own dowels

If you need dowels in unusual sizes, make your own from lengths of hardwood rods cut to length.
1 Clamp a sabersaw blade or handsaw in your vise, then score grooves in a length of hardwood dowel rod. The grooves will release compressed glue and air when the dowels are driven into a workpiece.

2 Cut the rod into pieces of the desired length, then slightly bevel the ends of each dowel on a stationary sander. Beveled ends will make the dowels easier to insert.

Veneer Basics

With hardwood supplies dwindling, veneering is a skill every woodworker should know.

Veneer expands the range of usable wood types. We applied the walnut burl veneer *above* to plywood to make a striking tabletop. Solid burl walnut would be too weak for this use.

Veneering is the art of applying very thin flexible layers of premium, decorative wood to a base layer of less expensive material to simulate the look of solid wood. The ability to use veneer effectively and with some artistic flair has been a valued woodworking skill for more than 4,000 years. In recent years, the use of veneer has taken on more importance because it allows us to stretch our dwindling resources of fine and exotic hardwood so more people can enjoy them. Veneer also lets woodworkers use wood types and grain patterns that would not be usable (much less affordable) if they were solid wood.

About veneer

Fine woodworker's veneer is sliced with a razor-sharp knife from the choicest hardwood logs available, usually to a thickness of ⅟₂₈". The grain pattern and figure of the veneer depends on the type of wood, of course, but also on the cutting method used by the veneer maker (see *photo,* lower right).

To make it easier for woodworkers to match the grain patterns on separate pieces of veneer, the manufacturers are careful to keep all the veneer from a single log (called a flitch) together in one bundle, packed in the order the pieces were cut. Always purchase veneer in consecutive pieces from the same flitch, rather than picking and choosing randomly.

Most woodworker's supply stores carry many different varieties of veneer, ranging from common oak to rare, very expensive kinds, like Macassar ebony. The product is sold either in pre-cut, standard sizes, or in random sizes, priced by the square foot. Mail-order suppliers also sell veneer. For special projects, custom-sized or very unusual types of veneer may be ordered to meet your needs.

Recently, furniture and cabinet makers have begun relying almost exclusively on veneer with a heat- or pressure-sensitive backing that's applied at the mill. Woodworkers have been slow to accept backed veneer, perhaps because it's very thin (usually ⅟₆₄"), and the wood types are limited. However, heat- and pressure-sensitive products are very popular for edging strips.

Always buy a little more veneer than you think you'll need, and make sure you have enough fine-grade veneer for all the exposed surfaces of your veneering project.

BUYER'S TIP

Knife checks are thin cracks that occur on the back face of veneer as it is sliced. In most cases, a few knife checks are unavoidable, but don't buy veneer with checks that run more than halfway through the thickness of the layer.

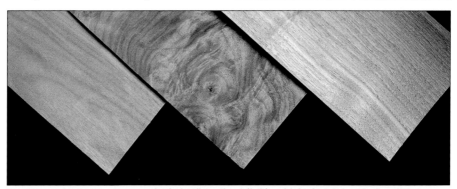

Three common types of veneer include: flat-sliced (left), which shows a varied grain pattern; quarter-sliced (right), which displays the narrow grain pattern typical of quarter-sawn lumber; and flat-sliced specialty veneers, such as burl (center).

Application methods

Along with selecting a veneer you think is suitable for your project, you also must choose a method of applying the veneer.

There is considerable debate among woodworkers over the best application method. In one traditional method, called hand veneering or hammer veneering (because the veneer is smoothed out with a veneer hammer), the veneer is bonded with hide glue that's heated in a glue pot until the moment it's applied. The veneer is rolled and smoothed as the glue cools, forming a fast, solid bond.

Hand veneering offers some advantages. It requires no clamping or pressing, and hide glue can be reheated by ironing the veneer with a household iron, loosening the glue bond enough to let you make adjustments or repairs. These properties make hot hide glue an excellent product for small projects and repairs. But on the down side, the glue and the wood being joined require close attention and quite a bit of preparation.

Most veneering projects are larger in scale, involving the lamination of veneer onto a panel. For such projects, using a veneer press to clamp your work yields the best results.

Even if you don't own a veneer press, a creative woodworker can usually dream up some system of clamps and cauls for laminating (see *TOOL TIP*, page 135). Hot glue is neither necessary nor recommended for use in a veneer press. Instead, use plain white carpenter's glue, because white glue has a relatively long set-up time, giving you more time to get the veneered project into the press.

For smaller projects, some people prefer to use contact cement, which is applied to both the veneer and the groundwork (the surface being veneered). Then the veneer is positioned and rolled flat. But if you use contact cement, be aware that you'll have no margin for error in laying the veneer, and that contact cement is broken down by some oil-based finishing materials.

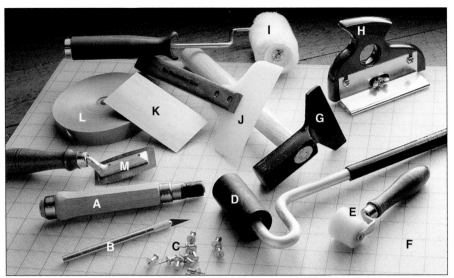

Specialty tools for veneering include: veneer punch (A), craft knife (B), stainless veneer pins (C), J-roller for rolling corners (D), seam roller (E), cutting mat (F), veneer hammer (G), veneer cutter (H), glue roller (I), veneer smoothing blade (J), cabinet scraper (K), veneer tape (L), and a veneer saw (M).

Veneering tools

As with any project, veneering can be done more easily and accurately if you have the right tools for the job.

Cutting tools: *Veneer saws* have thin, double-sided blades with small, very sharp teeth that have no set. When used with a straight-edge, veneer saws produce straight, clean cuts with no tearout. For trimming curves and cutting inlays, a simple *craft knife*, like an X-acto knife, works very nicely.

For edging and cutting straight splice joints, a *veneer cutter* gives you very precise control. Equipped with a saw-type handle and a fence for following edges, veneer cutters can slice through any grain pattern without leaving a kerf or causing tearout.

Hand veneering tools: Its name is a little deceiving, but a *veneer hammer* is primarily a smoothing tool. The broad, flat "claw" of the veneer hammer is used to smooth out the just-glued veneer. A *veneer smoothing blade* serves the same purpose as the veneer hammer (at a fraction of the cost) but unlike the veneer hammer, it can't be used to tap out air bubbles.

Seam rollers and *J-rollers* (for corner areas) are used frequently in hand veneer work, especially by those who use contact cement.

Miscellaneous veneering tools: *Veneer punches* are used to cut out defects in veneered surfaces, as well as to cut plugs from good veneer to fill the cutout. *Veneer pins* have very fine points so they don't leave visible holes when the pins are used to secure veneer to groundwork while the pieces are matched. *Veneer tape* holds seams together while glue dries. *Cabinet scrapers* are used to remove veneer tape residue and to smooth out uneven seams. A *glue roller* spreads glue evenly, and a *cutting pad* lets you do precise work without damaging tool blades.

Preparing veneer & groundwork

You may be surprised at what you find the first time you go shopping for veneer. The thin, rumpled sheets of wood that are sold in stores bear little resemblance to the flawless veneer surfaces that are achieved when the veneer is applied carefully.

Most veneer needs flattening

WOODWORKER'S TIP

Glycerine, sold in drug stores as a skin softener, is a chemical that veneer workers should know. Brittle veneers are softened and made more workable for cutting by coating them with liquid glycerine.

before it can be glued to a surface. Lightly dampening veneer with a sponge, then clamping it overnight between two pieces of particleboard or plywood will straighten out most problems. Be careful not to get the veneer too wet, or you will have to let it dry for several days after removing it from the press, during which time it's likely to buckle again.

For a successful veneering project, it's crucial that the groundwork be flat and free from defects like knots or chips. Generally, manmade materials like plywood and particleboard make a better groundwork than solid wood, but use only top-quality, filled, plugged, and sanded plywood, or cabinet-grade particleboard.

If simple sanding will not take care of a problem area, chisel out the defect (if it's above the plane of the surface) then fill the area with putty. Sand the putty smooth after it's dried.

If you plan to lay the veneer by hand, instead of using a veneer press, some extra groundwork preparation is recommended. First, score or "key" the surface of the groundwork with a toothing plane or a rasp to provide crevices for any excess glue. Blow off the dust, then "size" the surface by applying a thin coat of sealing material, such as thin wallpaper paste, over the entire surface. This prevents too much glue from being absorbed. Sand the entire surface lightly with 120-grit sandpaper, then clean thoroughly.

If you're gluing up several pieces of solid wood to form the groundwork, as is often done to make arches and curves, use quartersawn wood wherever possible because it's less likely to warp.

Lay out the pattern

Before you begin cutting and gluing your veneer, select a veneer pattern that complements both the grain of the wood and the scale of the project. Choosing a pattern then matching the individual strips of veneer together to come up with the best possible arrangement has a huge impact on the success of your project.

The most common (and easiest) patterns for veneering are slip matching and book matching. Both of these patterns are made

Slip match (usually used with quarter-cut veneer) and book match (usually used with face-cut veneer) are the two most common veneering matching patterns. To make a slip match, simply try to align the grain pattern of one panel as closely as possible with the grain pattern of the next panel. To make a book match, arrange adjacent pieces in a mirror image of one another, like two open pages of a book.

simply by butting strips of veneer edge-to-edge. There are an infinite number of veneer patterns to experiment with, but until you master the basic veneering techniques, you're much better off sticking with a simple arrangement. Trying to get veneer pieces square is enough of a challenge.

After you've matched veneers, you'll understand why manufacturers and storekeepers are so careful to keep the sheets in order when they ship and sell each flitch. Carefully matching the grain pattern of each strip to the one next to it makes the seams disappear.

For the best matching results, cut all the veneer strips to the same width as the narrowest strip. Make a shooting board by cutting two scrap boards slightly smaller than the veneer strips, using your jointer and tablesaw to make sure the boards are square.

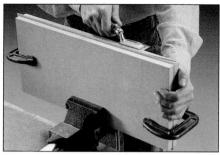

Two square pieces of scrapwood serve as a a shooting board-type guide for trimming all the veneer strips evenly with a veneer saw or bench plane.

To use the shooting board, sandwich the veneer pieces between the boards, making sure the boards are aligned exactly. There should be a slight veneer overhang on all sides. Secure the shooting board in a bench vise, then trim the edges of the veneer to the size of the shooting board, using a veneer saw or a bench plane.

Lay out the veneer pattern by arranging the strips of veneer on the groundwork, or any flat surface, to check the pattern and the fit. Inspect each joint by lifting up the sheets and pressing the veneer strips together, then holding them

up to a light. If any light gets through, trim the mating edges with an edge trimmer or a veneer cutter, using a straightedge as a guide. Once you've settled on a finished pattern, label all the strips in sequence, using chalk.

Taping veneer strips

Carefully matched veneer strips are of no use if the strips slip out of place when they're glued to the groundwork. For this reason, most woodworkers use special veneer tape to join all the pieces together prior to the glue-down. Veneer tape is a gummed tape, usually 1½" wide, with very low adhesion.

1 Set the first veneer strip in position on the groundwork or a flat surface, then dry-fit all the strips for the panel.

2 Position the next veneer strip (for three or more strips, use a weight to hold the first strip in place), and attach it to the first strip with low-adhesion masking tape laid across the seam.

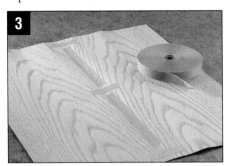

3 Moisten the gummed veneer tape, then carefully lay pieces of the tape over the seam, between the strips of masking tape. Lay a thin, flat board over the taped strips and set a weight on top.

4 Tape the remaining strips in position, covering the tape with weighted-down boards.

5 After the veneer tape dries completely (two to three hours), carefully remove the boards and the strips of masking tape lying across each seam.

Making a veneered panel

For most veneering projects, a veneer press will give you a flat, flawless surface that doesn't require a lot of smoothing, rolling and adjusting. When making veneered panels, begin with the back side of the project and save the face for last.

1 Prepare the groundwork, then lay out and tape the veneer strips, as shown in the previous sections. Make alignment marks on the groundwork if the veneer panel will be centered. The taped veneer panels should be ½" larger than the groundwork on all sides.

2 Lay the taped veneer panel for the back tape-side down on your workbench or gluing table. Set the groundwork next to it, face-side up.

3 Apply a thin coat of white carpenter's glue to the groundwork

only, using a small paint roller. Be sure to cover the entire groundwork, with no bare spots.

4 Lift the groundwork and set the glued-side down on top of the veneer for the back.

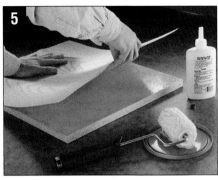

5 Apply glue to the surface of the groundwork, then place the veneer strips for the panel face, tape-side up, onto the groundwork.

6 Set sheets of wax paper on the clamping surface of the veneer press and on the veneered surface, then carefully slip the panel into the press (see *TOOL TIP,* below).

7 Slowly tighten the wing nuts until the cauls have flattened out and are locked into position.

8 Let the panel set overnight, then remove it from the press. Check for areas where the glue didn't hold by rapping with your finger. If you find a hollow area, make a slit in the veneer and inject glue from a glue syringe into the slit, then roll the area until it's flat.

9 Trim the excess veneer from the edges, using an edge trimmer or a veneer cutter.

10 Remove the veneer tape and smooth out any rough or uneven joints with a cabinet scraper.

11 Cut out defects and damaged areas in the veneer with a veneer punch or a craft knife, then cut plugs of the same size and shape, and glue them into the opening. Set a weight on the patch and let the glue dry.

12 Sand the veneered surfaces with 180-, then 220-grit sandpaper, until the seams are undetectable.

13 Cover exposed panel edges with strips of veneer or edge trim. Edge strips can be cut from the same veneer as the panel sheets, or you can use heat- or pressure-sensitive strips.

TOOL TIP

Build a simple press for making veneered panels. The press shown here was made using scrapwood and a few pieces of hardware. Our press uses a series of caul frames to apply even pressure to sheets of plywood and hardboard that sandwich the veneer workpiece. Our press, as shown, can be used to laminate panels up to 24 × 36", but you can lengthen it simply by adding more caul frames and a longer bed.

The chief advantage to the caul system is that it pushes glue away from the center as you tighten the

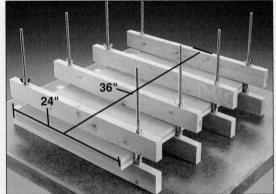

Construction details: Each caul (top and bottom) is crowned from 3½" width at the center, to 3⅜" at the ends. The anchor nuts and lock washers at the bottom ends of the threaded rods are set into ¾ × ¾" counterbores so the cauls can lay flat on your worksurface; the hardboard panel is glued over the plywood to provide a smooth surface. Cauls are 9" apart.

threaded rods, preventing excess glue buildup between the veneer and the groundwork. When using the press, separate the workpiece from the hardboard beds with a flat layer of wax paper. Begin tightening with the center cauls, and work your way toward the ends. Hand-tighten the wing nuts first, then tighten them with pliers (being careful not to overtighten) in the same sequence used when hand-tightening.

Dovetail Joints

Crisp, tight dovetail joints are a hallmark of fine woodworking.

In the many centuries that have passed since the first dovetail joint was made, no other joint has been created to match its sturdiness. With or without glue, a good dovetail joint uses the strength of the wood to bring two workpieces together.

Creative woodworkers have developed countless variations of the basic *through* dovetail, but all types of dovetail joints have a few things in common: the characteristic interlocking wedge shapes; the ability to withstand expansion and contraction without losing any strength; and an attractive appearance that quickly identifies any project as a fine piece of work.

Named for its resemblance to the wedge-shaped tail of a dove, the dovetail joint is composed of two interlocking boards, called the *tail member* and the *pin member*. The tail member contains the wider wedge-shaped tails, which are fitted together with the narrower pins in the pin member.

Because dovetails are a visible design element in any project, the size and spacing of the individual tails and pins is very important. The joint layout is often symmetrical, but the ability to vary the layout in ways that complement the project is a source of pride for experienced woodworkers.

In past years, dovetail joints were cut exclusively by hand, and many advanced woodworkers still prefer the control and design flexibility offered by hand-cutting. But due to the advent of dovetail router bits and fancy dovetailing jigs (see page 139), even beginners have access to tools for power-cutting dovetail joints quickly and with guaranteed precision.

Tail member Pin member

Through dovetails are simple to make, and they can be used in most wood-joining situations.

Tail member Pin member

Half-blind dovetails are used mostly in drawer fronts and other projects with hidden sides.

Tail member Pin member

Mitered dovetails offer strength and invisibility. Uses include small boxes and cabinet frames.

Dozens of different joints can safely be classified as belonging to the dovetail family, but a few basic types will do the job for most of your projects. Among them are the basic through dovetail (top), the half-blind dovetail (middle), and the mitered dovetail (bottom).

Planning a dovetail joint

The key to making tight, attractive dovetail joints is to do careful, precise work and to design a layout that's scaled to fit the proportions of the project. There are few limitations to the sizes of the workpieces or even the size of the tails and pins you can use, but keep a few basic rules in mind:

Pull on the pin members. Because the pin members do most of the work in a dovetail joint, put them in the front and back of drawers and other projects where directional stress is applied. For decorative reasons, however, you may prefer to put the tail members in front, where the dovetail shape will be most visible.

Start with a half-pin. The top and bottom of the joint should be created by a pin (called a *half-pin*) that's straight on the outside edge and tapered on the inside edge. At its narrowest point, the half-pin should be at least ¼" thick. For symmetrical joints, make the thin ends of the half-pins half the thickness of a full pin.

Select the right slope. The *slope* of a dovetail joint refers to the angle of the pin and tail sides. When hand-cutting, use a ratio to calculate the slope. For example, a ratio of 1:6 will give you tails that taper one unit for every six units in height. As a general rule, use a

TOOL TIP

Below is a list of the tools you'll need to cut most dovetail joints.

Hand-cutting tools:
- *T-bevel*
- *Cutting gauge*
- *Ruler*
- *Try square*
- *Sharp pencil and craft knife*
- *Dovetail saw*
- *Wood chisels*
- *Shoulder plane*
- *Drill and Forstner bits*

Router-cutting tools:
- *Dovetail template or jig (with guide bushing)*
- *Router with bits—dovetail and straight*

WOODWORKER'S TIP

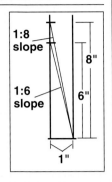

Make a guide for laying out the slope of the tails and pins. On a piece of scrapwood, draw a pair of parallel lines 1" apart near one corner. Draw an endline across the lines, then mark points on one of the parallel lines, 6" and 8" from the endline. Draw diagonals from the endline to the 6" and 8" marks to create slopes of 1:6 and 1:8. Transfer the slopes to your T-bevel.

1:6 slope when joining softwood, and a 1:8 slope (which is more gradual) when joining hardwood. The slope of dovetail router bits is given in angles (7°, 9°, and 14° are common). Use the higher slopes for softwood.

Visualize the joint. Sketch the pin member and the tail member on paper before laying out the joint. Experiment with several spacing arrangements, and different tail and pin widths. The primary goal of visualizing the joint is to decide how many pins and tails to cut into each workpiece.

Through dovetail joints

When cutting dovetail joints, lay out and cut the tail members before the pin members, then use the tail members as templates for laying out the pin members. Always make test pieces before cutting the actual joints.

1 Mark the *shoulder lines* of the joint at the depth of the tails and pins—usually the thickness of the

workpieces. Mark both sides of all workpieces with a cutting gauge.

2 On the end of one tail member, mark half-pins at each edge. Use a ruler to divide the space between the half-pin marks into equal sections (one for each tail). Draw parallel pin lines, half the thickness of a pin, on each side of each section line, to mark pin locations.

3 Set a T-bevel for the appropriate slope (see *WOODWORKER'S TIP*, left), then use the T-bevel as a guide to draw angled lines from the pin lines to the shoulder lines, on both faces of the tail member. Shade the pin areas between the tails with a pencil.

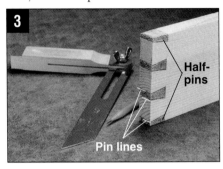

4 Clamp the tail member into a vise, tilted slightly so one set of parallel side lines is in a vertical position. Cut the lines on the waste side, using a dovetail saw, down to the shoulder line.

5 Move the tail member in the vise so the other set of parallel side lines is vertical, then cut along the lines with a dovetail saw.

TOOL TIP

For greatest accuracy, use a craft knife to mark dovetail outlines. A cutting gauge (a special marking gauge equipped with blades above and below) will mark the shoulder lines on both faces at one time.

6 Remove the tail member from the vise, then use a Forstner bit to remove waste material from the shaded cut-out areas.

7 Chisel away the rest of the waste material between the tails, using a sharp wood chisel. Don't try to remove all the waste at once—chisel out a little at a time, working both sides of the tail member, until the cutouts are smooth.

8 Use the tail member as a template to lay out the remaining tail members, if you're making more than one joint. Cut the other tail members.

9 Pair up the tail members with stock for pin members and label each pair.

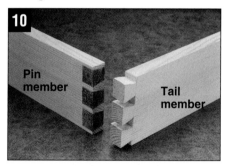

10 Use the tail members as templates to mark the layout of the joints onto the ends of the matching pin member pieces. Make sure the edges are aligned and the boards are at a right angle to one another. Connect the side lines on

> ### WOODWORKER'S TIP
>
> *Use a scrap piece of 2 × 4 as a saw guide to ensure straight cuts. Align the scrap piece with the pin or tail cutting line, and clamp it in place so it just touches the line. Make sure the top of the scrap won't interfere with the spine of the dovetail saw.*

the end of each pin member to the shoulder lines on the faces,

using a try square. Shade in the waste areas.

11 Clamp each pin member in your vise, and cut the sides of the pins down to the shoulder lines with a dovetail saw. Remove waste material the same way you did for the tail members.

12 Test the fit of the mating pieces by partially assembling them (don't fully assemble the joint, or you may have some difficulty getting the boards apart without damaging them). Apply a light layer of glue; interlock the pins and tails so the joint is smooth. No clamping is required.

Half-blind dovetail joints

For projects where you'd prefer not to see the joint from the front, as when making drawer fronts, half-blind dovetails are a common choice. The pin member in a half-blind joint has a lap area, usually about one-third of the board thickness, that is left uncut so it hides the joint.

There is little difference between a through dovetail and a half-blind dovetail. Hand-cutting half-blind joints requires more chiseling to remove waste material, however, and the layout is more complex.

1 Make shoulder lines on the tail member stock, using your cutting gauge. (For most half-blind dovetails, the depth of the tail shoulders is two-thirds the thickness of the workpieces. For example, with ¾"-thick stock, the tails should be ½" deep.) On your pin member stock, make shoulder lines equal to the full thickness of the workpieces.

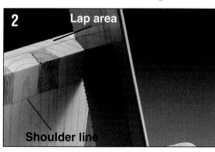

2 Lay out and cut tails for the tail members (see *Through dovetails, page 137,* steps 2 to 8,). Angle your dovetail saw when cutting and cut on the waste side of the

line. Be careful not to cut past the shoulder line, or into the lap area.

3 Use the tail members as templates for marking the layouts of the pin members. Set each tail member on the end of the matching pin member stock, so the shoulder lines of the tail members align with the inside face of the pin member. Trace the tails onto the end of the pin member.

4 Use a try square as a guide to connect the side lines of the pins with the shoulder lines, and shade the waste areas with a pencil.

5 Clamp a pin member into your vise. Remove as much waste material from the cut-out areas of the pin member as you can, using a drill and Forstner bit.

6 Carefully chisel out the remaining waste material, using a sharp wood chisel, until the cut-out areas are smooth.

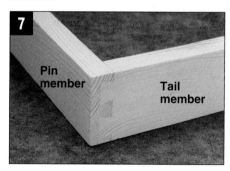

7 Dry-fit the joint partially and make any necessary adjustments. Apply glue and assemble the joint.

Mitered dovetail joints

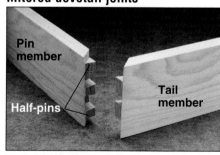

When making mitered dovetails, the top and bottom of the joint are formed by mitered laps, not by half-pins.

Nearly inseparable miter joints can be made using dovetailing techniques. Unlike most other dovetail joints, the mitered dovetail is easier to make if you lay out and cut the pin member first.

TOOL TIP

Advancing tool technology has brought constant improvement to the centuries-old search for an accurate, adjustable dovetail jig. Most router dovetail jigs sold in stores are a little intimidating in their complexity at first, but once you've mastered the technique you'll find them to be very handy workshop helpers.

The adjustable dovetail jig: *The jig shown here (Model D-1258R by Leigh Industries Ltd.) will cut just about any type of dovetail, including sliding and angled dovetails. The fingers that guide the router bit can be arranged in any pattern, then locked down to create a reversible assembly that will cut both tails and pins. Scaled settings can be set easily to very high tolerances, making the jig well suited for production work. Retail cost is about $350.*

The fixed dovetail jig: *This jig (Model 5008, by Porter-Cable) lets you adjust dovetail layouts by switching cutting templates and is fairly simple to learn. Its ability to cut pins and tails at once is an added advantage, but the templates offer no flexibility for varying the spacing of the dovetails. Retail cost is about $110 (templates, $20 to $30).*

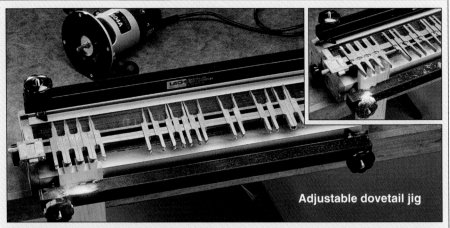

Adjustable dovetail jig

The adjustable dovetail jig *(above)* is used to make a wide variety of dovetails in any size and configuration you want. The narrow fingers serve as guides for cutting tails with a router and dovetail bit. The wider fingers guide a straight bit for cutting matching pins (inset photo). The fixed dovetail jig *(below)* has a much more limited adjustability range, but it can be used to cut the tails and the pins at the same time, and it's also less costly.

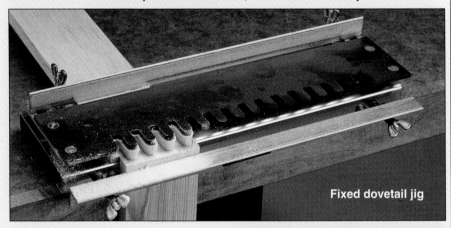

Fixed dovetail jig

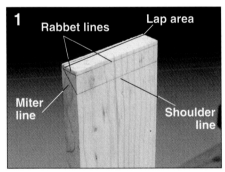

1 Rabbet lines Lap area

Miter line Shoulder line

1 Outline identical cutting areas on the pin and tail members. Make the shoulder lines equal to the thickness of the wood, then mark 45° miter lines on the edges of the workpieces, starting at the ends of the shoulder lines. On the end of each piece, mark a line for the lap area about one-fourth the thickness of the workpiece. Outline a rabbet the same depth as the thickness of the lap area, beginning at the lap line.

2 Using a dovetail saw, make a ⅛"-deep cut along the lap line on the pin member, to form the back of the rabbet, then flip the workpiece and carefully cut the ⅛"-deep rabbet with the dovetail saw.
3 Mark lines on the bottom of the rabbet, ¼" in from the edge, for the side lap part of the joint. Beginning at the ¼" line, measure and mark outlines for the pins.
4 Cut the sides of the pins with your dovetail saw tilted at an angle (see *Half-blind dovetail joints, opposite,* step 2), then remove the waste material with a drill and Forstner bit. Trim the pins to the outlines with a wood chisel, then cut along the miter lines on the edges of the pin member, removing material to form the side laps.
5 Cut a backer board the same width as the pin member, with the end trimmed at a 45° miter.

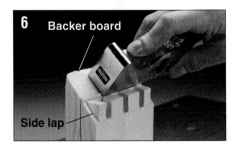

6 Backer board

Side lap

6 Align the backer board with the sloped edge of the side lap, then clamp both pieces into your vise. Use a shoulder plane to miter-cut the back edge of the pin member.
7 Mark side laps on the tail member; set the end of the pin member on the tail member so the inside faces of the pins are aligned with the shoulder line.
8 Outline the tails, then cut the tails and side laps. Remove the waste and plane the miter.
9 Test-fit, then glue and assemble the joint.

Mortises and Tenons

One of the oldest and sturdiest ways to join wood, using mortises and tenons can strengthen and beautify your wood projects.

Pinned mortise-and-tenon joints provide your projects with strong and attractive joinery.

Mortise-and-tenon joints have been used for thousands of years to tie together projects as large as barns and as small as chairs. Mortises and tenons can attach walls to ceilings, to floors, and to each other. Mortises and tenons are used for stile-and-rail construction of raised panel doors. Cabinet shops and furnituremakers also use mortises and tenons to build strong joints into their wares.

The mortise-and-tenon joint is strong and durable, sometimes requiring additional fasteners and sometimes not. Wedges and plugs provide extra security in mortise-and-tenon joints. Wedges driven into the end of the installed tenon spread the tenon in the mortise, preventing the tenon from slipping out of the mortise. Plugs inserted into holes through the tenon also keep the tenon from slipping out.

In the past, the mortises and tenons were chiseled out using a chisel and a 4- to 10-pound wooden maul. Now mortises can be cut using a drill press with a mortise attachment or a router with a mortise jig, while tablesaws and routers are most often used to cut tenons.

Parts of the joint

"Mortise" and "tenon" refer to different parts of the mortise-and-tenon joint. The mortise is the hole cut in a piece of wood to receive the tenon. The tenon is the pin cut in the piece of wood to be joined with the mortise member.

When laying out mortise-and-tenon joints, remember that it's always easier to adjust the tenon to the mortise than the mortise to the tenon, so cut the mortise first.

The weight and stress distributions for mortise-and-tenon members differ according to use. In a vertical use, the tenon rail shoulder takes all the weight bearing down. In a horizontal use, the mortise takes the weight.

Types of mortise & tenon joints

Through mortise & tenon: This type of joint's mortise goes all the way through the mortise member. The tenon member is visible through the end of the mortise. Instructions for creating this type of joint are shown under *Cutting mortises with power tools* and

Different types of mortise-and-tenon joints include through (A), twin (B), loose-pinned (C), double (D). Also see stopped (E) and corner (F).

Cutting tenons with power tools, page 142. Tenon members can be wedged for added holding power (see *Wedging tenons, page 143).*

Double mortise & tenon:

This joint is used when the required width of the mortise and tenon is greater than can safely be cut from the wood. Instead of cutting one large mortise which would remove more than ⅓ of the mortise's mass, use the double mortise and tenon joint where two smaller mortises allow the mortise member to remain strong while the two tenons allow the weight to be spread out over a wide surface area.

Twin mortise & tenon:

This joint is the same as a double mortise and tenon except that the mortise and tenons are cut into the face of the mortise member rather than into the edge of the mortise member.

Stopped mortise & tenon:

This joint is the same as a through mortise and tenon except that the mortise is stopped before it cuts all the way through the mortise member. The tenon does not extend through the mortise and is not visible through it.

Corner mortise & tenon:

These joints involve two tenons entering a mortise member on adjacent sides, as in chair rails that meet in a chair leg. The mortises for the tenons usually meet in corner mortise-and-tenon joints, and

the tenons, to avoid pushing each other out of the joint, should be mitered to fit against each other inside the mortises. Do not cut the tenons short rather than miter them, for shorter tenons weaken the joint.

Loose-pinned mortise & tenon:

This joint includes a through mortise in the vertical structural member and an extra-long tenon in the horizontal member. The extra-long tenon sticks out beyond the mortise in the vertical member by at least two thicknesses of the mortise member. In that extra-long tenon, a through mortise is cut adjacent and ½" in toward the vertical structural member. A wedged pin, often of contrasting color, fits into the tenon's mortise, keeping the tenon in the vertical structural member's mortise. This joint can be disassembled.

Establishing the dimensions of mortises & tenons

The relative thicknesses of mortises and tenons vary greatly due to a variety of factors. Acquaint yourself with accepted mortise-and-tenon guidelines before using them in your projects.

Mortises should not cut out more than ⅓ of the mass of the thickness of the mortise member. If you need to distribute a heavy weight over a larger surface area than that, use a double mortise and tenon. By cutting two smaller mortises farther apart you can remain within the ⅓ thickness guideline yet spread the weight out over more space.

Usually tenons are ⅓ the thickness of the wood when two members of wood the same width are being joined. Tenons can be up to ½ the thickness of the tenon member if they are being joined to a thicker mortise member. Tenons should not be thicker than they are wide. Tenons are usually as wide as the entire width of the tenon member.

The length of the tenon is determined by the type of joint you use. If the joint is a through joint, the tenon should be as long as the mortise member is wide. If the joint is a stopped joint, the mortise and tenon should be ¾ the width of the mortise member.

Cutting mortises with power tools

There are many different ways to cut mortises and tenon joints. If the mortise is to be cut with home power tools, use a drill press with a mortise attachment to cut the mortise. A mortise attachment for a drill press is a drill bit that spins within a hollowed-out chisel.
1 Lay out lines for the mortise. The mortise should be large enough to accommodate the tenon with very little extra room around the tenon.

2 Set up the drill press with a mortise-attachment bit the size of the mortise opening. Cut the mortise only ¾ of the way through the board. Then turn the stock over and finish the mortise by drilling through the other side.
3 After drilling hole for the mortise, use a chisel to square up edges.

Cutting tenons with power tools

Before cutting a tenon, measure the width and length and the gap of the mortise. Using those measurements, mark out the cutting lines for the tenon member. Shade in the waste area of the tenon to facilitate cutting out the right material. Cut the tenon to fit snugly into the mortise.

When making multiple tenons facing the same direction on the same piece of wood, cut one large tenon that encompasses all of the tenons required. Then use a bandsaw or coping saw to cut the waste between the tenons.

Most mortises and tenons can be cut by hand using chisels and chisel hammers and backsaws, tenon saws, and coping saws.

There are two ways to cut a tenon on a tablesaw: the single pass method and the multiple pass method.
Single pass: This method involves making cuts to slice away excess lumber.
1 Place the tenon in a jig with the tenon pointing down toward the saw table.
2 Pass tenon through saw blade and cut one cheek on each pass.
3 Then extract the tenon from the jig to make the shoulder cut. Cutting a shoulder will produce a good gluing surface.

Multiple pass: With this method, excess stock is plowed out using a crosscut blade or a dado-blade set on the tablesaw.
1 Then place the tenon flat on tablesaw, lengthwise against the miter gauge on the tablesaw.
2 Begin to cut the tenon on the tablesaw. The first pass should cut the shoulder line, indicating both the length and the thickness of the tenon. Turn over the piece and cut shoulder line on the other side.

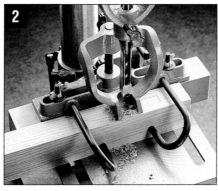

3 After cutting the shoulders, plow out the rest of the stock around the tenon. A crosscut blade will require more passes to plow out waste around tenon.

Cutting mortises by hand

Use a chisel and a mallet to cut a mortise by hand. To withstand the pounding of the mallet on the chisel, put the workpiece on a strong flat surface. A piece of plywood between the workpiece and worktable will prevent chipping.
1 Clamp down the workpiece with C-clamps. Putting yourself in line with the workpiece makes it easy for you to check the mortise cut as you proceed.

2 Starting in the middle of the mortise with the chisel's bevel edge facing away from you, use the mallet to drive the chisel and carve out the mortise, progressing about ⅛" deeper with each hit of the mallet. Work backward to one edge of the mortise. Then turn around and work backward to other edge of the mortise.

3 Turn the workpiece over to clear any loose chips out of the mortise. Put the workpiece back down and finish the mortise by trimming the end and squaring the hole.

Cutting tenons by hand

Cutting a tenon by hand requires more expertise than cutting a tenon with power tools.

1 Measure the width and length of the mortise. Then measure and mark the cutting lines for the tenon member to fit the mortise.

2 Set workpiece in clamp or vise at a 30 to 45° angle to the workbench with the tenon end away from you. Try to keep the cutting edge parallel to the workbench.

3 Using a tenon saw, cut the shoulder lines first. Make sure that you do not cut past the shoulder line.

4 Take the workpiece out of the vise or clamp, turn it 180°, and cut the other side of the tenon, sawing down level with the shoulder.

5 Remove any remaining waste. The tenon should fit the mortise. If the tenon is too large to fit into the mortise, pare or sand the cheeks of the tenon until it fits snugly into the mortise.

Wedging tenons

To expand the tenon in a mortise, especially a through mortise, wedge the tenon through the end

of the mortise.

1 Cut a through mortise-and-tenon joint.

2 Before installing the tenon, cut slits in the tenon down the full length of the tenon. These can be either straight cuts or diagonal ones, depending on whether you want the wedge to be decorative or not.

3 Cut tenon wedges from either matching or contrasting wood. Tenon wedges can be either flat or wedged (thicker at the top than the bottom). In either case, the wedges should be cut along the same long grain as the tenons. The tenon wedges should be as wide as and a little longer than the slit in the tenon.

4 Install the tenon in the mortise. Then add glue to the tenon wedge and insert it in the slit on the tenon. Pound the wedge into the tenon using a wooden mallet. Cut off excess length of the tenon wedge with either an offset dovetail saw or a chisel. Sand to finished smoothness.

Pinning mortise & tenon joints

Another way to strengthen the bond between mortise-and-tenon joints is to pin them. Plugs can be cut from matching or contrasting wood. For more information on plugs and other decorative elements, see *Finishing Wood*, pages 154 and 155.

1 Cut and assemble a mortise-and-tenon joint. It can be a through or stopped joint.

2 Cut a dowel to slightly longer than the depth of the mortise-and-tenon joint.

3 Drill a hole through the mortise-and-tenon joint. The hole should be the same diameter as the dowel.

4 Apply glue to the dowel and the hole in the mortise-and-tenon joint. Then drive the dowel into the hole to pin the mortise-and-tenon joint together. Be sure that the dowel is driven all the way through the joint and sticks out of the bottom of the hole at least a little bit.

5 When the glue has dried, cut or sand away the end of the plug.

WOODWORKER'S TIP

To cut tenon wedges, cut along the same direction of grain as the tenon. Cut wedges from a similar piece of lumber by marking off adjacent triangles on the end grain of the wood. Then run the wood through a bandsaw. Discard the wedges cut from the edges of the lumber. But all of the wedges cut from the interior of the lumber should be well suited for use as tenon wedges.

CHAPTER 7

Finishing Wood

The Final Touch

Your woodshop project is constructed. The china hutch, or the children's wagon, or the picnic-perfect table stands ready for paint or stain, and a final buffing. Don't let your enthusiasm carry you away. Before you touch a brush or buffing cloth, review the finish options discussed in this chapter. Perhaps your hutch deserves a hand-rubbed tung-oil finish. Maybe that wagon needs a liquid sanding sealer application before you paint it red.

You've invested hours of time in the shop to ensure that every cut is smooth, every joint is perfect, every wood screw is concealed. Invest a little more time to select the ideal finishing procedure and product. You'll be glad you did when your masterpiece is finished to perfection.

Water-Based Finishes 146
Finishing Products 148
Sandpaper...150
Painting Basics 152
Working with Plugs 154
Finishing with Oil..156

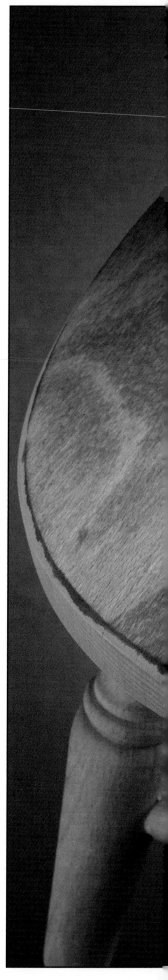

Water-Based Finishes

*Friendly to the environment—
and to the woodworker.*

Water-based stains and top-coat finishes were introduced in the 1960s in response to clean-air legislation restricting the use of oil-based solvents in paints and finishing products. The early water-based finishes behaved much differently than traditional oil-based products, and won few fans among experienced woodworkers.

Today, however, manufacturers have improved the chemistry of water-based stains and finishes, and woodworkers have learned new techniques that let them use these convenient products to full advantage. Even the most tradition-bound woodworkers use water-based finishes from time to time, and an increasing number have grown to prefer the performance of water-based stains and top-coat finishes.

Oil-based finishing products contain a high percentage (up to 80%) of petroleum-based solvents, such as mineral spirits. These solvents, categorized as VOC's (volatile organic compounds), are what make these finishing liquids smelly, flammable, messy, and toxic. More than 35 states now restrict the use of VOC's. By contrast, the water-based finishing products currently available, including premixed stains, sanding sealers, and so-called "polyurethanes" and "lacquers," consist of about 60% water. Although they contain a small amount of oil-based solvent, which serves as an emulsifier for the inert solid materials, these water-based finishes are for the most part nonflammable, odorless, and easy to clean up.

Apply water-based surface finishes to large surfaces with a short-napped painting pad or paint roller, then smooth out the finish by dragging a brush across the surface with light, slow strokes. Because water-based finishes dry quickly, avoid repeated brush strokes that will likely leave lap marks in your finish.

Characteristics

Chemically, water-based stains and top-coat finishes are much different from oil-based finishes, and have distinctly different properties.

Water-based top-coat finishes, for example, dry completely clear, with none of the warm, amber-colored tones associated with oil-based finishes. If you want to achieve this warm color, you'll need to first color the wood with a light stain.

Water-based stains and top-coat finishes also dry much faster than their oil-based relatives. This allows you to apply additional coats within an hour, but it also means you have less time to smooth out wet surfaces with a brush.

Water-based finishes have a ten-dency to hold air bubbles, especially if they are shaken or stirred too vigorously. Newer products have improved flow enhancers and debubbling agents to minimize the problem. Water-based finishes should be mixed by gentle stirring and should be applied with slow strokes, using a good-quality polyester brush with feathered bristles.

Because these finishes contain a high percentage of water, they will raise the grain of some woods,

> **WOODSHOP TIP**
>
> *Water-based finishes can cause a metal container to rust, leaving debris in the liquid. To avoid this problem, transfer water-based finish to a plastic bottle or glass jar.*

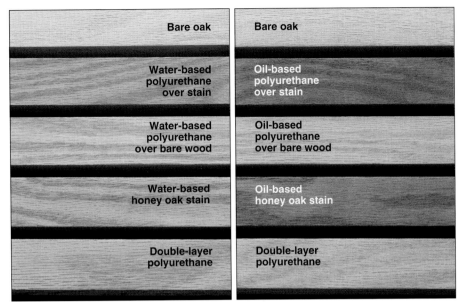

Water-based finishes perform differently than oil-based stains, so it's a good idea to test the finish and hone your techniques on scrapwood before applying it to your project. As shown *above*, water-based stains and finishes have more noticeable color differences than oil-based products.

especially those with open grain patterns, like red oak. You can minimize this problem by moistening and sanding the wood before you begin finishing, by applying finish in very thin coats, and by using sanding sealers where possible. Still, there may be instances where, for the best possible appearance, you'll want to color wood with an oil-based stain, then apply a surface coating of water-based finish.

If you choose to apply water-based finish with a sprayer, you can use either a conventional spray system or a newer high-volume low-pressure (HVLP) system. With a conventional system,

DESIGN TIP

Depending on the manufacturer, a water-based surface finish is sometimes called "polyurethane," or "lacquer," even though it is chemically much different than the traditional oil-based products bearing these names. Other manufacturers refer to their water-based products as "coating," or "finish"—a more accurate, if less familiar, label. Like oil-based finishes, water-based products are available in flat, matte, and gloss finishes.

use a 6 to 8" spraying pattern, and set the sprayer at 20 psi. With an HVLP system, set the gun at 5 psi.

Surface preparation

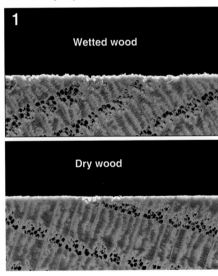

1 Moisten the wood surfaces lightly with a damp rag to raise the wood grain.
2 Let the wood dry completely, then sand it smooth with 220-grit sandpaper. Premoistening and sanding away the raised grain makes it less likely that water-based stain or top-coat finish will alter the wood grain.
3 Clean away all sanding dust with a brush and vacuum.

Applying stain & top-coat finish

1 Apply water-based stain using a lint-free cloth or staining pad.
2 Let the stain dry completely (one hour), then apply a thin coat of water-based sanding sealer to provide a smooth base for the surface finish.
3 Let the sealer dry for at least one hour, then sand lightly with 220-grit sandpaper. Apply additional coats of sanding sealer, as needed, until the surface of the wood is perfectly smooth to the touch. Make sure to vacuum the surface clean after sanding.
4 Apply a thin coat of water-based surface finish. Apply the finish using slow brush stokes, making sure not to overload the brush. For large surfaces, apply finish with a thin-nap painting pad, then smooth out the surface by lightly drawing a brush across the surface (see *opposite page*).
5 Let the surface finish dry for at least one hour, then sand lightly with 220-grit sandpaper.
6 Apply additional thin coats of water-based finish, sanding between coats, until the finish reaches the desired thickness. Because they must be applied in very thin coats to avoid bubbling, you probably will need to apply at least three coats to achieve a thick, durable surface finish.

Finishing touches

When properly applied, water-based finishes dry to a smooth, hard surface that is suitable for most uses. However, for the best possible appearance, you may want to wet-sand the finished surface with water and 400-grit wet-dry sandpaper to remove brush marks and any dust particles. Wipe the surface clean with a cloth, then, if you wish, polish the finish with buffing compound.

WOODWORKER'S TIP

Prolonged exposure to air can cause lumps to form in finishing liquids; if necessary, strain the finish through cheesecloth or a nylon stocking before using it.

Finishing Products

New products make it easy to achieve a fine finish.

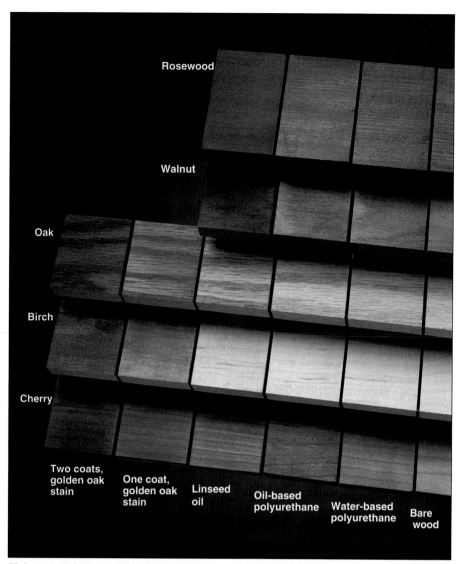

Rosewood
Walnut
Oak
Birch
Cherry

Two coats, golden oak stain | One coat, golden oak stain | Linseed oil | Oil-based polyurethane | Water-based polyurethane | Bare wood

Make test sticks from strips of scrap wood to evaluate how different stains and finishes will look on different types of wood. Make sure to test multiple coats of stains, as well as different combinations of stains and finishes. Label the back sides to identify the finishes used, and keep the strips for reference.

Gone are the days when finishing a woodworking project was laborious drudgery. Twenty or thirty years ago a woodworker had to blend powdered stain pigments in careful ratios with oil-based solvent to achieve a desired color, but today's woodworker can choose from hundreds of premixed oil- and water-based stains. To achieve lustrous surface finishes, woodworkers once routinely ground solid flakes of shellac, mixed them with alcohol, then hand-rubbed many coats onto the workpiece over a period of several weeks. Today, even the most discriminating of woodworkers can get picture-perfect results in a few days, using synthetic varnishes and polyurethanes.

But modern convenience carries its own price. Choosing the right stains and finishes is more complicated these days. New products differ dramatically in their chemical composition, often making them incompatible with each other and with the old-time classic finishing products. Brushing synthetic polyurethane over a seal coat of boiled linseed oil, for example, causes the finish to bubble and blister almost immediately. Choosing the right product is fur-

ther complicated by inconsistencies in the way manufacturers label and market new products. Depending on the manufacturer, virtually identical products that blend tinted stain with penetrating oil might be marketed as "Penetrating Oil," "Danish Oil," "Danish Finish," "Rubbing-Oil/Finish," or "Penetrating Finish & Stain."

Read manufacturers' labels carefully for information on compatibility, and if you can, use stains and finishes from the same product line and manufacturer.

New products give you extra options and may make your finishing work easier, but they may require

you to learn some new terms and techniques. The summary, on opposite page, although by no means complete, will introduce the most commonly used finishing products, both old and new.

BUYER'S TIP

A growing number of water-based stains and finishes are now available (see Finishing Wood, *pages 146 and 147). Because the primary ingredient in these products is water rather than oil-based solvents, water-based products are nonflammable, nontoxic, and easier on the environment.*

SHELLAC

A traditional resinous top-coat finish, now largely replaced by instant gloss finishes, such as synthetic polyurethane varnish.

Composition: natural resins derived from a variety of scale insects, dissolved in alcohol.
Uses: creates a classic French-polished surface when applied in several thin, hand-rubbed coats; used as a sealer under hand-rubbed wax finishes or lacquer.
Advantages: gives a warm-colored, lustrous finish.
Drawbacks: slow application; poor resistance to moisture and alcohol; forms a brittle film that is easily cracked.
Compatibility: good over tung-oil based rubbing oil and water-based stains; poor over oil-based stains that contain linseed oil.

LINSEED OIL

Composition: plant oil derived from flax extract.
Uses: hand-rubbed finishes.
Advantages: easy to apply.
Drawbacks: poor resistance to moisture, easily scratched.
Compatibility: poor under shellac or lacquer.

SALAD-BOWL OIL

Composition: an oil-based finish containing only nontoxic additives.
Uses: as a top-coat finish for turned bowls, children's toys, and other projects that require nontoxic finish.
Compatibility: should not be used with other types of stains and top-coat finishes.

LACQUER

A long-time favorite among old-time cabinet-makers, lacquer is available in two forms: one for brushing, one for spraying.

Composition: nitrocellulose (chemically derived from wood pulp) dissolved in alcohol.
Uses: clear surface finish over shellac or other sealer; especially good for relief carvings, where a thin finish layer is essential.
Advantages: easily applied with sprayer; dries very quickly.
Drawbacks: poor resistance to moisture, alcohol, temperature variations; brittle and easily cracked; extremely fast drying time makes it difficult to avoid brush marks.
Compatibility: good over shellac, tung oil, and penetrating oil; poor over oil-based stains that contain linseed oil.

PENETRATING OILS

Often known as rubbing oil or Danish oil, penetrating oil is available in a yellowish clear tone, or premixed with stain for easy one-coat application.

Composition: small amount of alkyd resin blended with a large ratio of linseed oil or tung oil; many types also have tinted staining agents added.
Uses: low-gloss, penetrating finish for furniture, trim, and other interior woodwork.
Advantages: very easy to apply; good resistance to moisture.
Drawbacks: minimal sheen; less durable than varnish or polyurethane top-coat finishes.
Compatibility: poor under synthetic top-coat finishes, like oil-based polyurethane; good under natural top-coat finishes, like tung oil and shellac.

TUNG OIL

A yellowish oil, also known as China wood oil, tung oil is a standard ingredient in many varnishes. Blended tung oil has become increasingly popular for hand-rubbed top-coat finishes.

Composition: natural (and poisonous) oils from the tung tree, usually blended with mineral spirits and drying agents. Often premixed with tinted staining agents for easy, one-coat application.
Uses: rubbed on as a stand-alone surface finish over bare wood, or as a top-coat finish over stained or oiled wood.
Advantages: easy to apply; good resistance to moisture and alcohol.
Drawbacks: slow to dry; not as durable as polyurethane varnishes.
Compatibility: good as a top-coat finish over stain and penetrating oil, or as a sealer under lacquer; poor with polyurethane.

OIL-BASED STAINS

Composition: finely ground color pigments mixed with linseed oil or petroleum-based mineral spirits.
Uses: changes wood color prior to top-coating with varnish, tung oil, or polyurethane.
Advantages: does not raise wood grain.
Compatibility: good under tung oil, varnish, and polyurethane; stains that contain linseed oil are poor under shellac and lacquer.

WATER-BASED STAINS

Composition: finely ground color pigments blended with water.
Uses: changes wood color prior to applying a top-coat finish.
Advantages: nonflammable; easy cleanup.
Drawbacks: may raise wood grain.
Compatibility: good under any top-coat surface finish.

VARNISH

A clear top-coat finish over stained or bare wood.

Composition: alkyd resins mixed with oils, with thinning agents added; outdoor varieties use phenolic resins.
Uses: top-coat finish for furniture, floors, outdoor projects.
Advantages: slightly flexible, will accommodate temperature expansion and contraction; good resistance to moisture.
Drawbacks: slow-drying; difficult to brush smooth; may yellow with age.
Compatibility: good over penetrating oil or tung oil; poor with shellac, lacquer, or polyurethane.

OIL-BASED POLYURETHANE

A synthetic varnish used as a clear top-coat finish over stained or bare wood.

Composition: synthetic plastic resins mixed with drying oils and thinning agents added; low-gloss, matte-finish types have silica mixed in to refract light.
Uses: top-coat finish for interior furniture and floors.
Advantages: very hard surface; dries clear.
Drawbacks: may crack if wood experiences wide temperature variation; slow-drying, difficult to brush smooth.
Compatibility: good with water- or oil-based stains; poor with most other penetrating sealers or top-coat finishes.

WATER-BASED POLYURETHANE

Composition: plastic resins mixed with water and small amount of oil-based solvent. Low-gloss, matte-finish types have silica mixed in to refract light.
Uses: brushed on as a clear top-coat finish over bare or stained wood.
Advantages: nonflammable and nontoxic; dries very quickly to a completely clear finish that is very hard and durable; easy cleanup.
Drawbacks: fast drying time can trap air bubbles in the surface and makes it difficult to brush surface smooth; dried surface is somewhat brittle.
Compatibility: good with all penetrating stains and oils.

Sandpaper

Achieving a fine finish is impossible unless you choose the right sanding materials.

Sandpaper is the generic term for a number of finishing products made by bonding abrasive particles to a flexible backing. The original sandpaper, also called "glasspaper," used small particles of flint as the abrasive material, but flint has long since been replaced by more efficient, longer-lasting chemical compounds and synthetic materials.

All sandpaper comes in many different grades of coarseness, usually categorized by a numbering system which assigns progressively higher numbers to finer grades of coarseness. For example, 40-grit sandpaper is a very coarse product designed for grinding away large amounts of wood, while 1500-grit paper has extremely fine abrasives and is normally used for burnishing to a finely polished finish.

Manufacturers also categorize their products alphabetically, according to the thickness of the paper or cloth used as backing. Grade "A" is thin, flexible material; "B" is somewhat thicker and less flexible, and so on.

Better sandpapers use a resinous adhesive to bond the abrasives to the backing. The resins are more flexible and stronger than traditional glues, like those used with the old glasspapers.

General sanding guidelines

In addition to whatever rough sanding is needed for general shaping (usually done with sandpaper between 60- and 100-grit), wood surfaces require three rounds of finish-sanding with progressively finer sandpaper. You may need more sanding if the

Sanding products are available in many specialized forms to match different sanding tools. The samples shown above include: belts for portable power sanders (A), triangular adhesive paper for corner sander (B), flap sanding wheel for use with a drill or drill press (C), sanding cord for sanding grooves in turned pieces (D), small belt for loop sander (E), self-adhesive discs for a disc sander (F), rubber eraser for cleaning sanding belts (G), perforated sanding discs for use with random-orbit sanders with dust-collection bag (H), self-adhesive pads for orbital sander (I), sheet sandpaper (J), and self-adhesive roll sandpaper for hand-sanding block (K).

wood is very rough to start with, or if you desire a burnished look.

1 Do the preliminary finish-sanding with a belt sander and medium sanding belt (120- to 150-grit). Tools should be used, and sanding should be done, parallel to the grain.

2 Change to a pad sander with 180-grit sandpaper for the intermediate sanding.

3 Sand the wood to finished smoothness with fine sandpaper (220- to 280-grit). On hardwood, you can sand with 300-grit paper for extra smoothness. Apply finish to the workpiece within 24 hours so the wood does not absorb moisture from the air.

4 Between coats of finish, hand-sand the surfaces with extra-fine paper (400- to 600-grit). For an extremely smooth finish, some woodworkers like to use extra-fine silicone carbide sandpaper to "wet-sand" the finish with water or finishing oil.

WOODWORKER'S TIPS

- *To check the quality of your sanded surface, hold a light low against one edge of the surface. Scratches, dips, and rough spots will be easy to spot under direct side light.*
- *Extend the life of sandpaper by frequently brushing sanded surfaces clean to reduce the dust that clogs the surface of the sandpaper. Clogged sandpaper can sometimes be cleared with a brush or vacuum cleaner.*
- *Use an "open-coat" sandpaper with widely spaced abrasive particles when sanding softwoods like pine. Open-coat paper will not clog as easily as closed-coat paper.*
- *On open-grained wood like red oak, lightly wet the wood just prior to finishing to raise the grain slightly. Hand-sand the surface with fine sandpaper to smooth away the raised wood fibers and ensure a glass-smooth final finish.*

GARNET

Type of abrasive: *natural garnet mineral, heated and crushed.*

Availability: *available in sheets ranging from coarse (60-grit) to medium (150-grit).*

Characteristics: *gives somewhat uneven results, because the sharp abrasives easily break away from the backing paper, especially if used with moderate to heavy pressure. Garnet paper is rather brittle, making it difficult to fold.*

Uses: *sanding by hand or with a pad sander set at low speed. Works well for sanding end grain, because the abrasives break away easily, preventing burning.*

ALUMINUM OXIDE

Type of abrasive: *powdered bauxite, heat-fused with silica and iron to produce a hard, durable oxidized surface. Aluminum oxide is the most widely used sandpaper.*

Availability: *sanding belts and drums ranging from coarse to medium (60- to 150-grit); sheet papers from coarse to fine (60- to 320-grit).*

Characteristics: *a very durable and uniform product that cuts evenly with little burning.*

Uses: *sanding by hand or with virtually any type of power sander.*

ZINC STEARATE

Type of abrasive: *standard aluminum oxide, with a coating of dry zinc stearate powder that serves as a dry lubricant and keeps the abrasive coating from becoming clogged with wood dust.*

Availability: *sheet paper from coarse to fine (60- to 400-grit).*

Characteristics: *does not cut as fast as standard aluminum oxide paper, but lasts longer, especially in the finer grits.*

Uses: *sanding by hand or with pad sanders.*

Garnet

Aluminum oxide

Zinc stearate

Silicone carbide

Synthetic mineral

SILICONE CARBIDE

Type of abrasive: *silica and carbon heat-fused, then ground into very fine, sharp granules.*

Availability: *sheets ranging from fine (220-grit) to ultra-fine (1500-grit).*

Characteristics: *very consistent abrasive particles; most types are coated with zinc stearate to reduce clogging; abrasive and backing paper are resistant to moisture.*

Uses: *finish-sanding or wet-sanding by hand or with a pad sander; works well on glue-filled composite products, like particleboard, because the abrasive material resists clogging.*

SYNTHETIC MINERAL

Type of abrasive: *a ceramiclike material (known by the trade name* Regalite*) that is much harder than any natural abrasive.*

Availability: *sanding belts ranging from coarse (50-grit) to medium (150-grit).*

Characteristics: *more expensive than other sanding belts, but much more durable; belts are bidirectional: the seams are butted, not overlapped, so the belt can be reversed.*

Uses: *quick rough-sanding of hardwoods and softwoods.*

Metal sandpaper is a recent development. It is made from tiny tungsten carbide fragments heat-bonded to a metal backing. Available in sheets or in discs, and in grits ranging from 32- to 320-, metal sandpaper is extremely long-lasting.

Painting Basics

Add lively flair to your projects with color finishes.

Although many woodworkers prefer clear finishes for their projects, there are times when an opaque color finish—paint—is the best choice. For example, a colorful painted finish can make a dramatic design statement. Paint also can be used to dress up modest woods that have uninteresting grain patterns.

Chemically, latex and oil-based paints are remarkably similar to the brush-on transparent finishes—lacquer, varnish, and polyurethane. Paints use many of the same solvents and base materials as transparent finishes, but have colorful, opaque pigments included.

As with other types of finishes, paints are available in both water-based (latex) and oil-based (alkyd) types. Each type has advantages and drawbacks. Latex paints are nontoxic and easy to apply, but are not as durable as alkyd paints. Alkyd paints are somewhat messy to apply and more difficult to clean up, but many woodworkers feel that they provide a smoother surface because alkyd paints dry slower.

Both latex and alkyd paints are available in different reflective formulations, ranging from flat (sometimes called matte) paints that reflect little light, to high gloss paints that produce a very shiny finish. Because the painting technique we use on this project will be covered with a clear protective top coat of varnish for extra luster, we chose a semi-gloss or matte paint, because it will bond better to the top coat.

Many woodworkers, including many who are quite skilled at the patient art of using stains and clear finishes, know surprisingly little about the proper methods for applying paint to woodworking projects. As with many finishing techniques, a good paint finish is achieved by applying several coats of sealers, primers, and top coats—as many as five layers, for the best possible finish. Many of the same techniques used for clear finishes—including wet-sanding—also can be used for applying a painted finish.

For our basic technique, we'll apply the paint with a brush. Wet-sanding the painted surface and covering it with a layer of varnish will give you an extremely smooth, lustrous surface without visible brush marks.

Like clear finishes, paint can also be applied with a sprayer, a method that requires skillful use of expensive equipment. However, spraying can result in a very smooth, uniform surface.

TOOL TIP

Good-quality paintbrushes have chisel-shaped tips and bristles that are frayed (flagged) at the ends to reduce brush marks. Brushes with synthetic polyester bristles are good for applying both latex and alkyd paints. Brushes with natural china bristles should not be used with latex paints, because the bristles will absorb water and go limp. Use the largest brush that is practical for your job, but use a small sash brush with an angled tip to paint molded areas and inside corners.

Preparation

As with any other type of finish, the quality of a painted finish depends on careful preparation of the surfaces. Except for very rough utility projects, never paint directly over bare, unsealed wood. Two or more preparatory coats of sanding sealer are essential for a fine, smooth finish.

1 Sand the surfaces to finished smoothness with 120-, then 180-grit sandpaper. (For painting, you don't need to use sandpaper finer than 180-grit, because the sanding sealer and paint will fill in these fine scratches.)

2 Clean the surfaces thoroughly, then brush on liquid sanding sealer to fill the grain.

3 Let the sealer dry completely, then apply a second coat of sanding sealer. (On woods with very open grain, such as red oak, you may need to apply several coats of sanding sealer; or, you can fill the grain with paste filler.) Let the sealer dry completely.

4 After the last coat of sanding sealer dries, sand the surfaces lightly with 320-grit sandpaper to give the surface "tooth" for bonding with the paint. Wipe away all sanding dust before applying paint.

WORKSHOP TIP

Airborne dust is the arch enemy of the painted finish. Avoid painting a project in an area where woodworking tools have recently operated, and wipe off sanded surfaces with a tack cloth to completely remove all sanding dust.

Applying paint

Your choice of water-based (latex) or oil-based (alkyd) paint is basically personal preference. Whatever type you choose, you'll get best results if you apply at least two coats. Because we'll be applying a protective varnish top-coat to our painted finish, make sure the paint you choose is compatible with varnish.

BUYER'S TIP

*Some alkyd paints that have **polyurethane** (a synthetic clear finish) mixed into them do not bond well to the varnish top-coat finish we recommend for painted surfaces. Traditional alkyd **"enamel"** paints, however, have natural varnish mixed into them, and can be successfully top-coated with varnish.*

1 Apply a thin undercoat of paint to all surfaces, brushing first against the grain, then with the grain. With thick-bodied paints, you may want to thin out the paint for smoother application (use Penetrol to thin alkyd paints, and Floetrol for latex paints).

2 Let the undercoat dry completely, then sand it lightly with 320-grit sandpaper. Wipe the surfaces clean, then apply a moderately heavy coat of paint, brushing in the same direction as the wood grain. To minimize bristle marks, brush from dry areas into wet areas. Let the paint dry completely.

Top-coat

Wet-sanding painted surfaces and coating them with clear varnish creates a smooth, lustrous finish that is durable as well as beautiful. Oil-based varnish is a better choice than the newer water-based varnishes, because the oil-based varnish leaves fewer brush marks and will accept a hand-rubbed polish better than water-based varnishes. Low-gloss (satin) varnish generally polishes better than high-gloss varnish.

1 Moisten a sheet of 320-grit wet-dry sandpaper and use it to lightly wet-sand the painted surfaces. Rinse off the sandpaper frequently and use light hand pressure to avoid sanding through to bare wood. Dry the surface completely with a cloth.

2 Apply a medium-heavy coat of varnish over the paint, being careful to smoothly brush out the surface. Let the finish dry for at least two days.

3 Lightly wet-sand with 400-grit wet-dry sandpaper to remove any airborne dust that has settled on the varnished surfaces. Dry the surfaces completely.

4 Polish the surface to a deep, lustrous sheen with a buffing cloth and automotive polishing compound.

Plugs not only conceal screws but also can provide decorative contrast in woodworking projects.

Working with Plugs

Add a decorative touch to your woodworking projects with contrasting plugs or buttons.
Or highlight the uninterrupted wood surface of your projects with matching plugs.

Plugs fit into counterbores to cover screws in joints. You can use plugs that match perfectly the wood of the rest of your project, giving it a seamless quality and almost completely concealing the screw hole.

But using plugs can be more than just a cover-up technique. You can add contrast to your woodworking projects with plugs. Rotate the plug to place its grain perpendicular to that of the project. Use plugs made of contrasting wood. Or use rounded-top plugs called screw hole buttons. All of these kinds of plugs can turn some or all of the screw holes in your woodworking projects into decorative accents.

Precut plugs and buttons are available in woodworkers' supply stores. Manufactured in a range of materials such as oak, birch, cherry, and walnut, plug sizes range from ¼ to ¾" in diameter. Precut plugs are usually inexpensive.

Or you may make your own plugs even less expensively out of scrapwood. This is particularly helpful if you can't find an exact match of your wood or grain in commercially available plugs. Make your own plugs with a plug cutter installed in your drill press. Plug cutters are available in a range of sizes and types. You can use them to cut into face grain or end grain, making plugs that best match or contrast with your project's surface.

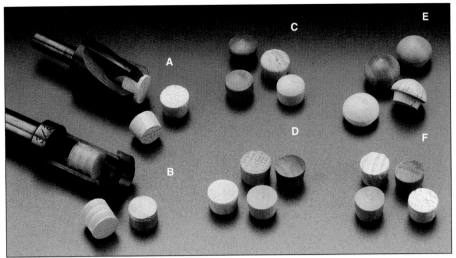

Make your own plugs, either tapered (A) or straight-edged (B). Or choose from the variety of commercial plugs and buttons available: wood plugs (C), face grain plugs (D), screw hole buttons (E), and flat top plugs (F).

BUYER'S TIP

• *Wood plugs have slightly rounded tops and tapered plug bodies.*

• *Face grain plugs, when installed correctly, require no sanding yet still blend in with wood grain.*

• *Screw hole buttons' rounded tops are wider than the plugs' diameter.*

• *Flat top plugs can be sanded flush to blend in with your project's wood grain.*

Making your own plugs

Making plugs doesn't take much time, and the results are well worth the effort, particularly if you've invested a lot of time and money building a project using imported or expensive woods.

Plug cutters produce the best results when mounted in a drill press, where they create perfectly aligned plugs. Some plug cutters create plugs with chamfered or tapered ends, making the plugs easier to install. Other cutters eject the plugs as they are cut, speeding up the process.

Purchase a plug cutter whose diameter matches the diameter of the holes you're filling. Typical plug cutter diameters are ¼, ⅜, and ½". Also make sure the plug cutter shank fits your drill press.

To cut plugs, drill into the face or the end grain of the wood by positioning the drill press work-table and the workpiece accordingly (see *Woodworking Tools*, pages 54 and 55). If the plug cutter does not eject the plugs as they are cut, cut or pry the plugs out of the workpiece.

1 Install the plug cutter in the drill press and position the work-piece below it.

2 With the drill press turned off, check the depth of the cut by lowering the plug cutter next to the workpiece. Set and lock the depth stop.

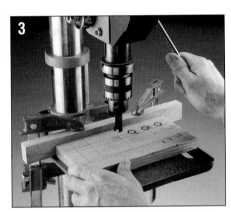

3 Turn on the drill and let it reach full speed. Then lower the plug cutter into the workpiece.

4 Raise the cutter and shift the workpiece over to make another plug. Continue until you've cut enough plugs. Turn off the drill.

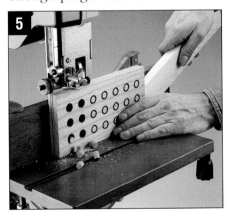

5 Remove the plugs from the workpiece. Either trim them off using a bandsaw, creating even, flat ends, or use a screwdriver to pry and snap the plugs out.

Installing plugs

To install most plugs, drill the counterbore slightly shallower than the length of the plug so the plug can be cut and sanded flush with the surface of the workpiece. To install face grain plugs, cut the counterbore to match exactly the length of the plug. To install buttons and other rounded-top plugs, cut the counterbore to allow only the rounded surface of the plug to rise above the surface.

1 Drill a counterbore hole, using a counterbore bit or a brad point bits in a drill or drill press.

2 Drive a screw. The screw head will rest below the surface of the wood at the bottom of the counterbore cylinder.

3 Apply glue to the plug and insert it in the hole. Set a piece of scrapwood over the plug and tap the scrapwood with a hammer or wooden mallet to set the plug. The board protects the plug and the worksurface from damage.

4 Let the glue dry. Then trim off the plug with a chisel or offset dovetail saw. Sand the surface smooth.

Finishing with Oil

These easy-to-use finishes help highlight the natural beauty of wood.

All types of oil finish form a relatively flat finish without the shine of gloss polyurethane (A). Linseed oil (B) and penetrating oil (C) soak into the wood, leaving almost no shine. Tung oil (D) penetrates the wood, but also creates a slight build-up film that creates a moderate gloss. Because tung oil dries to a relatively hard surface, it is more durable than the other oils.

Hand-rubbed oil finishes are increasingly popular as alternatives to top-coat finishes, like varnish and polyurethane. But unlike these brush-on top-coat finishes, which coat the wood fibers with a high-gloss film, oil finishes penetrate the wood fibers, producing a low-gloss surface that lets you readily see and feel the texture of the wood grain. Oil finishes are a good choice whenever you want to highlight, rather than hide, the wood grain.

Oil finishes dry relatively quickly, and are very easy to apply. Because the wood is saturated with oil, then wiped dry, dust does not have a chance to settle on wet surfaces.

Although oil finishes are not as hard or durable as varnish and polyurethane, they do form an excellent moisture barrier. Minor surface damage on oil-finished wood is easily repaired simply by applying additional oil. Oil is an acceptable finish for most wood surfaces, but for heavy-use surfaces, like steps, floors, and countertops, polyurethane is a better choice.

The term "oil finish" is used to describe a number of different products, but the oils most commonly used for woodworking include linseed oil, penetrating oil, and tung oil.

Linseed oil: Boiled linseed oil, derived from flax, is a traditional rubbing oil that has been largely replaced by penetrating oil and tung oil. Because it does not harden completely, linseed oil can hold dust and dirt. Surfaces finished with linseed oil will darken slightly with age.

Penetrating oil: Commonly marketed as Watco Danish Oil, penetrating oils are made by combining refined linseed oil resin with a penetrating solvent/drier solution. The resulting oil dries within 6 hours (not several days, like linseed oil) and is very easy to apply.

Tung oil: Also known as China wood oil, tung oil is a natural drying oil obtained from the tung tree. Tung oil has unique properties that make it much different from the other rubbing oils.

Like linseed and penetrating oil, tung oil soaks into the wood fibers. But unlike these oils, tung oil also forms a semi-glossy build-up layer similar to that created by some varnishes. In fact, tung oil is an ingredient in many commercial varnishes and can be applied by brush. Its short drying time, however, makes tung oil a good candidate for hand-application. Tung oil often is applied over a penetrating oil finish to harden the surface and make it more durable.

WOODWORKER'S TIP

Many woodworkers avoid using stains or tints together with oil finishes because the colors tend to mask the natural appeal of the wood. However, if some tinting is required (for example, if you need to match the color of existing furniture or woodwork), you can save time and avoid a separate staining step by using a precolored penetrating oil or tung oil. A better method is to mix powdered universal colors with natural-tone oil. Universal colors, available at woodworking stores and art-supply outlets, give you better control over the color, but to accurately judge the tint, you will need to experiment on scrapwood to find the correct blend of powders.

Using penetrating oil

Sealing and filling wood grain is rarely necessary, even with open-grained woods like red oak, if you wet-sand the surface during the first application of oil.

1 After finish-sanding the surfaces with 150-grit sandpaper and wiping them free of dust, apply a uniform coat of natural-tone penetrating oil to the surfaces.

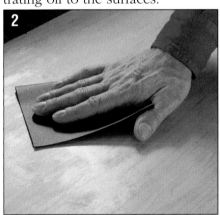

2 Use a folded sheet of 320-grit wet-dry sandpaper to sand the entire surface, using a figure-eight pattern. Wet-sanding creates an oil-sawdust slurry that is packed into the wood pores, filling the grain.
3 Wipe off the excess oil-dust mixture with a clean, lint-free rag.
4 Lightly sand the wood with fresh 320-grit paper, first sanding across the wood grain, then with the grain. Wipe the wood clean with a lint-free rag.

5 Let the oil dry for at least 4 hours, then apply another coat of natural-tone oil. Rub in the oil with a rag, using heavy hand pressure to warm the surface, improving the penetration of the oil. Let the surface dry for at least 4 hours.

WOODWORKER'S TIP

Manufacturer's directions often instruct you to apply two very heavy coats of penetrating oil, but you'll have better results if you apply several thin coats.

6 Apply additional thin coats of oil, spaced at least 4 hours apart. Open-grained woods, like red oak, may require as many as 5 coats of oil, but fine-textured woods, like maple, usually need no more than 3 coats. To color the wood, add powdered universal stain (or use precolored oil) for the last 1 or 2 coats of oil.
7 For a harder, more protective surface, top-coat the oiled finish with a thin coat of tung oil or water-based low-gloss polyurethane.

Applying tung oil

Tung oil is rubbed in by hand, much the same way as penetrating oil, but because tung oil dries so quickly, it can become gummy and sticky if applied too thickly. As with any finish, several thin coats will give better results than a single heavy coat. Sand the wood to finished smoothness and clean away all sanding dust before applying tung oil: Do not try to wet-sand with tung oil.

1 If applying tung oil to bare wood, apply the first coat in a thick layer to form a sealing layer, then rub it in by hand.
2 Wipe the surfaces dry with clean cloths. If the surface becomes too sticky to wipe, moisten your wiping cloths with mineral spirits.
3 Let the surface dry for at least one hour, then apply a second thin coat of tung oil, applied by hand-rubbing.
4 Let the surfaces dry for at least one hour, then apply a thin, final coat of tung oil.

5 Let the last coat of oil dry overnight, then burnish with 4/0 steel wool to create a smooth, even sheen. Take care not to scour through the finish.

BUYER'S TIP

Tung oil and penetrating oils sometimes contain small amounts of heavy metal, such as mercury or lead, as part of the drying agent. These products should not be used on children's toys or eating utensils. A good alternative is to hand-rub the wood with vegetable oil or olive oil, then polish it with a cloth impregnated with soft paraffin wax.

Abrasive wheels, 19
Alkyd paint, 152-153
Backsaw, 61, 110
Baltic birch, 126-127
Bandsaw, 36-39
    blades, 31, 37
    cutting multiple pieces, 102
    resawing, 104-105
Bar compass, 11
Belt sander, 52-53, 150
Bevels, cutting, 33, 39, 41, 43
Bird's-eye maple, 72
Birch, 73, 148
Biscuit joint, 117, 121, 124-125
Black walnut, 76-77
Blades, saw, 30-31, 32, 34-35, 37-38,
    40, 42
Bowl-turning, 94-95
Box joints, 108-109, 128-129
Brace and bit drills, 58-59
Buffing compound, 147
Butt joints, 124, 130
Calipers, 11, 50
Carbide blades, 31, 71
Carver's stone, 21
Carving, 71, 73, 75, 77, 79, 98-101
Casters, 89
Cauls, 120-121
Cherry wood, 78-79, 148
Chip carving, 98-101
Chisels, 49, 66-67, 98-101, 112, 142-143
Circles/Curves
    cutting, 38-39, 43, 47, 60-61
    templates, 11, 14
Circular saws, 32-33
    blades, 30-31, 32
Clamps, 119-121
Compass, 11, 14
Compass saw, 60-61
Compound miter, 115
Coping saws, 60-61
Crosscut fence, 116
Crosscut guide, 115
Crosscut saws, 60-61
Crosscutting, 28-29, 33, 38, 41, 60-61, 77
Crown molding, 41
Cutting multiple workpieces, 39, 102-103
Dado blades, 109, 110-113
Dadoes, 110-113, 123, 128-129
Danish oil, 148-149, 156

Disc sander, 52-53
Dividers, 11, 50
Dovetail joints, 47, 128-129, 136-139
Dovetail saw, 60-61
Dowel joints, 117, 121, 130-131
Drafting tools, 12
Drawer hardware, 86-87, 128
Drawer, making 126-129
Drawing table, making, 14
Drills
    bits, 55, 56-57
    depth stop, 59
    doweling jig, 59
    drill press, 54-55
    guides, 59
    portable, 58-59
    sanding, 59
    screwdriver bits, 59
Dust collection, removal, 8
Edge-cutting, 46
Edge-gluing, 118, 120
Endangered forests, 83
Enlarging patterns, 16-17
Face-gluing, 120-121
Fasteners, 88
Featherboards, 24-25, 105, 112-113
Fiddleback maple, 72
Finger joints, 108-109
Finishing wood, 71, 73, 75, 77, 79,
    146-157
    painting, 152-153
    plugs, 154-155
    preparation, surface, 147, 153
    sanding products, 150-151
    stain and sealers, 146-149
Flatsawn, 82
Frame-and-panel construction, 122-123
French curves, 11,14
Fret saw, 61
Gang-cutting, 102-103
Glues, 118-121
Gouges, 49, 94-95, 98-101
Grinder wheels, 19
Groove, 110
Hand planes, 62-65
Handsaws, 60-61
Hardware, 86-91, 128
Hardwood grades, 80-81
Hinges, 90-91
Japanese tools
    chisels, 67
    planes, 64
    saws, 61

Jigs
    adjustable crosscut guide, 115
    adjustable taper, 96, 117
    box joint, 108-109
    crosscut fence, 116
    dovetail, 129, 139
    doweling 130-131
    miter-gauge extension, 116
    router, 47
Joining wood, 108-143
Jointer
    cutting tapers, 97
    dadoes and rabbets, 110-113
Keyhole saw, 61
Knives, 98-101
Knobs, 87, 88
Lacquer, 149
Laminating, 120-121
Latex paint, 152-153
Lathe, 48-51, 94-95
Linseed oil, 149, 156
Lumber grades, 80-82
Maple wood, 72-73, 157
Marking tools, 10
Measuring tools, 10-11
Medullary rays, 71
Miter box, power, 40-41
Miter gauge, 109, 112, 114-117, 123
Miter-gauge extension, 38, 116
Miter joints, 33, 37, 41, 114-117, 121
Miter shooting box, 115
Mortises and tenons, 140-143
Nails, 88
Nuts, 88
Oak, 70-71, 147, 148
Oil-based finishes, 146-147, 148-149, 152-
    153
Oilstones, 18, 20-21
Paint, 152-153
Pattern transfer
    carving, 101
    enlarging grids,16-17
Penetrating oils, 148-149, 156-157
Plain sawn, 70-71, 73
Planes, 62-65
Plate joinery, 124-125
Plough, 110
Plug cutter, 154-155
Plugs, 154-155
Plunge cutting, 33, 43
Plunge router, 45, 113

Plywood grades, 81-82
Polyurethanes, 146-147, 148-149, 156
Portable tools,
    drills, 58-59
    saws, 26
Power miter box, 40-41
Project drawings, 12-17
Protractor, 11, 114
Pushsticks, 24-25, 112
Quartersawn, 70-71, 73, 82
Quilted maple, 72
Rabbets, 110-113, 128-129
Red oak, 70-71, 147, 148, 150, 157
Redwood, 74-75
Relief carving, 98-101
Repeat cuts, 102-103
Resawing techniques, 38-39, 104-105
Riftsawn, 70-71, 73, 82
Ripcutting, 28-29, 33, 38-39, 61, 71, 77
Ripsaws, 60-61
Rosewood, 148
Roughing, 50
Routers, 44-47
    dadoes and rabbets, 110-112
    edge-cutting, 46
    frame-and-panel construction, 122-123
    multiple workpieces, 102-103
Rubbing oil, 148-149
Sabersaw, 42-43
Safety, 9, 24-25, 38, 50
Salad-bowl oil, 149
Sanders, 52-53, 150-151
Sanding, finish, 50, 147, 153
Sandpapers/belts, 150-151
Saws
    bandsaw, 36-39
    blades, 30-31
    circular, 32-33

    hand, 60-61
    portable, 26
    power miter box, 40-41
    sabersaw, 42-43
    scrollsaw, 34-35
    tablesaw, 26-29
Sand papers/products, 150-151, 153
Scrapers, 49, 95
Screws, 88, 154-155
Scrollsaw, 34-35, 43
Sculpting, 98-101
Shaping, 71, 73, 75, 77, 79
Sharpening tools/stones, 18-21, 100

Shelf hardware, 89
Shellac, 149
Skew, 49
Softwood grades, 81-82
Splines, 117, 121
Sprayer, applying finishes, 147, 149, 152
Stains, 146-147, 148-149
Stationary power sanders, 52-53
T-bevel, 11, 114, 137
Tablesaw, 26-29
    cutting tapers, 97
    cutting tenons, 142
    dadoes and rabbets, 110, 112-112
    frame-and-panel construction, 123
    resawing, 104-105
Tannic acid, 79
Tannins, 71
Tapers, cutting, 96-97
Templates
    bandsaw, use with, 39
    circles, 11, 14
    dadoes and rabbets, 110-113
    multiple cuts, 102-103
Tenon saw, 60
Tools, 24-67 *see also specific tool*
    advanced shop, 9
    beginner shop, 9
    carving, 98-101
    cutting, 26-47, 60-61
    drills, 54-59
    intermediate shop, 9
    measuring and marking, 10-11
    sanding, 52-53, 150-151
    sharpening, 18-21
    turning, 48-49, 94-95
    veneering, 133
Tung oil, 149, 156-157
Turning, 49-51, 71, 73, 75, 77, 79, 94-95
Varnishes, 149, 153
Veneers, 77, 126-127, 132-135
Walnut, 76-77, 148
Water-based finishes, 146-147, 148-149,
    152-153
Waterstones, 19
Whetstones, 19
Whittling, 98-101
Wobble blade, 112
Wood, 68-83 *see also specific kind*
    carving, 100
    grading, 80-82
    moisture content, 82
    storage of, 82-83
Workshop, 8-9
Workstations, 9

INDEX OF TIPS

Bandsaw
    blade storage, 38
    buying tips, 36
    cutting curves, 38
    L-shaped pivot block, 38
Biscuit joinery, 125
Carving
    finish, 101
    router, 101
    shadows, 101
    sharpening tools, 100
    wood scraps, 100
Casters, mounting on tools, 9
Cherry
    finishing, 79
    working with, 79
Chisels, honing, 67
Circular saw
    buying tips, 32
    reduce tearout, 33
Clearances, workshop, 9
Construction drawings, 12
Copyright design, 14
Crosscutting, 41
Curing wood, 94
Cutting capacity, increase, 41
Dadoes and rabbets
    dado-blade set, 112
    marking with insert board, 110
    safety, 113
Dovetail joints
    guides, making, 137, 138
    jigs, 139
    marking outlines, 137
    tools, 137
Dowel joints, 131
Drawers
    parts, precut, 127
    kicker, 87
    stop, 87
Drill bits
    buying tips, 57
    sharpening, 20
Drill press, buying tips, 54
Dust collection, 52
Gang-cutting, 35

Grinding wheels
    cleaning and truing, 19
    cooling blade, 21
Hand planes, problems, 63
Handsaws, how to use, 61
Heights, workstations and
        shelves, 9
Honing guide, 20
Lathe,
    buying tips, 48
    corner shock, 50
    sanding, 50
    turning speeds, 51
Maple, shrinkage, 73
Measuring tools, 10
Miters, 115
Mortises and tenons, 143
Oak, red, finishing, 71
Oil finishes
    coats, number of, 157
    safety, 157
    tinting, 157
Paint
    brushes, 152
    dust elimination, 153
    types, 153
Pattern transfer, 35
Plugs, 155
Power miter box
    buying tips, 40
    platform, 41
Project drawings, 12
Pushsticks, grip, 25
Rainforest protection, 83
Red oak, finishing 71
Redwood
    conserving, 75
    restoring, 75
Router
    bits, care of, 45
    buying tips, 44
    edge-cutting, 46
    edge-routing, 46
   removable base, casting, 44
Sabersaw
    buying tips, 42
    tearout, prevention, 43

Sanders, buying tips, 52
Sanding, finish work, 150
Saw blades
    cutting curves, 31
    disposable, 37
    scrollsaw, 31, 35
    sharpening, 20
    teeth, number of, 30
Scrollsaw
    blades, 31, 35
    buying tips, 34
Surface, uneven, detecting, 65
Tablesaw
    accessories, 29
    buying tips, 27
    cutting problems, 28
    rip fence, 103
    safety, 27
    shaping head accessories, 31
    surface polishing, 27
    techniques, 29
Uneven surface, detecting, 65
Veneers
    buying tips, 132
    face, determining, 134
    glycerine, 133
    grain, 134
    press, building a, 135
Walnut, buying tips, 77
Water-based finishes
    debris in liquid, 146
    labeling, 147
    lumps, removing, 147
    safety, 148
Wood
    air drying, 82
    buying tip, 82
    grading system, 81
Workshop
    casters, mounting on tools, 9
    clearances, 9
    heights, workstations and
        shelves, 9

METRIC CONVERSIONS

U.S. Units to Metric Equivalents

To convert from	Multiply by	To get
Inches	25.4	Millimeters (mm)
Inches	2.54	Centimeters (cm)
Feet	30.48	Centimeters (cm)
Feet	0.3048	Meters (m)

Metric Units to U.S. Equivalents

To convert from	Multiply by	To get
Millimeters	0.0394	Inches
Centimeters	0.3937	Inches
Centimeters	0.0328	Feet
Meters	3.2808	Feet